Better Sailing

With Bob Fisher

First published 1980 by Octopus Books
Limited, 59, Grosvenor Street, London W1
© 1980 Octopus Books Limited
ISBN 0 7064 1009 2
D. L.-TO-8-80
Printed in Spain
by Artes Gráficas Toledo, S.A.

Contents

8 Foreword by Ted Hood

9 Introduction by Bob Fisher

10 Dinghy Sailing

36 Day Keelboat Sailing

64 Offshore Boats Sailing Inshore

88 Ocean Racing

112 Multihulls

130 Overall Tactics and Strategy

154 Glossary

156 Index

FOREWORD by Ted Hood

Competitive sailboat racing has occupied a considerable portion of my life. Striving to maintain a position at the front of any fleet has become more and more difficult as more and more people are learning the finer arts of racing. Yet there exists a considerable gap between the club sailor and the international circuit racer.

Bob Fisher has spent much of his life involved in competitive sailboat racing and with this book has found a way to bridge the gap. His sailing and racing experience in all sorts of boats from dinghies, daysailors and keel boats through catamarans to all sizes of ocean racers combined with his ability and experience as a trained reporter allows him to pinpoint and clarify the major issues.

In *Better Sailing* Bob's text is complemented by extensive illustration showing many of the best ways to tackle a race and the problems that occur in them.

If you can remember only ten per cent of what you read in this book, your sailing and racing skills will be improved and can lead you to new horizons.

INTRODUCTION by Bob Fisher

The standard of racing in all types of boats has increased by leaps and bounds during the past 20 years. During that period, I have been racing dinghies, keelboats, catamarans and offshore yachts at the highest levels. What I have set out to do in *Better Sailing* is to convey much of this experience.

Co-ordinating personal experience with that of the observation of others has produced a definitive idea on what is needed for success. In a book of this size it is not possible to investigate the foibles of each class but the generalizations will almost always hold true. Basic principles of sail trimming, boat handling and tactics will apply across the board; the skill comes in adapting them to the individual class or occasion. It is interesting therefore to note just how many of the world's top sailors are successful in whatever class they race. To them the basic skills have become instinctive and adaptation a matter of course.

The club sailor who intends to improve either to the top of his home fleet, or beyond that to international honours, must realize that practice is of paramount importance. Practice is not just sailing around, but concentrated, calculated hard work endeavouring to put sailing theory to practical use. This book helps to put forward sound theories; only regular practice will improve your sailing. Still the standards are rising and it's all too easy to be left in the fleet and not out with the leaders.

Dinghy Sailing

Handling must be almost instinctive,
an attribute that
comes only with experience under
all types of weather conditions.

To achieve maximum performance from a racing dinghy it is essential to appreciate the individual boat's potential. Each class of dinghy is very different in form and function and each reacts differently. Many general points are relevant to sailing technique but these alone will never take a helmsman and crew to the front of the fleet. To get there it is necessary to raise the boat to produce the ultimate in speed whilst at the same time concentrating on the tactics of the race.

To do this the handling of the boat must be almost instinctive, an attribute that comes only with hours of experience in the dinghy under all types of weather conditions. Helmsman and crew must be physically fit to promote concentration and psychologically they must be assured that their boat is properly prepared and thoroughly reliable. This is where teamwork begins; it is of paramount importance. No one should shirk the responsibilities of boat preparation, for the more man-hours put in on the job the better chances of success are likely to be.

Boat Preparations

A breakdown of gear during a race spells failure. There are occasions when minor breakages can be repaired without too much loss of time and races have been won by boats that have undergone some fairly hefty repairs during a race, but these are the exceptions to the rule. Breakdown should not, and will not, occur in a properly prepared and maintained dinghy.

Hull

No effort should be spared to ensure that the hull is as smooth and fair as possible; that it is down to the minimum weight allowed by the class rules; and that as much weight as possible has been kept out of the ends in order to reduce the radius of gyration.

A Glass Reinforced Plastic (GRP) hull poses perhaps fewer problems than a wooden one although it is easier to correct major faults in a wood-constructed boat. All the gouges in a GRP hull must be filled with gel coat just as soon as they appear. To save considerable time it is worth investing in some broad transparent adhesive tape. The gel coat is knifed into the gouge and allowed to stand slightly proud. The tape is applied over the top of the repair whilst the gel coat material hardens; when it is aired the tape is removed. This leaves little to do but to smooth the repair into the hull. Scratches in the gel coat allow water to penetrate the glass-fibre laminate and this makes the hull heavier.

Wooden hulls will need rather more care as they are more prone to bruising and scratching, but the same principles apply. All gouges and scratches must be filled and the paint

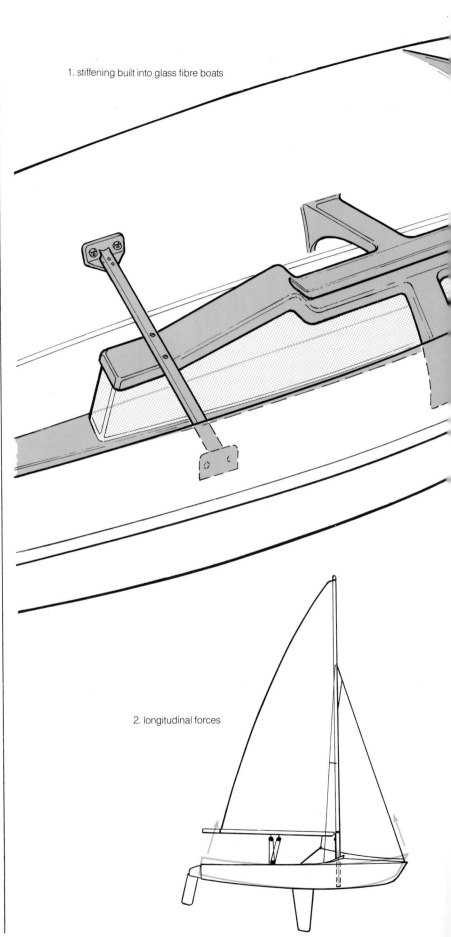

1. stiffening built into glass fibre boats

2. longitudinal forces

DINGHY RACING
Previous pages
Bunching 470s just
after the start. F10120

is going best in clear
undisturbed wind, with
room to accelerate
windward.

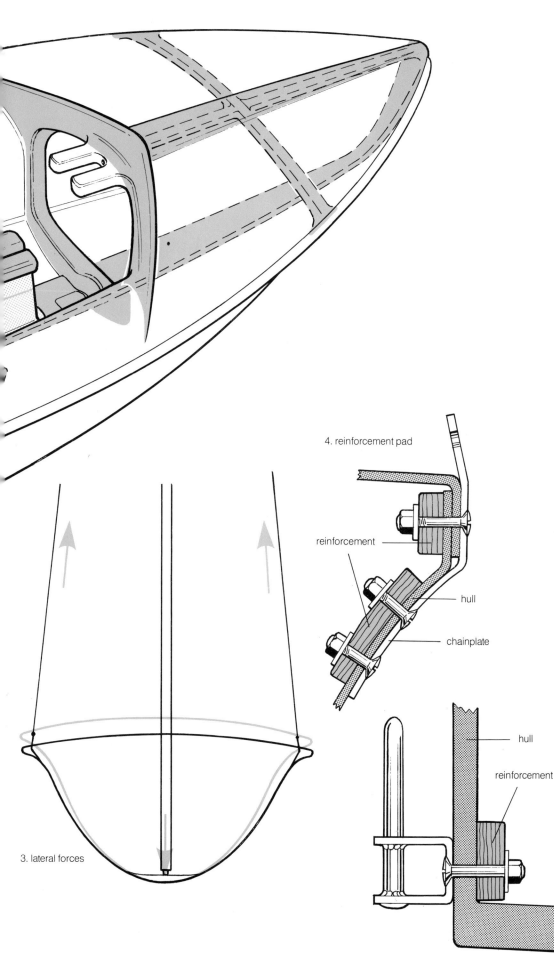

HULL STIFFNESS
Longitudinal forces trans-
mitted by the rigging tend
to bend the hull like a
banana. The forestay,
main sheet and backstay
pull the ends of the boat
upwards, while the mast
pushes down in the
middle. These forces are
opposed by the stiffness of
the keel-line members and
by stiffening under the
foredeck from the top of
the stem back to the mast
partners. The centreboard
casing is often tied into the
partners and thwartship
stiffening, which makes
the hull as hard to bend as
a ruler on edge. It is not
easy to greatly improve on
the longitudinal stiffness
originally built into the hull.
In the lateral plane the
mast pushes down in the
middle while the shrouds
tend to pull the sides of the
hull in and up. Normally
the hull is held stiff against
this sort of bending by
strong wooden or glass
fibre struts running across
the after end of the
foredeck, from the shroud
attachments (chainplates)
to the mast partners. The
natural rigidity of the hull,
deck and thwart also help
to prevent softness.
However where class rules
allow, it is fairly easy to
improve a soft boat in this
lateral plane by adding a
tubular alloy frame which
will tie together the
partners, the chainplates,
the maststep on the keel,
and perhaps also the
centreboard case. Ideally
it should be welded. It is
very important that load
bearing fittings such as
rudder pintles, chainplates
and sheet attachments be
soundly fitted. Usually this
means through-bolting
onto a hardwood pad.
Large washers also help to
prevent crushing which
often causes fittings to
work loose. The bolts
should be cut off close to
the nut and the end
peened over with a
hammer.

4. reinforcement pad

reinforcement

hull

chainplate

3. lateral forces

hull

reinforcement

surface brought back level. In all cases the final treatment for the hull should be a rubbing down with 600 grade wet and dry sandpaper to achieve a matt finish. A nice shiny finish may look good but it creates greater surface tension with the water. It is therefore better to take care of the boat after racing, by washing the hull down with fresh water and drying it off, as the flattening of the surface makes it more porous.

It is essential that the hull is as stiff as possible in all planes. This may require some additions to the structure, where the class rules allow, to assist in maintaining a rigid hull shape when loads of the rig are applied. It is especially important to tie the shroud anchorages to the mast step and partners so that there is no flexing; and also the whole of the midline so that the upward strain of the forestay and mainsheet working against the downward thrust of the mast does not distort the hull. Panel stiffness of the hull itself can be more difficult to improve and in most cases the only resort may be to buy a new hull. To battle on without a stiff dinghy hull is somewhat pointless.

All fittings must be through-bolted to the hull or deck with proper reinforcing backing pads. Too often screwed-on fittings decide to work loose at a time which causes the maximum embarassment. Even when they are through-bolted the fastenings should be checked before each race, particularly if there are strong winds. Rudder fittings are a particular cause of anxiety as they have to take relatively massive strains, and manufacturers appear to have begun to understand that weight in the ends is bad. They are often barely strong enough to stand the strain and then *only* when they are properly bolted to the stern or the rudder head. Once they work loose the fittings are in jeopardy. There is no exception to the rule that, however light the duty of the fitting, screws have a tendency to work loose through vibration – and then the hole becomes enlarged permanently. High-risk points are the shroud and forestay anchorages, mainsheet take-off point or track, and the rudder fittings. Careful cropping of the bolts and peening them over into the nuts is advisable for these items.

One area which is often overlooked is the centreboard slot. Considerable drag can be caused by inefficient keel strips and gasket and there have been many efforts made by leading sailors to find a suitable answer to the problem. It is necessary for the gasket to close off the centreboard slot completely, no matter what the angle of the centreboard. Many materials have been tried, and rejected, over the years. Plain rubber strip overlapping an eighth of an inch in the centre was for a long time considered to be the best, and those who tried to use cotton-reinforced rubber found themselves in trouble as soon as the cotton insert began to shrink.

To take its place came Mylar, a clear plastic film, but this had a tendency to become brittle

GRP REPAIRS
1) Open out the scratch with the sharp edge of a broken hacksaw blade.

2) Use a palette knife to spread gel coat into groove. Cover with transparent sticky tape.

3) When the gel coat is set, rip off the sticky tape. Then sand down with 600 wet and dry paper, used wet with soap in the water.

4) The bottom beautiful.

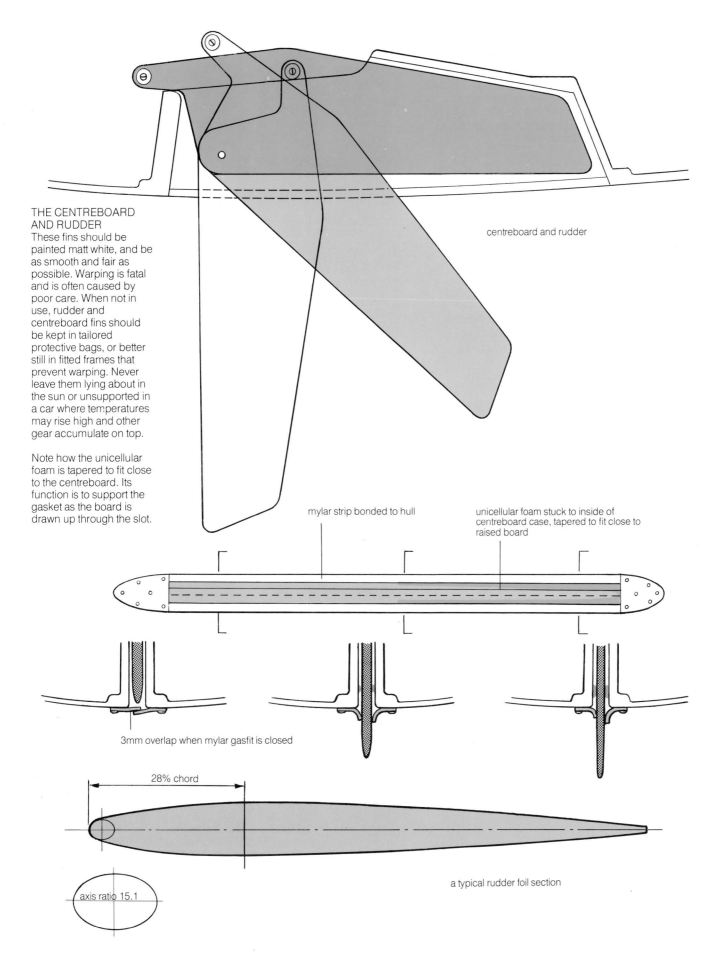

THE CENTREBOARD AND RUDDER

These fins should be painted matt white, and be as smooth and fair as possible. Warping is fatal and is often caused by poor care. When not in use, rudder and centreboard fins should be kept in tailored protective bags, or better still in fitted frames that prevent warping. Never leave them lying about in the sun or unsupported in a car where temperatures may rise high and other gear accumulate on top.

Note how the unicellular foam is tapered to fit close to the centreboard. Its function is to support the gasket as the board is drawn up through the slot.

centreboard and rudder

mylar strip bonded to hull

unicellular foam stuck to inside of centreboard case, tapered to fit close to raised board

3mm overlap when mylar gasfit is closed

28% chord

axis ratio 15.1

a typical rudder foil section

and crack and leave large sections scooping water up into the centreboard trunk. It was still better than the rubber, however, and for certain classes had the advantage that it could be glued in place and did not need a metal or plastic keel strip to keep it from moving.

A sailmaker then came up with another answer and this has proved one of the most successful so far. Taking a strip of 5oz. yarn-tempered Dacron sailcloth and folding it double and using one each side of the centreboard slot with an eight of an inch overlap proved highly effective. It is almost totally resistant to tear but has the disadvantage of losing its stiffness after a time. It does, however, need a capping strip to keep it in place.

The best solution is a combination of either the Mylar or sailcloth with an inside backing of foam rubber towards the back end of the slot. The foam rubber can be stuck to the inside of the centreboard trunking on both sides with a tapering slot between them to allow the centreboard to pass easily between. It provides support for the gasket and in use has shown to prolong the life of a Mylar strip gasket.

Spars

It might seem unnecessary to state that spars should be straight, yet too often they are not. Masts can become bent when trailing if they are not properly supported and, unless the step is directly between the partners, the mast can be bent in use. It is essential to check that the spars are straight and to correct them if they are not. Slight bends can be removed by using the corner of a building, suitably padded with wood, as a vertical 'bench' on which to force a spar straight. One needs to enlist the help of friends and the action has to be gentle; it is far better to move the spar back slowly into line than overdo the correction.

Booms tend to become permanently bent in use through the pull of powerful kicking straps and mainsheets. After one or maybe two corrections they should be discarded and replaced. A boom must be stiff laterally and longitudinally to provide a sound base for the mainsail to set correctly. Bendy booms, which were fashionable in the mid-1960s, no longer have a place in top-class racing.

The alarm points of masts are at shroud attachment, at the spreaders and the halyard sheaves. Wear can occur at both, although with increased use of T-bar terminals on standing rigging there is less chance of failure. Sheave cages and the pulleys therein are always suspect and should be kept well oiled to avoid any seizure, which will lead very quickly to the collapse of the sheave or pin and possible breakage of the halyard. The gooseneck and the kicker and mainsheet take-off points are the crucial points of the boom.

Standing and Running Rigging

This is all too frequently the source of break-down and should be examined regularly. High-risk areas in the standing rigging are at

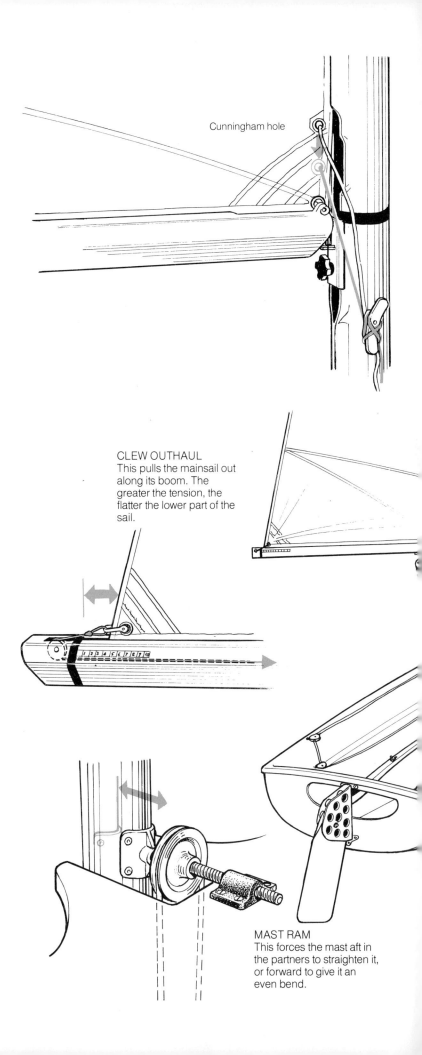

Cunningham hole

CLEW OUTHAUL
This pulls the mainsail out along its boom. The greater the tension, the flatter the lower part of the sail.

MAST RAM
This forces the mast aft in the partners to straighten it, or forward to give it an even bend.

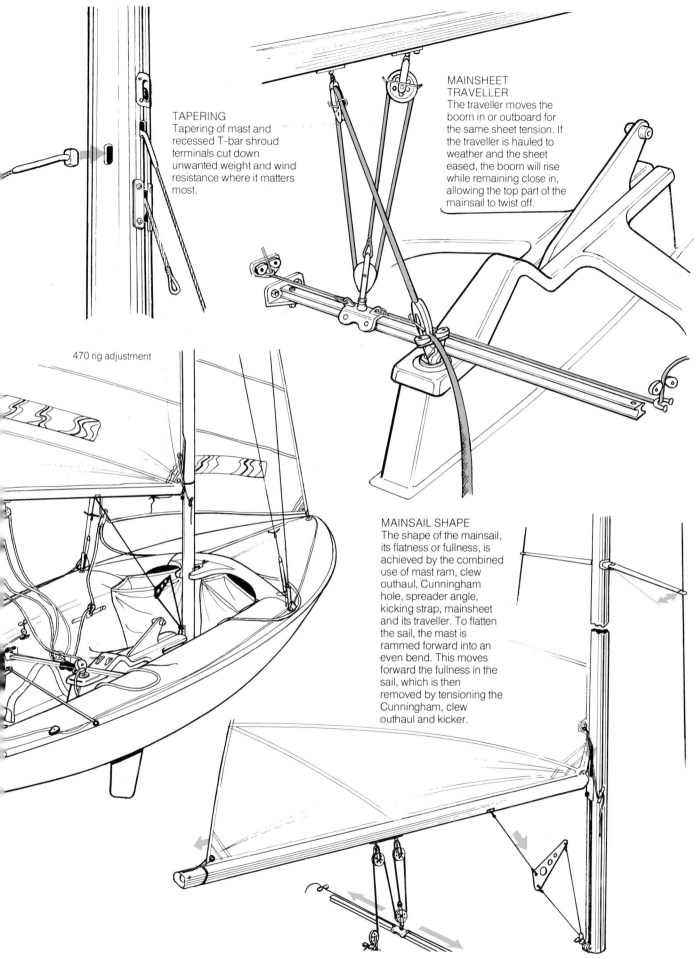

TAPERING
Tapering of mast and recessed T-bar shroud terminals cut down unwanted weight and wind resistance where it matters most.

MAINSHEET TRAVELLER
The traveller moves the boom in or outboard for the same sheet tension. If the traveller is hauled to weather and the sheet eased, the boom will rise while remaining close in, allowing the top part of the mainsail to twist off.

470 rig adjustment

MAINSAIL SHAPE
The shape of the mainsail, its flatness or fullness, is achieved by the combined use of mast ram, clew outhaul, Cunningham hole, spreader angle, kicking strap, mainsheet and its traveller. To flatten the sail, the mast is rammed forward into an even bend. This moves forward the fullness in the sail, which is then removed by tensioning the Cunningham, clew outhaul and kicker.

the terminals and where the shrouds pass over spreaders. Halyards and control lines are most susceptible where they pass over sheaves under load. Much of the problem can be eliminated by using the correct construction wires for the job, and one size larger provides insurance.

Centreboards and Rudder Blades

Perhaps the most overlooked part of any racing dinghy and yet one of the most important factors in success are the two foils. These should be properly sectioned, if the class rules allow, and regularly checked for warping. The matt surface finish should be the best it is possible to attain as these two items provide a large proportion of the wetted surface area of a racing dinghy.

Sailing to Windward

The windward leg, except in planing conditions, provides the greatest opportunity for gain. The degree of success depends on many factors; principally the skill of the helmsman and crew and the wind shifts. The ability to use the maximum power available from the boat whilst manipulating the wind shifts to advantage marks out the really good helmsman. It can only come with experience, but this can be gained faster than most people believe.

Racing is not the only occasion to achieve experience, although the more races he has entered the better a helmsman will be. In all other sports, competitors train for their events to achieve a higher standard of excellence; why not therefore train for sailing by sailing? Training for physical fitness is not enough; it is essential to clock up many hours on the water in order to more readily understand the boat, to be at one with it, so that corrective movements become instinctive and more time can be devoted to the tactical considerations of a race.

If a helmsman is very good he can get into almost any class of dinghy and win. His skills of boat handling and tactics – such as going the fastest way up the correct route – are of far greater importance than individual boat time. The majority of lessons learned by experience are pertinent to all dinghies and the very good dinghy sailor can soon appreciate the idiosyncrasies of tuning of a particular class. Of course he cannot win with thoroughly bad sails, gear or boat, but with all other factors being equal, he will be in with a good chance of success.

There are many individual factors which contribute to boat speed and the winners seem to get most of them right all the time. No-one is perfect and often there are compromises that just have to be made. It is all too easy, for example, at the end of two cascading planing reaches in a Laser, to round the leeward mark without adjusting the mainsail outhaul for the beat. Everyone who has sailed a Laser knows how difficult it is to make this adjustment whilst sailing to windward, since in any weight of wind it is a two-handed

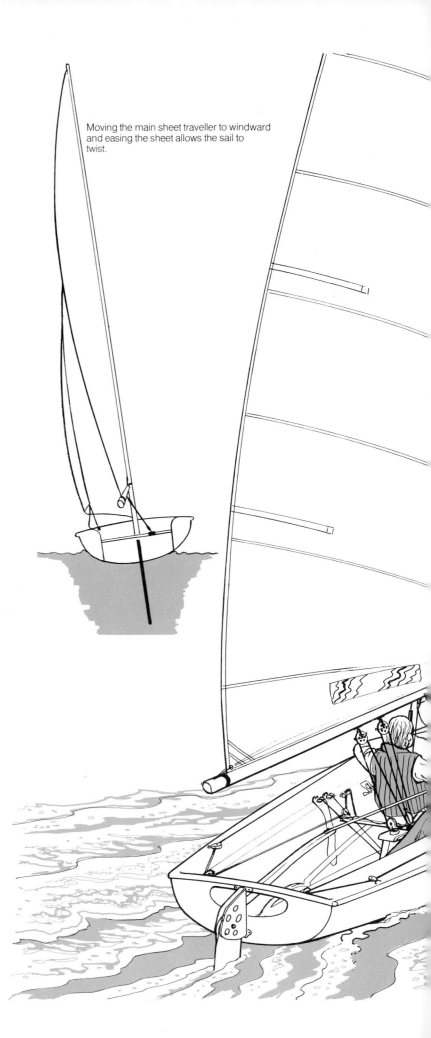

Moving the main sheet traveller to windward and easing the sheet allows the sail to twist.

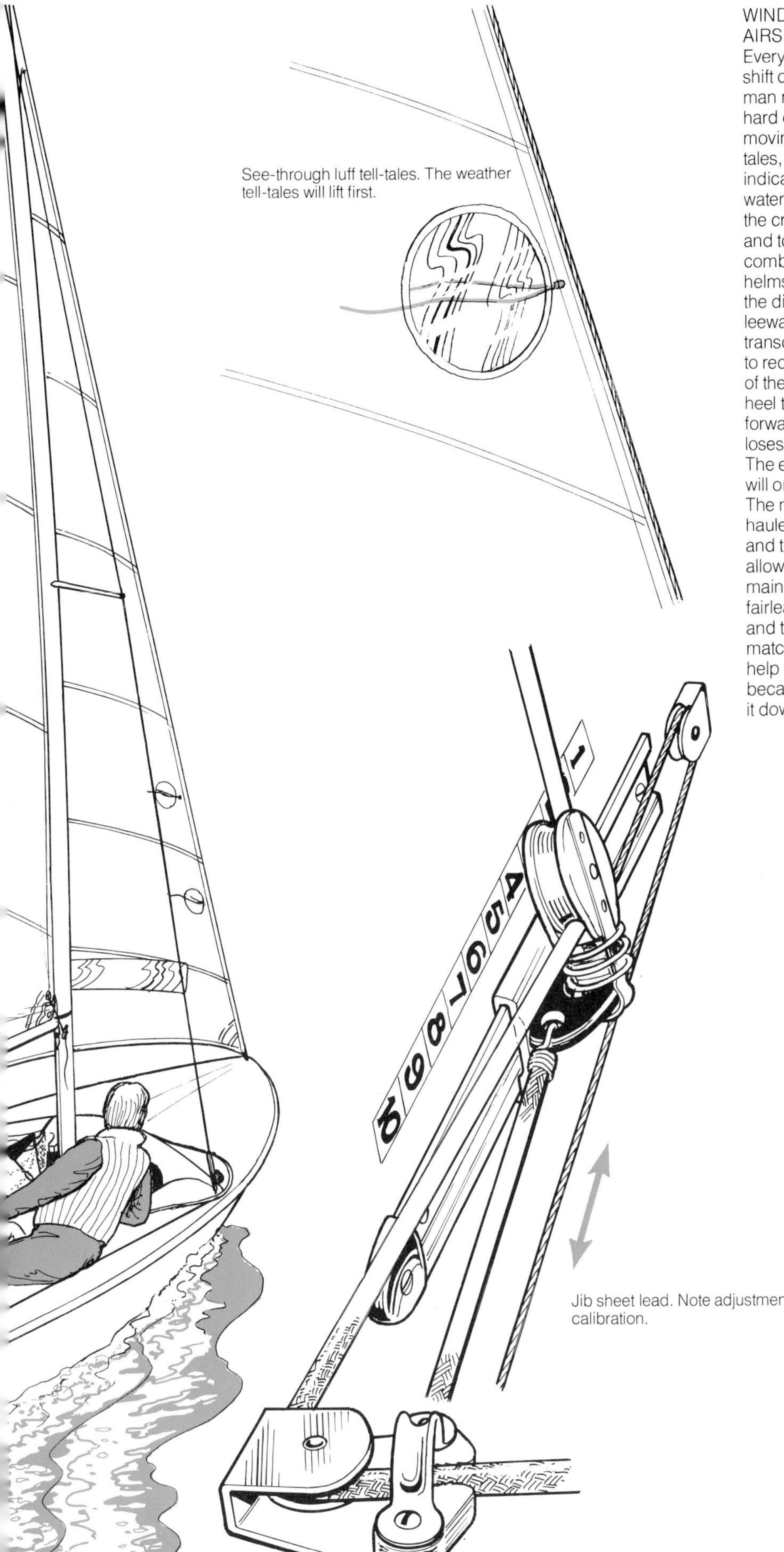

See-through luff tell-tales. The weather tell-tales will lift first.

WINDWARD IN LIGHT AIRS

Every little puff and wind shift counts. The helmsman must concentrate hard on keeping the boat moving, on the jib tell-tales, and on the indications of wind on the water surface. Note that the crew sits well forward and to leeward so that the combined weight of helmsman and crew heels the dinghy slightly to leeward and lifts the transom clear of the water to reduce the wetted area of the bottom. But do not heel the boat and sit so far forward that the rudder loses its grip on the water. The extra helm required will only cause more drag. The mainsheet traveller is hauled up to windward and the sheet eased to allow the upper part of the main to twist off. The jib fairlead is moved inboard and the sheet eased to match. Lightweight sheets help to keep the jib filling because they do not drag it down.

For light airs the sails should be kept flattened. The spreaders are pre-raked slightly aft and the mast ram applied to bend the spar forward. This together with some tension on the Cunningham hole and clew outhaul removes the fullness in the sail. The kicking strap is slack so that the boom may lift a little as the mainsheet is eased to give some twist to the sail. Never pinch the boat in light airs. Keep her moving, keep rudder movement to a minimum, and disturb the boat as little as possible by your own movements.
Sensitive jib trimming is all important as the apparent wind frees with the puffs and heads when it drops. Concentrate on the tell-tales on the luff of the jib, particularly those on the weather side of the sail which will lift first.

Jib sheet lead. Note adjustment and calibration.

operation. Far better then to forget it and sail the boat to its maximum speed rather than to stop, make the adjustment and continue. Maximize the plusses and take advantage of every beneficial situation. Above all do not be psychologically affected by some minute fault with the boat or rig. These do have a habit of providing a nagging worry for the helmsman, but they must be relegated to the back of the mind as quickly as possible. Try to remember that almost every race is won by someone who does not have their boat absolutely right. If this can be done the failure to achieve perfection may cease to affect you.

Where tactics and boat speed conflict is where the experience of the helmsman, and crew, become of the greatest value. It is up to them to decide which factor will produce the greatest possible benefit. In wind shift conditions the criterion is whether the benefit gained from tacking will outweigh the loss made through the action of tacking. It is a variable dependent on the particular class of dinghy. It is far quicker, for example, to tack a 470 with its small non-overlapping jib, than to perform the same manoeuvre with a Flying Dutchman, whose genoa controls the time taken to come about and pick up full way on the new tack. The Flying Dutchman helmsman will therefore often eschew many of the minor shifts from which the 470 skipper will reap benefits. Only practice in the class can help to make the all important decision as to whether or not to tack on a shift of wind.

Light Airs

An ability to sail well in light airs has generally been the prerogative of inland water sailors, simply because they get more practice at it. It is not perhaps the most enjoyable sailing but it requires equally as much skill as racing in heavy weather. The fundamentals are still the same: good sail and boat trim and an appreciation of the wind shifts. The accent shifts somewhat more often so that a preponderance of the time of both helmsman and crew is devoted to tactics rather than the technique of sailing the boat. Handling must be thoroughly natural and instinctive; any loss of rhythm will slow the boat dramatically. Movements of the rudder should be kept to a minimum and small, particularly on flat water. Concentration is all important and stillness of both the helmsman and crew in the boat imperative. Any movement of either person in the boat must be smooth otherwise the sails will shake and a loss of power result.

The flatter the water the higher the dinghy can be pointed towards the wind. The helmsman must sail with the jib just beginning to lift, which is not to say that the front half of the sail is stalled out but rather the weather tell-tale should show slightly broken flows of air across that side of the sail. The leeward tell-tales however will still be streaming properly. With the most delicate of rudder movements the helmsman must constantly explore the possibilities of the wind freeing as

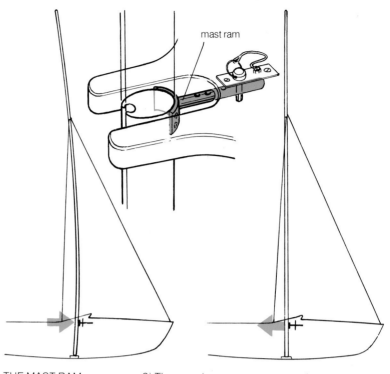

THE MAST RAM
1) This forces the mast forward in the partners, giving it an even bend from heel to mast head. The boom and mainsail also thrust it forward into a bend.

2) The ram also straightens the mast by shoving it back in the partners, against the thrust of the boom. The fore or aft position of the

spreaders will act in concert with the ram as pressure comes on the weather stay.

SPREADER ADJUSTMENT
The spreaders may be adjusted for fore and aft angle with a screw in the mast bracket. Swinging, and limited swing

spreaders do the same job but give less precise control.
The further aft the spreader is set the more it will push the upper part of the mast forward into an even bend.

As only the windward shroud will be under tension the whole mast will tend to twist around the outer end of the spreader. A tightly fitted mast heel counters this twist.

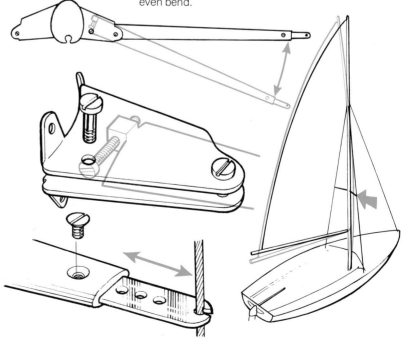

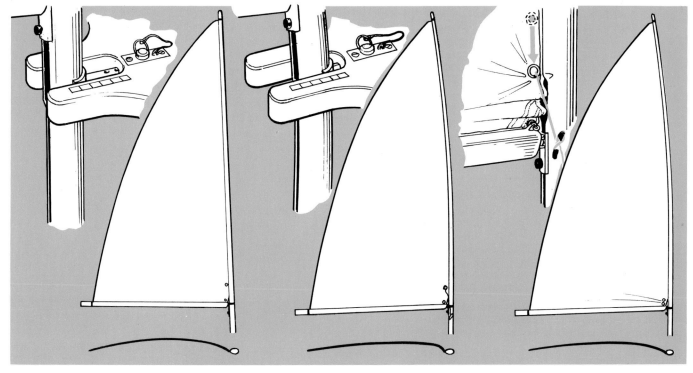

MAINSAIL SHAPE
To flatten the mainsail the mast is bent forward with the mast ram and the spreader angle, which moves forward and draws out the fullness in the body of the sail. This flattening is completed with a downward tension on the Cunningham hole, and with an outward tension on the clew outhaul. These controls must be used together to achieve the optimum airfoil.

Fullness is achieved by straightening the mast, ramming it back in the partners and by pre-setting the spreaders slightly forward. The Cunningham hole tension is released and the clew outhaul adjusted for the wind force. For either a full or a flattened main the adjustments will vary according to the wind speed. With the wind free the kicking strap may be used to keep the main flat if that is required.
Working out the correct adjustments of the rig for various conditions takes patience and care.

AIRFLOW
Flattening the sails allows the wind to flow faster over the surfaces when close hauled. Off the wind more fullness is needed.

However if the water is anything but calm more fullness will be needed to drive the boat through the extra drag. Allowing the sails to twist off in their upper section also speeds the flow of air across the sail surfaces.
Since the apparent wind frees with the gusts and the sheets are tightened, it is important to remember to ease them when the gust dies. Oversheeting the sails and choking the slot between jib and main slows a boat very quickly.

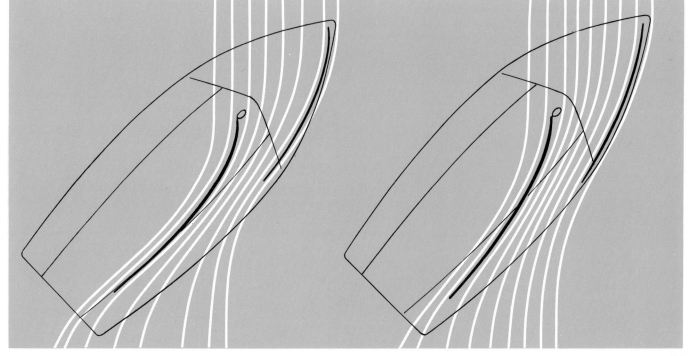

he sails to windward, keeping the jib on a fine line balanced between beginning to stall and being full. The shorter the waterline length of the boat the easier it is to maintain this balance perfectly as it will react faster to small helm movements. The longer dinghy, being heavier, will carry its way through the stalled period much better until the jib is full again.

However steady the wind appears to be it is never constant for long. The greatest changes at sea come when the wind is blowing offshore, and inland there are always obstructions to direct its flow. It is not only in direction that the wind will vary either; strength, too, will alter. Gusts consist of a downward movement of air and always provide a change to the previous direction of the wind. The importance of using each gust in light airs cannot be too heavily stressed; this is where the major gains are made.

In light airs the sails must be trimmed to encourage what little wind there is to flow across them fast. For this reason over-full sails are a disadvantage in light airs as the wind is bent further around them and loses speed. Yet off-wind the fullness is needed to pull the boat along. Therefore the rig must be able to adapt to sails for both purposes. The mast must be made to bend to remove the fullness in the luff of the mainsail, but without the use of the mainsheet.

Setting the rig up for light airs might see the spreaders raked slightly further aft and certainly more mast ram applied to the aft side of the mast at the partners. For this reason it is imperative that the control of the mast at the deck, in the case of a keel-stepped mast, should be positive in both fore and aft directions since it will be more efficient pulled slightly aft from the windward position when the boat is reaching. It must therefore be carefully calibrated so that it can be quickly returned to the optimum position at the start of each leg of the course. On no account should these positions be dogmatically adhered to, they are merely a guide. The helmsman and crew should make the fine adjustments to suit the weather conditions of the time. If, for example, a popple has started to disturb the surface of the water on the second beat, more fullness will be needed in the mainsail to help drive the dinghy through than would have been the case in flat water.

In order to encourage flow across them the sails are allowed to twist off considerably in light airs. Sheet fairleads are brought inboard and the sheet eased; the mainsheet traveller is to windward of the centreline so that the boom is in the midline with the sheet eased. In this way the slot between the two sails is kept equidistant and the effect of wind shear fully accounted for. It will be noted, however, that the angle of attack of the jib and the mainsail remains constant throughout their luff lengths. When the breeze increases because of say, a gust, there is more tension applied to the sheet. The main thing to remember then is to release this extra sheet tension after the

SAILING TO WINDWARD

The helmsman must be constantly searching for shifts in the wind and using them to advantage. The same applies to gusts which allow him to point higher, since the apparent wind moves aft a little. He must watch the surface of the water for signs of what wind is approaching, and he must watch the tell-tales on the luff of the jib, constantly edging up towards the wind until the tell-tale on the weather face of the sail begins to lift. Never stall the sail by coming up clumsily, but keep probing this fine line at the edge of a stall, luffing up until the tell-tale just begins to lift from the sail and then paying off a fraction. When the gusts arrive, make the best of them by heading as high as you can and tightening in the sheets. When it dies anticipate the heading shift in the apparent wind. Pay off and ease the sheets a little as you go to make the most of the reduced power available.

Remember to watch other boats, not only from the tactical view point, but to see what wind they are getting. Notice flags ashore, smoke from chimneys, areas of wind shadow from trees, buildings and ships. Remember the current and the effect of shoreline and shallows on its speed and direction – and yours.

gust has passed. Nothing stops a boat faster than over-sheeted sails as the forward force of the wind acting on the sails is considerably reduced by over-sheeting.

It will pay to sit further forward than normal when going to windward, and running, in light airs. The flatter after sections will then be lifted clear of the water, reducing the wetted surface area, and the hull centre of lateral resistance will be moved forward, encouraging a small amount of weather helm. The exception to this is with pram-bowed boats when moving forward would force the flat transom into the water where it would tend to act as a brake.

When the wind shifts sufficiently to tack in light weather, roll tacking is the only way to go. Done properly roll tacking will speed the boat in very light weather. It is possible to go faster by constantly tacking, using the rolling action to force wind across the sails, than it is to sail normally. Anyone doing so, and it is not too difficult to see when tacking is grossly unnecessary, can be protested under I.Y.R.U. Rule – unfair sailing. The unbeliever in roll tacking need only try to match a non-roll tack alongside a boat that roll tacks to be convinced of its efficiency.

It is not, contrary to general opinion, difficult to do. In a two-man dinghy it requires the coordination of both people in the boat, a coordination that comes with practice. In a single-hander there is no difficulty in judging the exact moment to shift the helmsman's weight. As the tiller is pushed down gently to begin the tack both helmsman and crew move their weight to windward. The crew will probably have moved from the lee side to the windward side and the helmsman leaned out. The sails then scoop up the wind as the boat is headed up and begins to heel to windward; the sails continue to remain full amost until the boat is head to wind. The dinghy then swings round to her new course but is heeling to leeward too much. As the helmsman, and if necessary the crew, move to the new weather side they again force the sails against the wind, creating forced flow across them and help the boat to accelerate on the new tack and assure a commanding position in the fleet.

In light weather therefore very, very little is lost in tacking a dinghy. A skipper should not be reluctant to put in more tacks if he feels the wind has shifted sufficiently and he is sure that he will not lose out simply by the action of the manoeuvre.

Accepting that roll tacking works in light winds and flat water, it can be seen that the same principles should be applied even as the wind increases until the point where it is necessary to rid the rig of some power on the windward legs. Acceleration away from a tack is important in terms of boat speed and tactics. The sheets should never be fully hardened-in until the boat has gathered speed, and some of this hardening-in should occur in sequence with the roll tack.

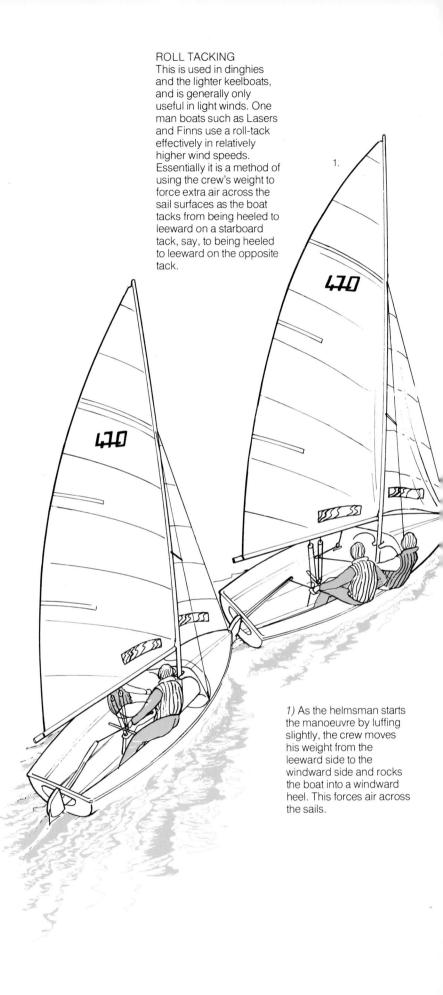

ROLL TACKING
This is used in dinghies and the lighter keelboats, and is generally only useful in light winds. One man boats such as Lasers and Finns use a roll-tack effectively in relatively higher wind speeds. Essentially it is a method of using the crew's weight to force extra air across the sail surfaces as the boat tacks from being heeled to leeward on a starboard tack, say, to being heeled to leeward on the opposite tack.

1) As the helmsman starts the manoeuvre by luffing slightly, the crew moves his weight from the leeward side to the windward side and rocks the boat into a windward heel. This forces air across the sails.

2.

3.

2) The helmsman now luffs up and leans inboard with the crew while remaining on the windward side. This heels the boat well to windward as she tacks, so that she arrives on the new tack already heeled to leeward.

3) Only when the boom has crossed over the centre line and begun to fill on the new tack will the helmsman move across to the new windward side to balance the boat. As his weight shifts the boat will rock back towards the upright and this will increase the wind flow over the sails. The roll-tack greatly reduces the time the sails spend flapping and they will be in the correct positions to take power from this additional draft. Moving the helmsman's weight from leeward to windward at the end of the manoeuvre, and so shifting the angle of heel also causes the apparent wind to move aft

immediately after the tack so that the sails fill more readily.
Done correctly in very light airs the boat will not only maintain most of her way, but can even increase speed.

Medium Airs

As the wind increases, so it is more necessary to make full use of the power available from the rig. Less twist is needed in the sails so the jib fairleads are moved outboard and the mainsheet traveller is eased off to the centre of the track. More sheet tension has to be applied and the shape of the sails altered with halyard tension or use of the Cunningham, and the outhaul of the mainsail. It may be necessary to have previously raked the spreaders slightly further forward and almost certainly the mast ram position will be altered. At first the mast ram should be pulled slightly aft to straighten the mast for slightly fuller sails will give optimum performance in light to moderate winds. As wind increases further the ram should be applied so that it forces the mast forwards at the partners, encouraging a regular bend. This will then help to flatten the sail and thereby reduce the heeling moment as soon as the boat is over-powered. As more mast bend is applied so more Cunningham tension will be needed to maintain a satisfactory equilibrium.

The crew will now be sitting to windward or beginning to use his trapeze. He then is in control of the lateral balance of the boat. He, and the helmsman, will have moved into a regular position, further aft than in the light airs and as close together as possible to reduce the radius of gyration of the boat.

With both the helmsman and the crew sitting out, or the crew out fully on the trapeze where one is fitted, the dinghy is sailing to windward at its fullest. Such trim as is necessary to the sails should aim to develop maximum forward power. Once again it is all too easy to over-sheet the sails, particularly the mainsail. If this is strapped into the centreline its resultant forward component will be very low whilst its lateral component, which heels the boat, will be high.

In these conditions there will be considerable weather helm, and the rudder at any angle to the fore and aft line will act as a brake. The boat may be difficult to control but the remedy is simple. The mainsheet traveller should be positioned further out along the track. Try to balance the boat with the sails so that the feel on the tiller is almost neutral. If you let go of the tiller on a properly trimmed dinghy sailing to windward in moderate airs it should begin to round up into the wind relatively slowly.

In medium breezes there is more to deal with than the shifting wind. Waves begin to appear on the surface of the water and these can have a dramatic effect on the speed of the boat and influence the way the boat is sailed to windward. Most small-boat sailors are aware of the manner in which waves help them downwind; but few are fully aware of the adverse effects of waves upwind, or how to avoid their worst consequences. Waves do not have to be very big to have a significant effect on a racing dinghy; one has only to see top sailors using 3-inch waves downwind to

MEDIUM AND HEAVY AIR SETTINGS
When the wind increases, the rig of a boat going to windward must be altered to accommodate both the weight of the wind and the increase in power needed to get through the waves.

IN MEDIUM AIRS
The crew will move across to the windward side and hook onto the trapeze in medium airs. Both helmsman and crew will move further aft, and they should stay close together to reduce the wind resistance of their own bodies.
The sails will have less twist, achieved by moving the jib fairleads outboard and the mainsheet traveller to about midships, and pulling the sheets tight. The mainsail must be fuller than for light airs, so the mast will be straightened with the mast ram pushing it back and with the spreaders pre-set further forward. The Cunningham will be slack.

HEAVY WINDS

The sails need to be flattened progressively in heavy winds. The jib sheet fairleads are moved aft, which allows the lower part of the sail to be flattened while the leech falls off, reducing the heeling moment. The mainsheet traveller is positioned to give the appropriate slot for the jib setting and the kicker bowsed down tight. The mainsheet controls the amount of twist. The mast is rammed forward again into an even bend and the Cunningham hole pulled down hard to free the leech. The clew outhaul is stretched taught to help flatten the lower part of the sail.

The helmsman and crew will move right aft together, and as far out as possible so that the dinghy is kept vertical on the plane. If the wind increases further the jib is kept drawing and the main feathered to avoid being overpowered.

The centreboard may be lifted slightly to counter excessive weather helm, but only after the mainsheet has been eased as far as is practical to obtain the maximum forward component from the wind.

understand that. The type of dinghy, or more particularly its bow sections, influence the way waves are tackled. The fuller the bows, the greater the angles of alterations in course.

The correct way to tackle waves of any size is to luff up the face of them, keeping the jib just on the point of stalling, until the boat reaches the crest and then bear away down the back. With small waves the sheet tension does not need to be altered. Complication occurs when the waves are very short and the boat is scarcely over one wave before it hits another. In such circumstances a compromise has to be made to avoid meeting a wave in the wrong manner. Yet even this may be impossible, in which case it is important to reduce this occurrence to the minimum. The more readily the lessons of sailing to windward in waves are understood and acted upon, the quicker the upwind leg will be mastered.

Heavy Airs
It is probably easier to steer a dinghy upwind as the breeze freshens because the boat creates more feel on the tiller. But there are many other factors to consider. The major problem is fear, resulting in a tenseness of both helmsman and crew which reduces their effectiveness and leads them to make mistakes. This anxiety is overcome with practice of sailing the boat in heavy winds.

Whenever it is blowing hard it is wise to go out and sail to get accustomed to the way of the boat and how to handle the sails and gear. The waves then are bigger and provide as much of a problem as the stronger wind, but these are far from insurmountable. Confidence in handling the boat is a prerequisite of success and this can be developed with constant practice. The value of this is borne out frequently in major international regattas when there is a heavy-airs race. Almost without exception the leading places are taken by those sailors who hail from an area of predominantly strong winds.

The rig can be adjusted quite easily to cope with the heavier airs by reintroducing twist into the sails and by flattening them. Whereas, in the past, it was always considered necessary to have a special suit of sails for light airs, it is now probably more essential to have a specialist suit for heavy airs. The cut should certainly be less full with the maximum draft further forward, but only slightly so; the cloth weight and construction also differ from light-air sails.

Twist is induced in a different way to that needed for light-air sailing. The jib sheet leads are moved aft which flattens the lower part of the sail and frees the leech, allowing it to fall off. This gives the boat a good pointing angle and keeps the power low down with a low heeling moment. The mainsheet has to be matched to this so that the slot between the two sails remains constant. Considerable tension on the Cunningham will help to free the leech of the mainsheet. The traveller must be further outboard, as far as the slot will

SAILING TO WINDWARD THROUGH WAVES
This is about finding the rhythm of the element.
1) The helmsman luffs up the face of the oncoming wave, as close to the wind as he can get without stalling the jib. This reduces the hull's resistance to the water by presenting the smallest area at the best angle. Usually the larger the waves the sharper the luff required.

2) As soon as the bow begins to break through the crest the helmsman bears away, accelerating across and down the back of the wave. With the acceleration the apparent wind moves forward. In larger or more awkward seas the sheets may have to be eased to get the boat to accelerate after the bow is knocked by the crest, and tightened in again as the apparent wind moves forward.

3) As the next wave approaches the helmsman prepares to luff up into the crest.
The whole secret lies in finding the rhythm of the waves and in anticipating the best action.
Waves are usually composed of two or more patterns coming from slightly different angles. The interaction of these patterns may be complicated by a current or tide running against the wind, or by shallows, all of which make for a shorter, steeper sea. Also a shoreline will bend the waves towards it.

reasonably allow, and the kicking strap must be tight. The sheet will then control the amount of twist in the sail.

At all times the boat must be sailed upright or it will make considerable leeway and be knocked off-course by further gusts. The best technique is to sail with the jib just drawing, and to feather the mainsail sufficiently to keep the mast vertical. On no account should the boat be excessively pinched. That will only result in slowing and lack of response on the tiller. In stronger breezes excessive weather helm may develop. This can be cured by raising the centreboard slightly so that the centre of lateral resistance is moved aft – but first try easing the mainsheet more to get a larger forward component of the force of the sail. Only when this does not cure the weather helm should the centreboard be lifted.

With more pronounced waves there is even greater need to deal with them correctly. To meet the crest of a wave in the right manner it is essential to luff quite sharply to present the best angle of the hull to the moving water, but as soon as the hull begins to break through the crest you must bear away as the boat will accelerate and bring the apparent wind further foward. The pattern of the waves is likely to be regular and a rhythm of luffing up the faces and bearing away through the crests and over the backs must be developed. To the top dinghy sailor this is instinctive.

Because boats move faster in heavy airs and there is no likelihood of 'holes' in the wind, covering to windward is very important. Gains made by wind shifts are amplified in the stronger breezes and you should not allow your closest opponents to get too far away from you, unless it is strikingly obvious that they are fighting the elements unnecessarily.

Reaching

The reaching legs are the most exciting ones in dinghy racing, especially in moderate or strong breezes when planing can be achieved. On these legs the waves can be made to assist the boat's progress, even in the lightest of airs, and proper use of them probably contributes more to success than any other single factor. The technique is similar to that used when going to windward except that everything is reversed. You luff up the backs of the waves and bear away down the faces, using the sheets to make the sails force air across themselves as the boat is borne away. Again, once through the crest and starting the slide down the face of the wave the apparent wind moves ahead, necessitating the trim of the sheet. When climbing up the back of the wave slows the boat, the apparent wind will move aft so that the sails can be eased. Once more it is a rhythmic operation, but the rhythm will be broken slightly as the waves become longer and the wind stronger and when planing down the faces of the waves becomes prolonged even to the point where you are able to plane up the back of the next wave and through the crest.

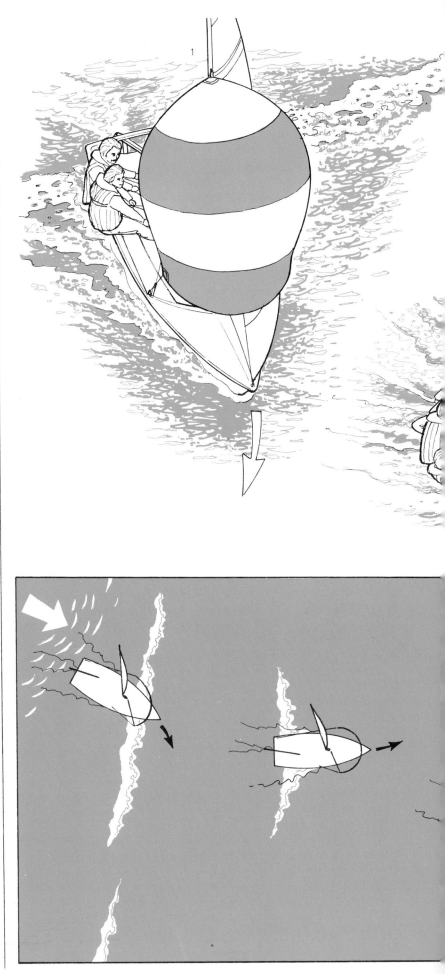

RUNNING WITH THE WAVES

This means using even the smallest wave to get the boat moving faster. The critical point is when with a little wave assistance the boat can be got onto the plane. The sooner you manage it the faster you go.

1) Watch the approaching waves, and watch the surface of the water for gusts.

2) Just before the gust hits luff up, and as the crest of the oncoming wave gets under the stern pump her onto the plane by sharply pulling in the main and spinnaker sheets.

3) Bear away down the face of the wave on the plane. The crew moves aft and the boat *must* be kept upright. The apparent wind moves forward as she accelerates. When the gust dies the helmsman should luff gently to maintain the same apparent wind.
In heavier winds the boat will plane on up the back of the next wave and into the crest. Here she should luff up to power through the extra resistance, and the crew can encourage her over the crest by moving forward. Pump and bear away as necessary at the crest of the wave to re-establish or maintain the plane.

Light Airs

It is of paramount importance to keep the maximum momentum on the boat at all times. To do so will involve constant sail trim and vigilance by helmsman and crew. With the spinnaker set the crewman must sit to windward to get the best view of the sail, and the helmsman will balance him leeward. It will be necessary to set the outboard end of the spinnaker pole lower in these conditions with the aim of keeping the two clews of this sail level. As the wind increases so it should be raised. The spinnaker must be trimmed as far aft as possible on the pole and with the weather luff just beginning to break. Because of this the sail will be constantly on the point of collapse and in light airs it will be difficult to fill again. Therefore the crew must not take his eyes off the spinnaker; the helmsman will steer the optimum course and it is the crew's duty to keep the sail set at all times. The one exception is when the wind comes too far ahead to make the sail set with any efficiency. The crew may then call for the helmsman to bear away from his course or even ask to take the spinnaker down. Very fine dark or contrasting threads set 6 inches in from the luff of a spinnaker make good light-air tell-tales and eliminate the need to let the luffs curl more than is absolutely necessary.

Clear air is important, but no-one should be involved in a luffing match which takes them way off-course and allows other boats to pass to leeward. Early course alteration towards a new, stronger wind will help to prevent this happening. If an overtaking boat is travelling noticeably faster, allow it to pass quickly and try to use the extra wind that it has got to your own advantage.

The mainsail should be as full as is reasonably possible for reaching with both the outhaul and the Cunningham released and the mast rammed back in the partners to keep it as straight as possible. Plenty of kicker tension will be needed except in very light airs when extra fullness can be gained by easing it.

Medium Airs

At a time of marginal planing great gains can be made. Then it is most essential to use the waves to promote planing and also to prolong it. Using the sails to pump the boat up on to a plane is permissable under the I.Y.R.U. rules and every opportunity to do so should be taken. Watch for the gusts of wind darkening the surface of the water and begin to luff slightly to take advantage of the gust just before it hits. Allow the boat to accelerate and use the crest of a wave to bear away on to a plane. As the gust dies the plane can be prolonged by luffing slightly and endeavouring to maintain the same apparent wind.

The sails should be trimmed in sympathy with the boat's movement by the 'pump' action on both the main and spinnaker sheets as the boat is borne away on to the plane.

The need to keep the boat as upright as possible cannot be too highly stressed. The boat

RIG ADJUSTMENT FOR REACHING

1) LIGHT AIRS
require full sails and lightweight sheets so that the sails are not dragged down out of shape. The mast is rammed back in the partners to straighten it, the Cunningham hole is released and the clew outhaul slackened. For very light airs slacken the kicking strap to give extra fullness to the main. The centreboard should be fairly well up, but not so far that the boat slides leeward.

The crew sits to windward to watch the luff of the spinnaker, the helmsman to leeward to balance the crew, and both sit forward to raise the stern and lessen the wetted surface resistance of the hull. The spinnaker clew will hang low in light airs and should be balanced by lowering the end of the spinnaker pole. The sail is trimmed as far aft as possible on the pole with the weather luff just beginning to curl and break. The spinnaker should have some light tell-tale threads about six inches in from the luff. As the luff begins to curl and break, the crew tweaks the sheet sharply which flips the luff back into shape. Immediately after doing this the crew eases the sheet because his tweak will have overtrimmed the sail. The spinnaker luff should be kept continually just on the point of curling.

2) MEDIUM AIRS
A flatter mainsail is required in medium airs and so the kicker is pulled tight. The crew will hook onto the trapeze and the helmsman move across to the weather side to keep the boat as upright as possible.

The end of the spinnaker pole should be raised to follow the clew of the spinnaker. The crew will play the luff as in light airs, watching the tell-tale threads.

3) IN HEAVY AIRS
The mainsail must be flattened further, in heavy airs, by ramming the mast forward into a bend, tightening down on the Cunningham hole, tensioning the clew outhaul and bowsing down the kicker. The mainsheet traveller should be right outboard and the centreboard a third to a half down.

With the boat planing the crew and helmsman will move right aft and get well out to balance the boat. The spinnaker should be set with the clew and the tack about level. A cross-section of the sail would be an even curve with the shoulders of the sail well opened up.

will plane faster and heel will only induce weather helm. The centreboard should be fairly well up for reaching in medium airs, and sufficiently down to provide resistance to leeway and to provide neutral helm.

Heavy Airs
Only practice can produce confidence, which is the essential ingredient for reaching in heavy airs. The crew and helmsman must be confident of their boat and their own ability. It will be less possible to set the spinnaker on close reaches and if there is any doubt it is better to sail high of the course and later bear away to set the spinnaker. That way the gybe can be taken with the spinnaker up and the second reach begun and sailed until it is perhaps necessary to take it down and reach up to the leeward mark.

Steering needs a firm hand but the movements should be smooth and deliberate, never jerky. In these conditions the seas provide much extra forward impetus, but care must be taken when reaching the troughs that the bow does not dig in and the boat take charge of itself. Both helmsman and crew must move aft in heavy airs, yet the crew can encouarge the boat through the crest of the wave and on to the face by moving forward and easing the boat on to the plane.

Gybing
The boat should be upright before a gybe is started; in light weather a slight heel to windward would be appropriate. The helmsman's actions must be deliberate and the crew aware of what is going on. Mostly it is a question of balance. The boat must not be allowed to heel excessively at any time during the gybe or it may take charge, broaching in either direction which in any weight of wind will almost certainly result in a capsize.

Gybe at the moment when the boat is travelling at its fastest – when it is going down the face of the wave. At this time there is least pressure on the sails and it is not difficult for the crew to swing the boom across as the helmsman steers through the gybe. In dinghies the spinnaker pole is best moved after the gybe, except in light airs when it may be possible to remove the pole and gybe and then reset the pole with the sail drawing all the while.

Running
This should present little difficulty except in the choice of the fastest course. In light airs it will be necessary to tack downward at quite a large angle in order to get adequate boat speed. Remember that the wind will continue to shift on the run and use must be made of these shifts. The opposite applies from beating; on the run you gybe when lifted and stay on when headed.

In stronger winds there is a danger of capsizing if running dead before the wind. It is safer to broad reach and therefore a technique of bearing away in the lulls should be developed in these conditions.

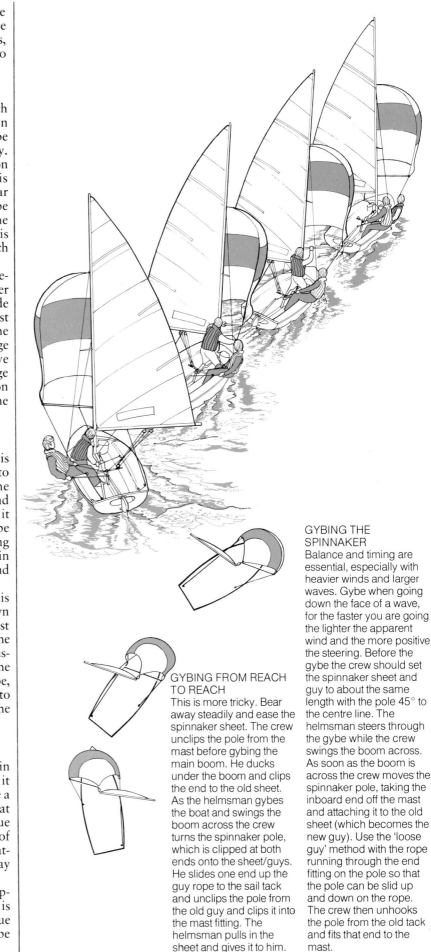

GYBING FROM REACH TO REACH
This is more tricky. Bear away steadily and ease the spinnaker sheet. The crew unclips the pole from the mast before gybing the main boom. He ducks under the boom and clips the end to the old sheet. As the helmsman gybes the boat and swings the boom across the crew turns the spinnaker pole, which is clipped at both ends onto the sheet/guys. He slides one end up the guy rope to the sail tack and unclips the pole from the old guy and clips it into the mast fitting. The helmsman pulls in the sheet and gives it to him.

GYBING THE SPINNAKER
Balance and timing are essential, especially with heavier winds and larger waves. Gybe when going down the face of a wave, for the faster you are going the lighter the apparent wind and the more positive the steering. Before the gybe the crew should set the spinnaker sheet and guy to about the same length with the pole 45° to the centre line. The helmsman steers through the gybe while the crew swings the boom across. As soon as the boom is across the crew moves the spinnaker pole, taking the inboard end off the mast and attaching it to the old sheet (which becomes the new guy). Use the 'loose guy' method with the rope running through the end fitting on the pole so that the pole can be slid up and down on the rope. The crew then unhooks the pole from the old tack and fits that end to the mast.

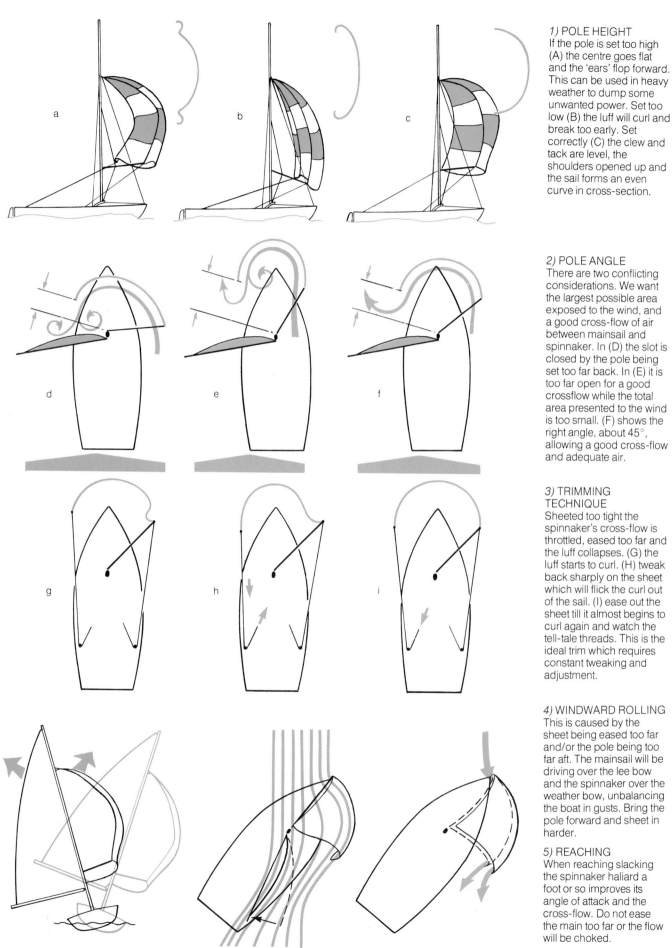

1) POLE HEIGHT
If the pole is set too high (A) the centre goes flat and the 'ears' flop forward. This can be used in heavy weather to dump some unwanted power. Set too low (B) the luff will curl and break too early. Set correctly (C) the clew and tack are level, the shoulders opened up and the sail forms an even curve in cross-section.

2) POLE ANGLE
There are two conflicting considerations. We want the largest possible area exposed to the wind, and a good cross-flow of air between mainsail and spinnaker. In (D) the slot is closed by the pole being set too far back. In (E) it is too far open for a good crossflow while the total area presented to the wind is too small. (F) shows the right angle, about 45°, allowing a good cross-flow and adequate air.

3) TRIMMING TECHNIQUE
Sheeted too tight the spinnaker's cross-flow is throttled, eased too far and the luff collapses. (G) the luff starts to curl. (H) tweak back sharply on the sheet which will flick the curl out of the sail. (I) ease out the sheet till it almost begins to curl again and watch the tell-tale threads. This is the ideal trim which requires constant tweaking and adjustment.

4) WINDWARD ROLLING
This is caused by the sheet being eased too far and/or the pole being too far aft. The mainsail will be driving over the lee bow and the spinnaker over the weather bow, unbalancing the boat in gusts. Bring the pole forward and sheet in harder.

5) REACHING
When reaching slacking the spinnaker haliard a foot or so improves its angle of attack and the cross-flow. Do not ease the main too far or the flow will be choked.

Day Keelboat Sailing

Keelboat racing is the sport for the student of yacht racing.

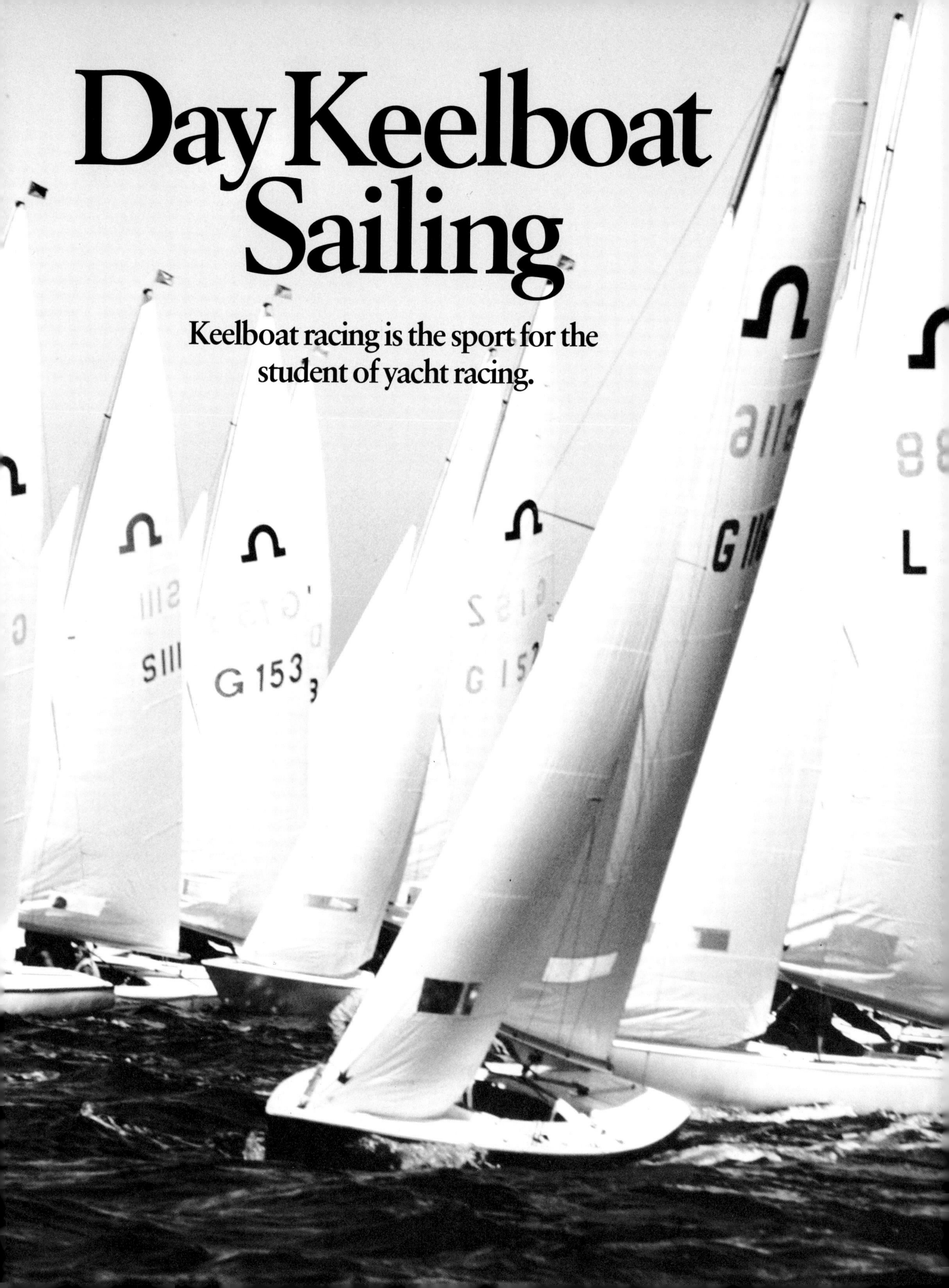

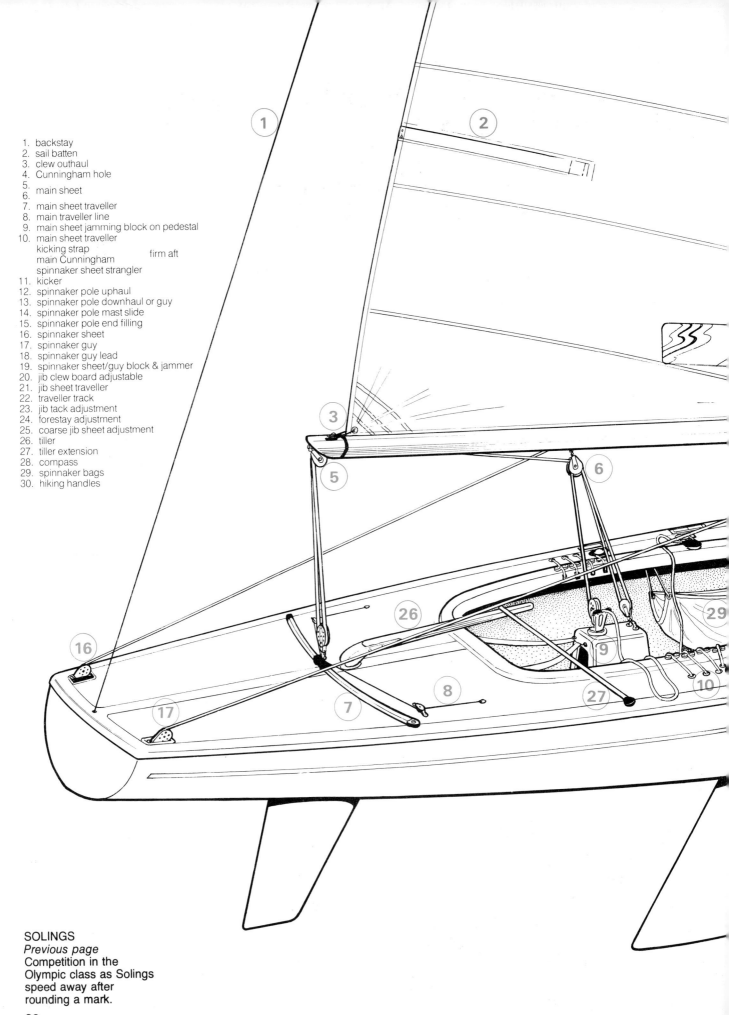

1. backstay
2. sail batten
3. clew outhaul
4. Cunningham hole
5.
6. main sheet
7. main sheet traveller
8. main traveller line
9. main sheet jamming block on pedestal
10. main sheet traveller
    kicking strap   firm aft
    main Cunningham
    spinnaker sheet strangler
11. kicker
12. spinnaker pole uphaul
13. spinnaker pole downhaul or guy
14. spinnaker pole mast slide
15. spinnaker pole end filling
16. spinnaker sheet
17. spinnaker guy
18. spinnaker guy lead
19. spinnaker sheet/guy block & jammer
20. jib clew board adjustable
21. jib sheet traveller
22. traveller track
23. jib tack adjustment
24. forestay adjustment
25. coarse jib sheet adjustment
26. tiller
27. tiller extension
28. compass
29. spinnaker bags
30. hiking handles

SOLINGS
Previous page
Competition in the
Olympic class as Solings
speed away after
rounding a mark.

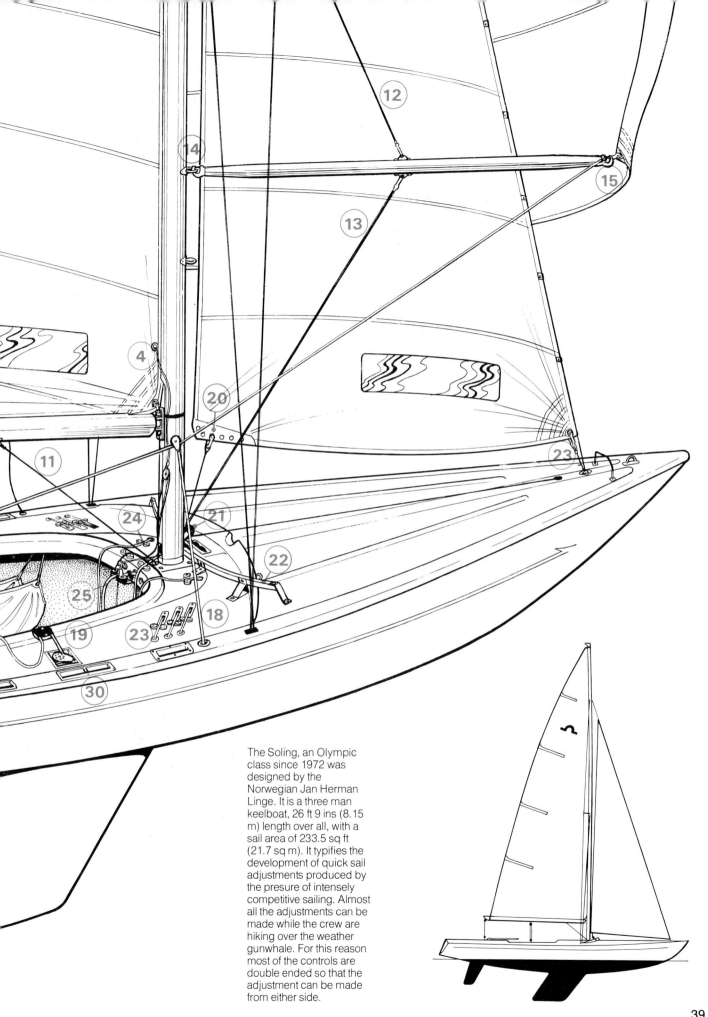

The Soling, an Olympic class since 1972 was designed by the Norwegian Jan Herman Linge. It is a three man keelboat, 26 ft 9 ins (8.15 m) length over all, with a sail area of 233.5 sq ft (21.7 sq m). It typifies the development of quick sail adjustments produced by the presure of intensely competitive sailing. Almost all the adjustments can be made while the crew are hiking over the weather gunwhale. For this reason most of the controls are double ended so that the adjustment can be made from either side.

Almost everything that applies to dinghy racing has relevance in racing keelboats. The degree of importance of the various facets differs, however, and sailors making the change from dinghies to keelboats find this hard to accept at first. None of the funamentals change and there is the security of knowing that only in rare circumstances is it possible to capsize a keelboat. It can, and does, happen even to the best if they are momentarily unwary but in the main it is something which can be put to the back of the mind.

Keelboat racing has its own undoubted appeal, but it must be remembered that to succeed requires as much determination as for dinghy racing – and probably more time. The logistics are greater to say nothing of the physical demands that keelboat racing makes. A keelboat is a larger, heavier craft to transport, to maintain and to tune. Each job takes longer to complete and each one is more exhausting. The gear is that much bigger and the effort required is much increased. Yet it does give more time for considered tactical planning and this most certainly becomes the major factor for success. In particular, one-design keelboat racing is the sport for 'the student of yacht racing'.

Boat speed differences are slight and can be negated by tactical decisions. Yet that is no reason to shirk the effort that is needed in preparing the boat for racing and trying to obtain an extra edge in boat speed. There will come a time when a fraction of a knot extra speed will be necessary to win. It is then that the hard work put in will pay dividends.

Some aspects of keelboat racing will take on even greater importance than they do in dinghy racing, simply because the boats are so alike in speed. Mistakes become more costly because there is less chance to recover. Mark-rounding is an area where several lengths can be gained, and advance plans must be made before reaching every buoy to take advantage of the situation.

The start is all important. It is in dinghy racing, too, but with keelboats an advantage at the start can put a boat in such a position that it can control the entire race. The opposition knows this too, and getting the best start is far more difficult in a top keelboat fleet than in a dinghy.

The acceleration of a keelboat is nowhere like that of a light centreboard and the helmsman must therefore commit himself to his plan of action much earlier than he would in a dinghy. The keelboat, however, does carry its way better and therefore less speed is lost during well-executed manoeuvres. More time is available for sail trim. There should be one man in a three-man boat whose job is constantly to review the sail trim, allowing the skipper to concentrate on steering. To help him he should have tell-tales on both the mainsail and the jib, more than are usually seen. Only by closely examining the flow over the sails can the trimmer have any idea of how close to perfection they are setting.

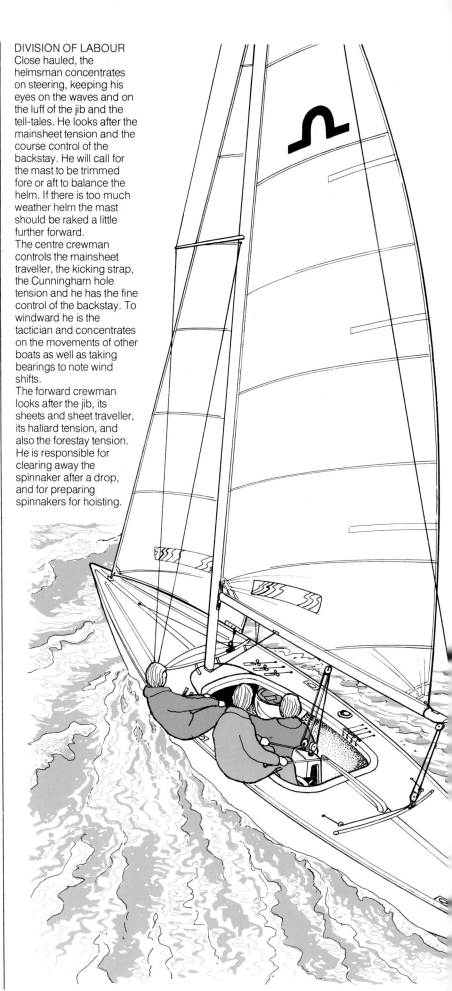

DIVISION OF LABOUR
Close hauled, the helmsman concentrates on steering, keeping his eyes on the waves and on the luff of the jib and the tell-tales. He looks after the mainsheet tension and the course control of the backstay. He will call for the mast to be trimmed fore or aft to balance the helm. If there is too much weather helm the mast should be raked a little further forward.
The centre crewman controls the mainsheet traveller, the kicking strap, the Cunningham hole tension and he has the fine control of the backstay. To windward he is the tactician and concentrates on the movements of other boats as well as taking bearings to note wind shifts.
The forward crewman looks after the jib, its sheets and sheet traveller, its haliard tension, and also the forestay tension. He is responsible for clearing away the spinnaker after a drop, and for preparing spinnakers for hoisting.

REACHING/RUNNING
The helmsman is now responsible for tactics as well as steering. He also hoists the spinnaker and uncleats it when it is dropped.

The centre crewman is responsible for the set of the spinnaker. He controls the sheet and guy and calls for alterations in the height of the pole. On a close reach he may move forward to get a good view of his spinnaker. The forward crewman controls the rake of the mast with the forestay and backstay, and alters the height of the spinnaker pole when asked to do so by the centre crewman.

He also looks after the jib if it is set, and he controls the mainsail with the sheet, mainsheet traveller, kicker, Cunningham and clew outhaul.

A division of labour is an efficient way of racing the boat to its maximum potential. I was made aware of this when, with John Oakley and Mike Fitzpatrick, I began an Olympic campaign late. We had only eight months to the selection trials and this period included the British winter. Each of us was familiar with the Soling and we broke down the various jobs and allotted them in such a way to obtain greatest efficiency. We found that it worked and we made few changes – and very nearly won the Olympic berth. We felt we might have done even better if one of us had not had to sail with a broken wrist.

The way in which we divided the labour is of sufficient importance to be included here. The boat's gear needs to be properly arranged and so we spent two long weekends re-arranging the gear on the boat which was supplied as standard from Paul Elvstrom. The duties of each man changed for various legs of the course although John was always at the helm and the final arbiter of any tactical decision.

Upwind

John concentrated on the steering and would call for any alteration of trim in order to balance the helm. His eyes were for the waves and the luff of the jib but he also had the mainsheet which gave him fine control on the sail trim. The coarser controls other than the backstay were handled by the two crew.

I had the control lines for the mainsheet traveller, kicking strap and Cunningham together with the fine control of the backstay, but I concentrated my efforts on watching the compass bearings and the relative positions of the other boats. I would make the basic tactical decisions and could call for a tack unquestioned.

Mike, the lightest of us, was the forward hand and had controls for the jib traveller, sheet and halyard. He set up the forestay at the start of the windward leg at a predetermined position. He was also in charge of clearing up the spinnaker and its gear after a takedown and preparing a new one ready for a hoist.

KEELBOATS
Previous page
Running keelboats dice for position. They are harder to work than dinghies, but less capricious. They also offer much more scope for tactical forward planning.

TIDAL OR CURRENT BIAS
Tides and currents run less strongly inshore. In this example, with the shore to port, a boat tacking inshore will make more over the ground than a boat tacking up from the committee boat end. Eddies in the tide or current often run counter to the general flow right inshore and behind obstructions such as headlands.

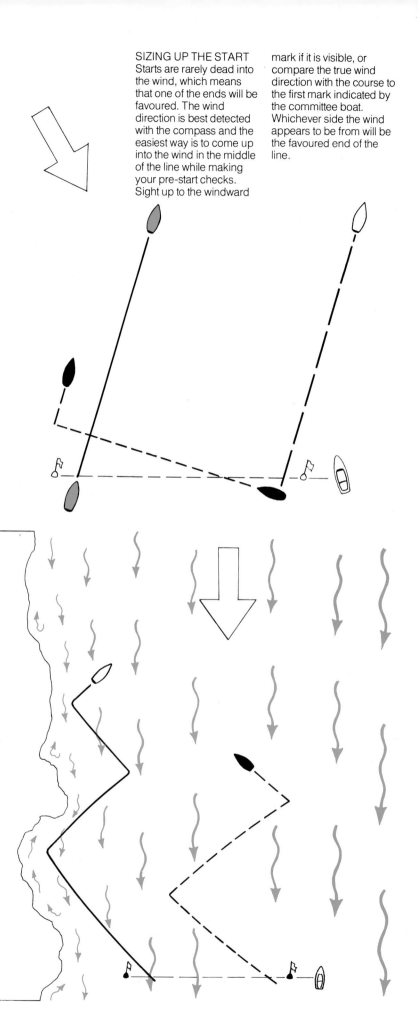

SIZING UP THE START
Starts are rarely dead into the wind, which means that one of the ends will be favoured. The wind direction is best detected with the compass and the easiest way is to come up into the wind in the middle of the line while making your pre-start checks. Sight up to the windward mark if it is visible, or compare the true wind direction with the course to the first mark indicated by the committee boat. Whichever side the wind appears to be from will be the favoured end of the line.

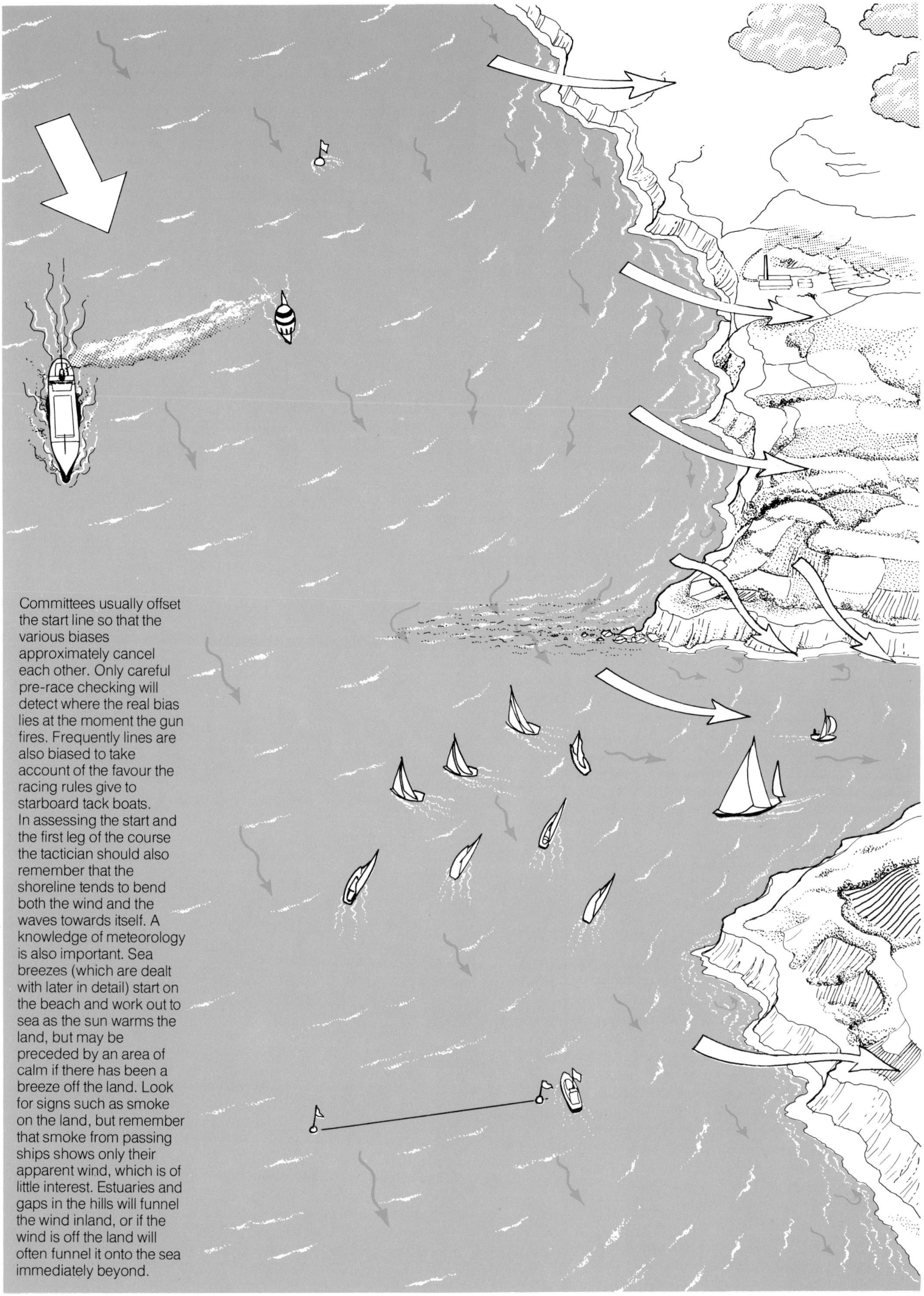

Committees usually offset the start line so that the various biases approximately cancel each other. Only careful pre-race checking will detect where the real bias lies at the moment the gun fires. Frequently lines are also biased to take account of the favour the racing rules give to starboard tack boats. In assessing the start and the first leg of the course the tactician should also remember that the shoreline tends to bend both the wind and the waves towards itself. A knowledge of meteorology is also important. Sea breezes (which are dealt with later in detail) start on the beach and work out to sea as the sun warms the land, but may be preceded by an area of calm if there has been a breeze off the land. Look for signs such as smoke on the land, but remember that smoke from passing ships shows only their apparent wind, which is of little interest. Estuaries and gaps in the hills will funnel the wind inland, or if the wind is off the land will often funnel it onto the sea immediately beyond.

Downwind

John now took on all tactical decisions and this, with the steering, was his share of the duties. The spinnaker halyard was led aft to his cockpit and he hoisted it and was responsible for uncleating it on the drop.

I had the spinnaker sheets and concentrated on that sail alone. I was not allowed to take my eyes off it at any time, except when approaching a mark when I would call for the takedown. I moved forward in the boat to get a better view of the spinnaker on the reaches but returned to the middle of the boat for the runs. I would get the spinnaker out of its canvas locker for the hoist and bundle it away fast on the drop.

Mike attended to the remaining jobs. He altered the position of the mast with forestay and backstay and was responsible for the spinnaker pole height when an alteration was called by me. He dropped and hoisted the jib as required and trimmed the mainsail with the fine controls, taking over the middleman role.

This arrangement worked efficiently and if ever we have another attempt in this class we would distribute the tasks in the same manner. Because the arrangement meant that we had to communicate constantly with each other we were the noisiest boat in the fleet.

Starting

Where the speed of the competing boats is close, as it is in keelboat racing, starting takes on added importance. One foot ahead at a close start can soon be two lengths clear of the fleet. The start requires the greatest concentration from all members of the crew. With the boats in close proximity the slightest mistake can turn a 1 foot lead into a 1 foot deficit, and that can rapidly become back position in the fleet. It is of paramount importance that the boat should be sailed from the start at maximum speed.

Many factors decide where one should start on any line. Rarely is a starting line set dead square to the wind so the resultant bias is a major consideration. Another is if one side of the course is favoured, and as often as not this will be the opposite to the favoured end of the line. In an oscillating wind the time of the start will be another factor that has to be considered and the tide can provide a fourth. All are subject to change with only the tide truly predictable in advance. It makes choice of a starting place on the line rather like a mobile game of chess – except that wherever you choose to go so will a lot of other top sailors. They too know exactly where the best place is and will be out to capture the pole position at the start. Because of this it is sometimes better to opt for a different position, a slight distance away from the bunch. Each of the top crews is likely to affect the other and the entire bunch sail quite slowly at first. From a judicious distance it is possible to get out into the clear air quickly and establish a lead over the boats that started from the most favourable position.

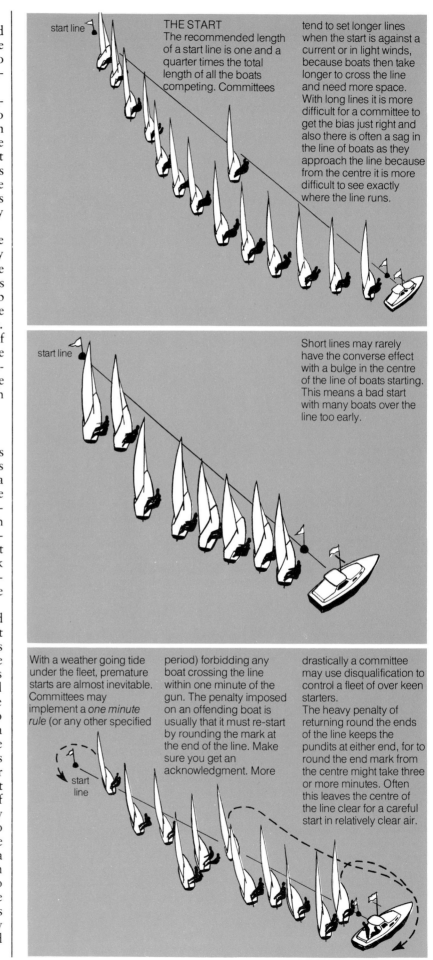

THE START
The recommended length of a start line is one and a quarter times the total length of all the boats competing. Committees tend to set longer lines when the start is against a current or in light winds, because boats then take longer to cross the line and need more space. With long lines it is more difficult for a committee to get the bias just right and also there is often a sag in the line of boats as they approach the line because from the centre it is more difficult to see exactly where the line runs.

Short lines may rarely have the converse effect with a bulge in the centre of the line of boats starting. This means a bad start with many boats over the line too early.

With a weather going tide under the fleet, premature starts are almost inevitable. Committees may implement a *one minute rule* (or any other specified period) forbidding any boat crossing the line within one minute of the gun. The penalty imposed on an offending boat is usually that it must re-start by rounding the mark at the end of the line. Make sure you get an acknowledgment. More drastically a committee may use disqualification to control a fleet of over keen starters.

The heavy penalty of returning round the ends of the line keeps the pundits at either end, for to round the end mark from the centre might take three or more minutes. Often this leaves the centre of the line clear for a careful start in relatively clear air.

COURSES

The modern Olympic course (left) consists of a start and finish into wind, the two lines normally being outside the course to prevent congestion when more than one race is held. The windward mark is rounded on starboard tack, followed by a broad reach to the second mark where the fleet gybes onto another broad reach. The second windward leg is followed by a dead run down to the third mark, and the final leg is to windward. If the legs are short the number of laps may be increased. The triangular course (right) has the start and finish line between the committee boat and the pin-end/third mark.

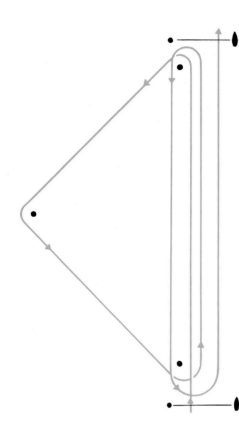

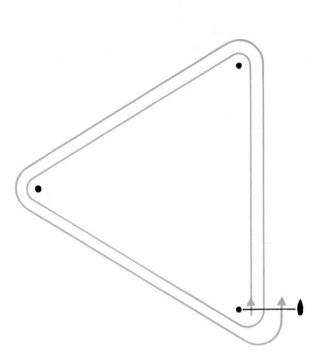

GATE STARTS

The Pathfinder E may take three minutes to open the gate B to G when there is a large fleet. He is usually selected from the bottom end of the top ten per cent of a previous race. He should sail as fast and high as possible, for he is racing from the moment the gate begins to open. The committee boat A and the starting mark B are at the port end of the line. The Pathfinder E is preceded by the guard launch F about 30 metres ahead and some 10 metres to leeward for dinghies. He is followed by the Gate Launch D at three boat lengths. Competitors may not pass between the committee boat and the start mark, or between the pathfinder, the gate launch or the guard boat.

To start you sail as close as possible under the stern of the Gate Launch D. The Pathfinder turns at the limit of the starting line G and also passes astern of the Gate Launch. Gate starts are less hectic and give indifferent starters a more even chance with the experts. They also make pre-planned strategy more likely to prove useful and there is much less likelihood of recalls and protests. On the other hand if conditions are fluky or very rough the precise sequence of events may go awry.

KEY

A Committee Boat
B Start Mark
C Other competitors
D Gate Launch
E Pathfinder
F Guard Launch
G Limit of Starting Line

The introduction of the rule stipulating a return around-the-ends of the line in the event of a premature start has put a premium for the aggressive starter on being near the committee vessel or the pin end buoy. It can take as long as five minutes to sail the length of a championship start line; from the mid-point it would take about three minutes to sail round the end and get back in the race. That makes any starting error fatal. It has had the effect of keeping the pundits away from the middle of the line and offers the careful starter an opportunity to make a pitch for the clear air he can get in the centre, safe in the knowledge that he can outsail the lesser helmsmen starting from there.

Contrary to general opinion there is not a bulge in the mid-field as has so often be said. My own experience as both a competitor and an observer at many world championships and Olympic regattas is that the converse is true – there is a sag of around three boat-lengths in the middle of the line.

Time must be found to plan the start, and that involves getting out to the course early, sailing hard at the edges of the course as well as up the middle. A plot of the wind oscillation should be made by checking its direction every three minutes. It is also important to note the headings and their variations on each tack, and to write this information down with a grease or chinagraph pencil where it can be seen by the helmsman and tactician, and as close to the compass as possible. The best and worst headings before the start will give an immediate indication on how the boat is sailing relative to the course at any time during the first or subsequent beats and the knowledge of a shift at any time when the leeward mark has just been rounded. The skipper can harden up around the mark and see if he is on a lift or whether he should tack immediately.

The plot of wind oscillation should enable a prediction to be made as to which will be the favoured tack at the start and how long the wind will last before it shifts direction. This can be done because the oscillations are generally regular in their timing and thus produce a regular pattern. Do not be fooled by a regular wind bend on the course. These do occur and have no connection with the wind shifts. If they are relatively permanent they should be exploited to the full on the first beat, and the only way that this can be done is to have foreknowledge defined from being on the course early. At least one hour before the start should be spent in order to get maximum benefit from such a reconnaissance. By then, too, the entire crew should be well into the rhythm of sailing the boat and should be able to drive it at maximum speed from the starting gun.

A helmsman cannot both look at a watch and steer the boat properly at a start, either in a keelboat or a dinghy. Keeping him apraised of the time should be the job of one of the crew, preferably the one nearest to him. A stopwatch with five 1-minute segments

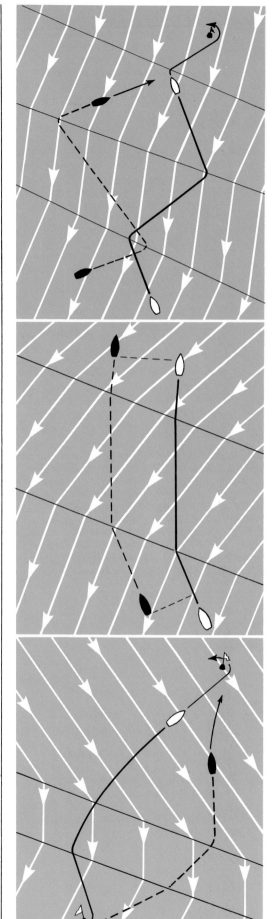

WIND SHIFTS
Winds are rarely truly constant. Shifts come in varying sizes, due to various causes. Forecasting, detecting and using these will win or loose races.

RHYTHMIC WIND SHIFTS
(left top) may occur in any steady wind and are often only detectable with a compass. The period of the rhythm may be only a minute, or may be more than fifteen minutes. The difference from the apparent mean wind may one or two degrees, or ten degrees. Much longer periods, or much larger shifts will be caused by more obvious factors such as a sea breeze or thunder clouds. The shifts caused by gusty unstable conditions such as commonly follow a cold front are not predictable in the same way. To establish a shift pattern arrive early on course. Sail to windward and watch the compass, noting the times and directions of shifts of more than a few degrees. Check for sea breeze and cloud effects. Be sure you know beforehand the general meteorological forecast. Using rhythmic wind shifts will get you round the course fastest. The rule is to tack when the shift heads, and stand on if it frees. But don't tack too soon. Make sure you have got a lasting shift by examining the water to windward. Watch out for a STEADY WIND SHIFT *(left centre)*. This is useful if you anticipated it and have placed yourself to windward. Other boats can only lose by it. The rule here is to sail towards the expected shift. However if you expect a really LARGE WIND SHIFT *(left bottom),* due for example to a cold front passing, so that the windward leg becomes a reach, then it may pay to keep to leeward. Correct forecasting, timing and orientation on the course are the key.

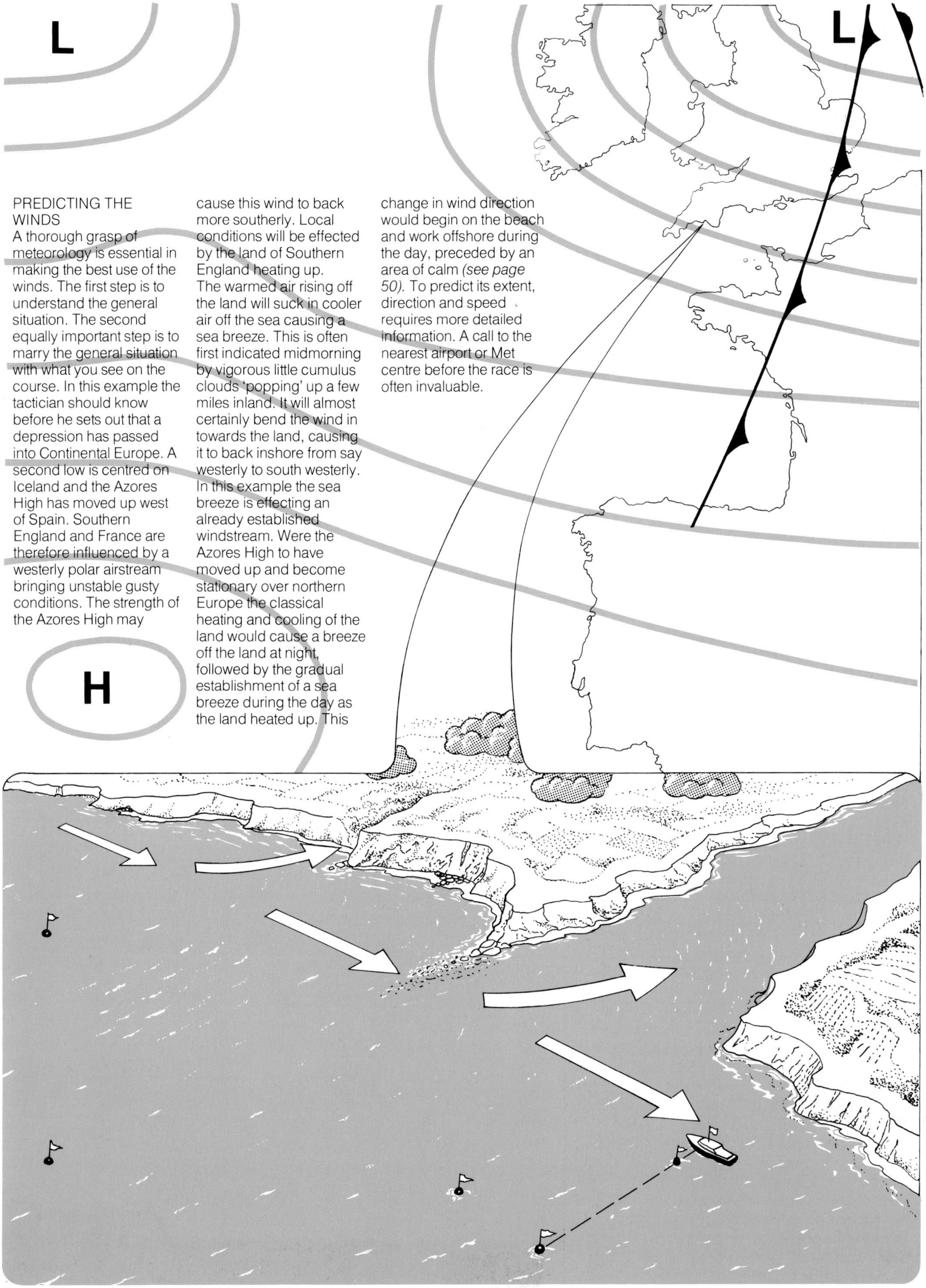

L

L

H

PREDICTING THE WINDS

A thorough grasp of meteorology is essential in making the best use of the winds. The first step is to understand the general situation. The second equally important step is to marry the general situation with what you see on the course. In this example the tactician should know before he sets out that a depression has passed into Continental Europe. A second low is centred on Iceland and the Azores High has moved up west of Spain. Southern England and France are therefore influenced by a westerly polar airstream bringing unstable gusty conditions. The strength of the Azores High may cause this wind to back more southerly. Local conditions will be effected by the land of Southern England heating up. The warmed air rising off the land will suck in cooler air off the sea causing a sea breeze. This is often first indicated midmorning by vigorous little cumulus clouds 'popping' up a few miles inland. It will almost certainly bend the wind in towards the land, causing it to back inshore from say westerly to south westerly. In this example the sea breeze is effecting an already established windstream. Were the Azores High to have moved up and become stationary over northern Europe the classical heating and cooling of the land would cause a breeze off the land at night, followed by the gradual establishment of a sea breeze during the day as the land heated up. This change in wind direction would begin on the beach and work offshore during the day, preceded by an area of calm (see page 50). To predict its extent, direction and speed requires more detailed information. A call to the nearest airport or Met centre before the race is often invaluable.

marked on the dial and a sweep second hand is useful; but even better is a reverse digital counter that gives the time left to the starting gun, which makes the tactician's countdown to the skipper a very simple process. Many more of this type of timer will appear in racing in the near future.

The tactician watches the committee boat closely for the starting signals and should know which flag or shape refers to this class and which for the class starting immediately beforehand. He will then be able to get a precise start to the countdown on the 10-minute gun; and he will be able to check this out at the 5-minute mark. During that period he should give 1-minute time-checks to the helmsman. After the 5-minute gun the countdown should be in quarters of a minute down to 1¼ minutes to go. Then the count is in 5-second intervals until the last 15 seconds when the countdown is every second. There should be no need for the tactician to shout this information to the skipper; if he does so the boats nearby will be able to use his timing and their crews will have one less job to do.

During the final 5 minutes before the start the helmsman will be manoeuvring the boat into the position he has chosen to start from, making sure that he keeps a space to leeward of the boat so that he can bear off to get some initial speed. His choice will have been dictated by the wind conditions and if he is going for the best position on the line he will have to display very positive attitudes as others will be trying to do the same. There is no use trying to start a keelboat by hovering close to the line without much way-on and the sails flapping. It takes some time for a keelboat to get to speed, and boats coming from behind with way-on have a huge advantage over a boat trying to start in that manner. You must cross the line at full speed for your starting tactics to have any value whatsoever.

The Windward Leg
Immediately after the start the whole crew must give all their effort to getting the best possible speed out of the boat. It will almost certainly be impossible to tack, unless you are the weather-most boat. But if you are the weather-most boat you tack as soon as possible because you have probably started at the right-hand end of the line because the right-hand side of the course is forward. The aim is to get into clear air going the way that is best. After a few minutes, when the fleet has spread, you can consider tacking. It may mean ducking one or two sterns, but if the other side of the course is the paying one then that should be the main consideration.

More often than not the starting line is laid with a bias towards the port end. With the entire fleet starting on starboard tack this does, theoretically, balance things up. The boat at the committee-boat end can tack earliest whilst the craft at the pin end have a slight territorial gain. If these are the conditions at the start, and there is not an over-

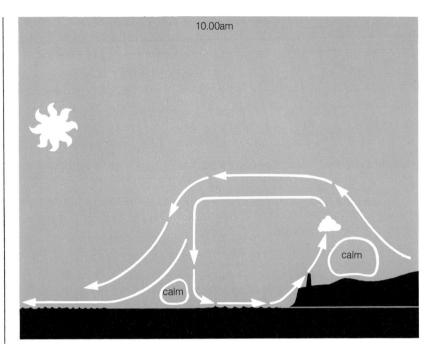

SEA BREEZES
Sea breezes can occur on almost any coast, but they are most marked where the inland areas are flat and the coast south facing (North facing in the Southern Hemisphere). They do not travel well over hills, but funnel through the gaps such as estuaries and valleys. They depend on the land heating the air immediately above it, which then rises. Even thin high cloud cover will prevent this, as will a temperature inversion which stops the warmed air rising through a usually invisible barrier. Hazy air to a few thousand feet overland, topped by blue

skies, often indicates an inversion. Where there is no established gradient wind, sea breezes begin with warmed air rising over the land adjacent to the coast and forming small vigorous cumulus clouds. These gradually build up until the land often looks covered in cloud while the skies are clear over the sea. The night breeze caused by cool air moving off the land will be pushed up over these mid-morning thermals and will reappear as falling cooler air out to sea. As the system develops the thermal clouds will suck in more air from further out to sea, which is replaced by

the cool air circulating over the top of the system and descending out at sea. An area of calm gradually moves offshore. This marks where the cool falling air spreads and divides, part of it continuing out to sea and part being sucked back into the system. On a good day the sea breeze may extend ten miles out to sea and build up to force four Beaufort. It will commonly switch off in mid-afternoon, sometimes suddenly. Where a sea breeze is combined with a gradient wind, both tend to shift in the same direction as the sun during the day.

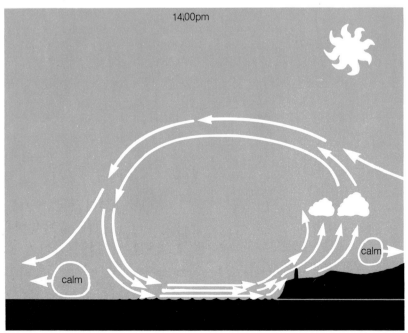

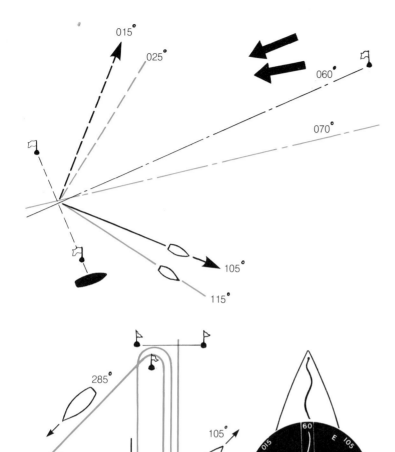

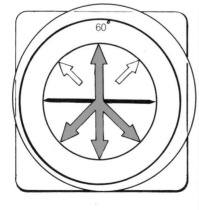

CALCULATING YOUR COURSE

Any shift in the wind·from dead ahead on the windward leg will alter not only the favoured tack on the windward leg, but also when, and on which gybe the spinnaker can be set. First you must establish just how close your boat will point to windward. In the *top* example the boat will sail 45° from the true wind, therefore the port and starboard tacks will be 90° apart. With the true wind bearing 060° the boat will sail 015° on the starboard tack and 105° on the port tack. A 10° veering in the wind will give you a starboard tack heading of 025°, and 115° on port tack. There are several types of course calculator for sale, two are shown *bottom left* and *right*. The simpler calculator, left, if set to the wind direction, will show the theoretical tacking angles to the windward mark, and of the start line. On a note board, *(centre left)*, or on the deck write down the start line bias and the actual direction to the windward mark, as well as the courses from mark to mark, and the current. On the more elaborate course calculator, *right*, the bearing to the windward mark and the true wind can be set up on the two revolving discs, and the tacking angles noted on the base board. This calculator also gives the gybe on the downwind legs.

A tactical grid compass can do all this as well as the needle indicating whether you are sailing into a lifting or heading shift. However some crews find them complicated and too easy to misread in the heat of a close race.

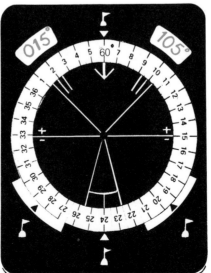

whelming need to go to the right-hand side of the course, I would go for the pin start every time. With the buoy there you have something to aim for and it does make arriving on the line at full speed much easier. Make the intention known to the opposition by early taking up a position that will ensure that nobody can creep up to leeward and luff, or peel down on top from windward. As long as a boat is moving forward with good steerage way, its helmsman can control the situation. Once clear of the line he hopes he has sufficient speed to pull fractionally ahead of the boat immediately to windward to obtain a lee bow-position and force it to tack. Then the pin-end starter can accept a few degrees of freeing in the wind without worry, as long as it is not a permanent shift or one that is going to continue to veer.

The pin-end starter hopes for a header after he has worked out ahead of the bunch immediately to windward. When the header comes he will have to sail into it for some time as he will be the first to encounter it, and for his tack to have maximum effect he needs the majority of the fleet to be similarly affected. When he sees that he can comfortably cross the nearby boats it is time to tack, and with luck the rest of the fleet will go by astern.

Sail trim is desperately important for the crew trying to get the most useable power from the rig. Just how they trim depends on wind strength and sea conditions. The flatter the sea, the flatter the sails can be trimmed and the higher the boat pointed effectively to windward. In lumpy seas the boat will need full sails to give it the power to force it through the waves; it cannot therefore be pointed as high to windward. The trim may vary on each tack as it is unlikely that the waves will come immediately down wind. Old winds and existing currents will affect the wave pattern so that on one tack the sails may be flatter than on the other because the waves are more oblique to the boat.

All other things being equal, the current flow can dictate which way a boat goes up the windward leg. If there is an adverse current every effort should be made to go where it has the least effect. If it is a favourable current then the maximum use must be made of it where it runs strongest. These are facts that can be established before the race begins. Charts of the area of the course together with all known sources of tidal constants can often be supplemented with knowledge acquired locally. Professional seamen and fishermen of the area are useful sources, but it is wise to check their folklore against large-scale local charts.

Light Airs

Sailing to windward in light airs needs intense concentration by the helmsman on the luff of the jib. The seas will be relatively flat but by no means, in the lightest of airs, should the boat be pointed exceptionally high. It pays to free off slightly and thereby increase the

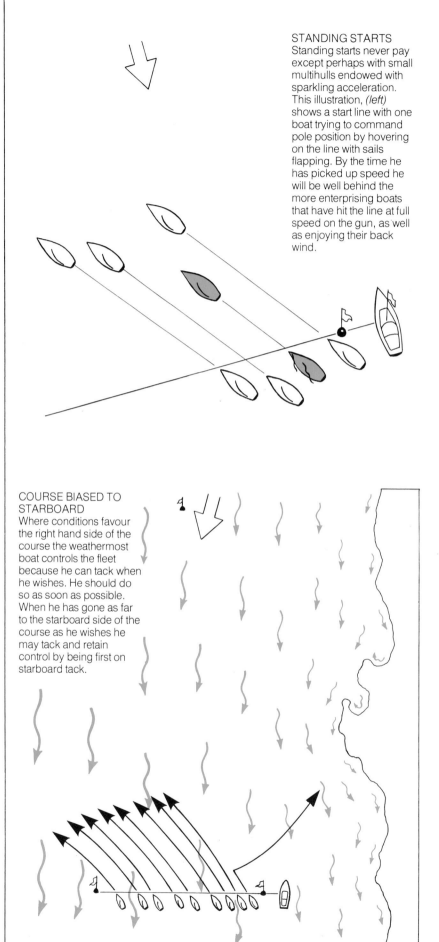

STANDING STARTS
Standing starts never pay except perhaps with small multihulls endowed with sparkling acceleration. This illustration, *(left)* shows a start line with one boat trying to command pole position by hovering on the line with sails flapping. By the time he has picked up speed he will be well behind the more enterprising boats that have hit the line at full speed on the gun, as well as enjoying their back wind.

COURSE BIASED TO STARBOARD
Where conditions favour the right hand side of the course the weathermost boat controls the fleet because he can tack when he wishes. He should do so as soon as possible. When he has gone as far to the starboard side of the course as he wishes he may tack and retain control by being first on starboard tack.

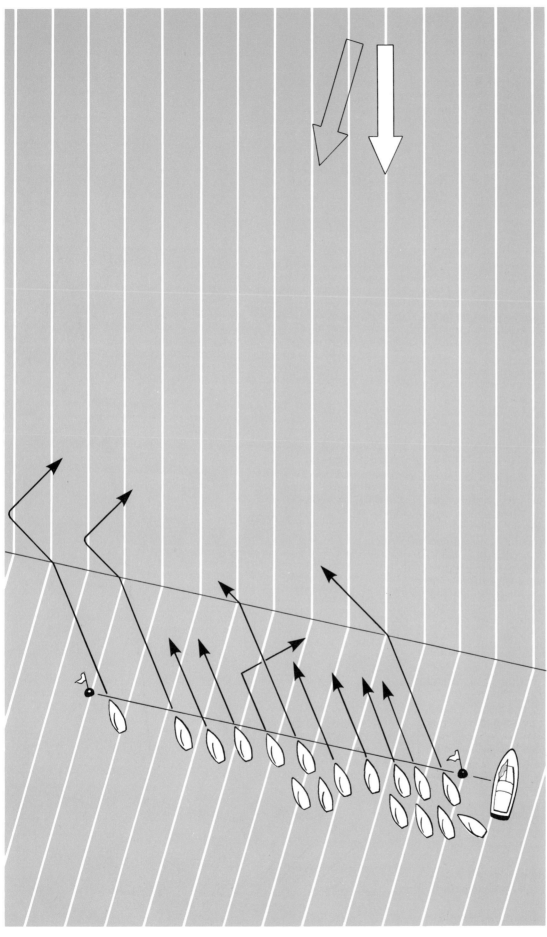

PIN END STARTS
The pin end start has several advantages. There is usually a small territorial gain because committees often lay the line with a slight bias towards the port end. This balances the advantage the starboard end starters have in being able to tack first. Once over the line the pin end starter hopes to pull a little ahead, preferably being able to establish a lee bow position on the nearest boat behind and forcing it to tack. A heading shift is what he is hoping for, as soon as he has worked out a little ahead. Since he will be the first to encounter it he should hang on to the starboard tack long enough to be sure that the rest of the fleet are getting the same wind. As soon as he sees he can cross comfortably ahead of the nearest boats he should go onto the port tack.

boat's speed and thus make less leeway. More boat speed will increase the apparent wind across the sails and thereby make them more efficient. Considerable twist should be induced in the sails with the jib fairleads well inboard and the mainsheet traveller up to windward with the sheets eased.

Many modern keelboats, like the Soling, have self-tacking jibs. In these boats the traveller takes care of the fairlead position laterally and the sheet is anchored to a variable position board in the crew instead of a normal single cringle. Moving the sheet forward on this board is equivalent to moving the fairlead position aft. Once underway it is possible to move the sheet along the board only if a relieving mini-sheet is used to hold the sail whilst the change is made. In addition to being able to alter the leech tension with the sheet, it is also possible to do so with the jib halyard, which may be necessary in light weather; the mast will be raked aft to its maximum to obtain the necessary amount of weather helm to sail the boat efficiently. For optimum effect of trimming the jib in these conditions an adjustable tack fitting is also needed. Then this, together with the halyard, sheet and clew position must be trimmed in sympathy.

Behind this the mainsail is trimmed similarly. The twist is controlled by the sheet and traveller and the shape of the sail by the backstay, kicking strap, halyard and Cunningham. Tensioning the backstay will bend the mast and flatten the sail but it will also require more tension on the mainsheet as there will be a further opening of the leech. Only just enough Cunningham is needed to remove the puckers in the luff of the sail and it is important to keep all the mainsail full without backwind from the jib. It is essential for the twist in the jib to match exactly that of the mainsail, and for the angle of attack of the jib to be constant to the wind throughout the entire length of the luff. It must be remembered that the angle of the wind to the luff will not be constant throughout the length of the luff because of wind shear. A jib that is short of tell-tales on the luff will therefore be impossible to trim correctly all the time.

The shifts will dictate the tactics of a light-airs beat but the winning helmsman is the one who plans his strategy to take the maximum advantage of the conditions. Tacking must be smooth, and the bigger the overlap of the jib the slower the tack will be. The crew members will probably have been crouched in the leeward bilge but there is no reason why they should not attempt to roll tack a keelboat as if it were a dinghy. In a Soling this is highly effective, speeding the tack and giving the boat extra speed to come out on the new tack. Getting the jib in on the new tack must be smooth and even those boats with 'self-tacking' jibs need attention.

On the tack the fine control of the sheet should be fully eased; it is not retensioned until the boat has begun to gather way on the

TO WINDWARD IN LIGHT AIRS
The sails should be fairly flat, and set with plenty of twist. For the self-tacking Soling jib this means moving the sheet forward on the clew-board to flatten the sail, hauling the traveller inboard and easing the sheet to allow twist. *(See insets)* The mast should be raked aft to give the right weight of weather helm, and at the same time bent slightly with the backstay to flatten the sail. The Cunningham and clew outhaul should both be tensioned just enough to take the puckers out of the cloth. The mainsheet traveller is hauled to windward and the sheet eased to allow twist in the sail. It is important that the twist in the jib matches that in the main, and that the jib does not back the mainsail. It is also essential that the luffs of the sails are at a constant angle of attack to the wind, with the right amount of twist to accommodate the shear in the apparent wind (see page 61). To get this adjustment right you need plenty of tell-tales, high up as well as in the usual places.

new tack. Then it will come in slowly and simultaneously with the mainsheet so that the slot between the two sails remains constant. With a large overlapping jib the crew must endeavour to keep the action as smooth as possible. It is therefore essential to clear the weather sheet in light weather so that the jib can be pulled round the mast with the least possible effort. Gains are made by the boats that tack smoothly and well. With shifts providing the incentive a helmsman should have sufficient confidence and skill so that there is no need for him to wonder whether or not to tack because of worries about the loss he might incur through a badly executed manoeuvre.

Medium Airs

In regular sailing breezes the crew's job is to obtain maximum efficiency from the rig while the helmsman uses it to gain the most boat speed. The tactical rules still apply and because of the conditions the boat will tack quicker; her greater speed before the tack will carry her through the tack better and when she emerges from the tack and begins on the new course she will be travelling at a higher speed.

The mast will not be raked as far aft as for lighter airs and the forestay will be considerably tighter. Allowing the forestay to sag to leeward does make the jib fuller but the increased breeze makes it necessary to point higher as the boat foots faster and makes less leeway. If the sheet leads are kept where they were for lighter airs the slot would tend to become choked, so the sheet leads should be slightly further outboard. The leech tension on both the main and the jib will be much greater and the sails will have only a small amount of twist – just sufficient to cope with the wind shear.

The crew must attempt to balance the boat against the wind, sitting out as far as the wind demands and the class rules allow. The hiking harnesses allowed by the Soling class have removed much of the hard work of sitting out in those boats, but the Star class refuses to pamper its crews. The 'mini-hike', as it is so inappropriately known, is a highly efficient way of adding righting moment to a keelboat in these conditions.

Heavy Airs

Once again twist is induced into the sails but this time the purpose is to disseminate power from the upper regions of the sails and thereby reduce the keeling moment while keeping the power low-down in the sails. The degree to which this is done depends on the amount of wind. Day-racing keelboats rarely reef – few in fact have the facility to do so – and therefore must adapt the rig to cope with a very wide range of wind strengths.

Waves now concern the keelboat helmsman much more as they have increased in size. He will tackle them in exactly the same way as the dinghy sailor: luffing up the face of

MEDIUM AND HEAVY AIRS
As the wind increases from light, to medium and heavy weather, the rig must be adjusted to deal with the higher wind speeds. For medium airs (left hand boat) the sails are fuller, with the mast less raked and straight. The forestay is tighter and both sheet travellers are moved outboard with tightened sheets to reduce the amount of twist in the sails. The Cunningham and kicker are slacked and the clew outhaul adjusted to give the right degree of fullness. On the self-tacking jib the sheet is led to the after hole on the clew-board to give extra fullness to the sail. This is the same as moving the fairleads forward on an ordinary jib sheet system. The crew move their weight to the weather side and may use a mini-hike, which means sitting with the calves of your legs hitched over the side deck and your bottom nearly in the water against the side of the hull.

IN HEAVY AIRS (right hand boat) twist is re-introduced and the sails flattened. To this end the travellers are moved to windward and the sheets eased a little to give twist. On the self-tacking jib the sheet is moved forward on the clew-board to give a slacker leech. This is the same as moving a normal jib sheet fairlead inboard and aft. The main clew outhaul and Cunningham downhaul are well tightened. The mast is bent to flatten the sail, but is upright to reduce weather helm.

56

Top right, light airs.
Centre right, heavy airs.
Bottom right, running under spinnaker the mast is allowed to lean forward by slacking the backstay. The kicking strap prevents the boom lifting and keeps the mainsail flat.

the wave as the boat slows slightly and bearing away down the back after he has broken through the crest. It is a skill that many dinghy sailors use in keelboat racing and the effect has been to leave established helmsmen of the class wallowing in their wake.

Trimming the jib will entail moving the sheet leads aft or, in the case of a 'self-tacking' jib, moving the sheet forward on the clew board. This way the lower part of the sail can be trimmed flat while the upper part, with the leech free, can twist and spill out air. The mainsail is similarly trimmed. The clew outhaul is pulled well out to flatten the foot of the sail and the Cunningham tensioned to move the fullness of the sail further forward. The mainsheet is well tensioned to help preserve the tension in the forestay and avoid sag. Twist is induced in the sail by considerable backstay tension which frees the leech of the mainsail and at the same time flattens the sail by bending the mast. Fine adjustment of the backstay can then keep the rig in balance. The mast will be further forward for windward work in heavy airs and this will reduce the amount of weather helm.

Reaching and Running

Once around the weather mark and away on a reach with a spinnaker set, there is much for the crew of a keelboat to do. The helmsman will have a known compass course to steer, but tactical considerations will decide exactly which way he will go. The crew have the sails to trim and the boat to prepare for any sail change that may be necessary with any sudden change in wind or tactics.

On an Olympic course, a backing wind may make the first reach very shy for the spinnaker. The tactician should be able to appraise the skipper of this as he will have noted bad headings on starboard tack increasing progressively towards the end of the windward leg. If this shift is constant, the tactics will be very different from those employed if it is thought that the backing is only temporary. In the former case it will pay to sail high on the reach away from the weather mark without the spinnaker set until one is high enough above the rhumb line to bear away and set it comfortably. In the latter case it will pay to set the kite immediately, sail low for a while and wait until the veer comes before heading up for the mark. A backing wind will broaden the second reach and a veering wind make it more shy when, as on true Olympic courses, the marks are left to port. For those highly dangerous, and ill-recommended, starboard-hand course the converse is true.

When reaching, the boat is under the control of the spinnaker trimmer. He calls for course alterations if he finds he cannot set his sail efficiently. As the wind increases, however, he has to compromise trim in conjunction with the helmsman if broaching looks a possibility. A good crew will be able to feel the boat begin to stagger as the helmsman

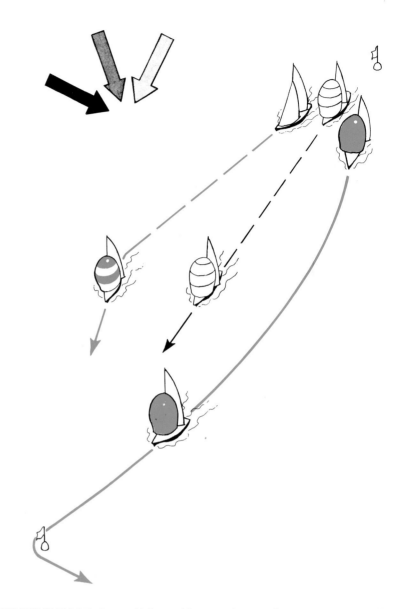

REACHING RUNNING LEGS
As soon as the weather mark is rounded you must decide which way to go to the next mark. Before rounding the windward mark the tactician should have noted any shift in the wind, and the crew should have prepared the spinnaker that will be used. If the wind is backing, the rhumb line course to the second mark of an Olympic course will be extremely shy for the spinnaker. If the shift is constant it will pay to sail

high, reaching away from the windward mark without the spinnaker until you can bear away and set the spinnaker comfortably. If you know the wind is going to veer it will be best to set the spinnaker immediately on rounding the windward mark, then sail low on the rhumb line until the veer comes, allowing you to head for the mark. In deciding which way to go, bear in mind that currents are stronger offshore, and that that is also where you will usually find the best waves

for planing. Also consider that by taking the inside course you may obtain an inside overlap at the next mark. One of the disadvantages of the inside course is that you can easily end up in the wind shadow of following boats. Whichever way you go, you may be sure that the one course that almost never pays is to go straight down the middle, unless you are on your own and it is a spinnaker ride the whole way.

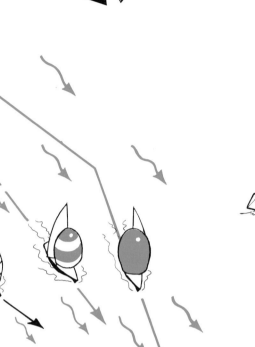

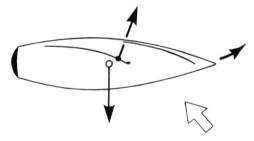

The mast raked right forward produces lee helm.

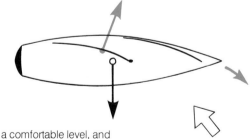

The mast raked aft produces weather helm.

RUNNING LEG

Much the same considerations apply on the running as on the reaching leg. There is always a tendency for the tracks of boats to bend to windward as the leading boats try to protect their wind by luffing, until they are finally forced to bear away to fetch the mark. In this example the boat that keeps offshore of the rhumb is in the stronger current and will arrive first at the third mark. However in the right sea breeze conditions a boat taking the inshore route could well get the best breeze, since the sea breeze begins inshore and is strongest there.

With either the second or third leg of an Olympic course, if the wind has shifted such that a spinnaker cannot be set on the rhumb line course, it is invariably best to either bear away under spinnaker and then close-reach the last part of the leg, or to close-reach the first part and then bear away with the spinnaker to the mark. Either way you will cover the ground faster than reaching without a kite. Which route will be the best on the day will depend on your position in the race, on your forecasting of future shifts, and on your estimation of current and wave effects.

WEATHER AND LEE HELM

The weight of weather or lee helm depends on the position of the centre of effort (CE) of the sails in relation to the point about which the boat pivots, known as the centre of lateral resistance (CLR). The position of the centre of effort can be moved by raking the mast. The CLR is fixed by the boat's design. Moving the mast aft will move the centre of effort aft too, and this produces weather helm. Rake the mast forward and you produce lee helm. Nobody wants lee helm, but you may rake the mast forward enough to reduce weather helm to a comfortable level, and this also reduces drag caused by the rudder. In a dinghy with a swinging centreboard the CLR may be moved aft by lifting the board a little and this too reduces weather helm.

WIND SHEER AND SAIL TWIST

The frictional drag of the sea's surface slows the wind near the surface. *(See graph opposite.)* Since the boat is moving through the water at an angle to the wind this means that the apparent wind will sheer between the bottom and top of the sails. The only way to detect this in practice is to have plenty of tell-tales high up on the luffs as well as low down. To accommodate the apparent wind sheer the sails must be twisted. Some twist is inherent in the cut of the sail. More can be introduced by moving the sheet travellers inboard, even to windward of the centre line, and then easing the sheets until the tell-tales fly true along the length of the luff, showing that the angle of attack is constant.

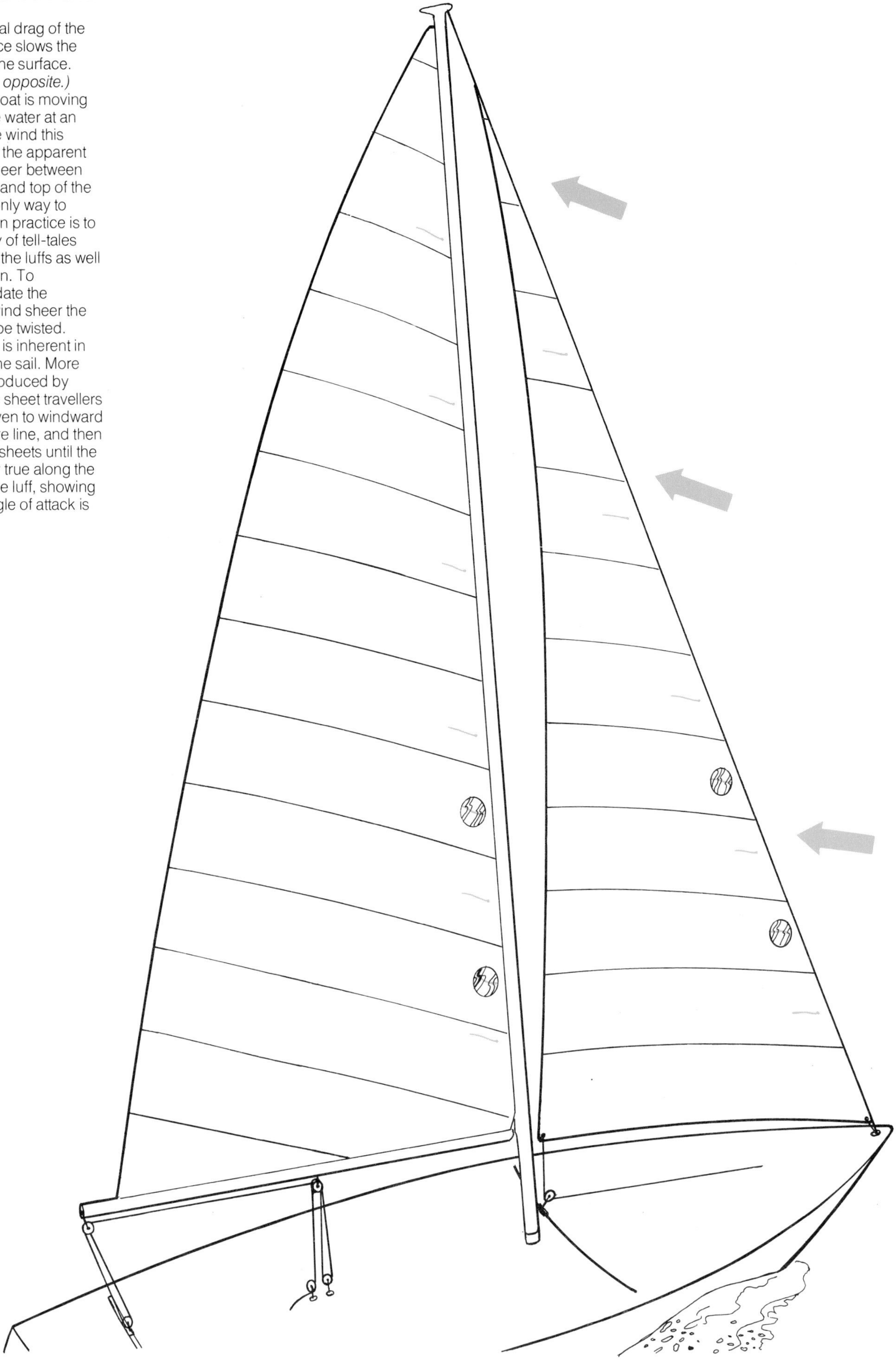

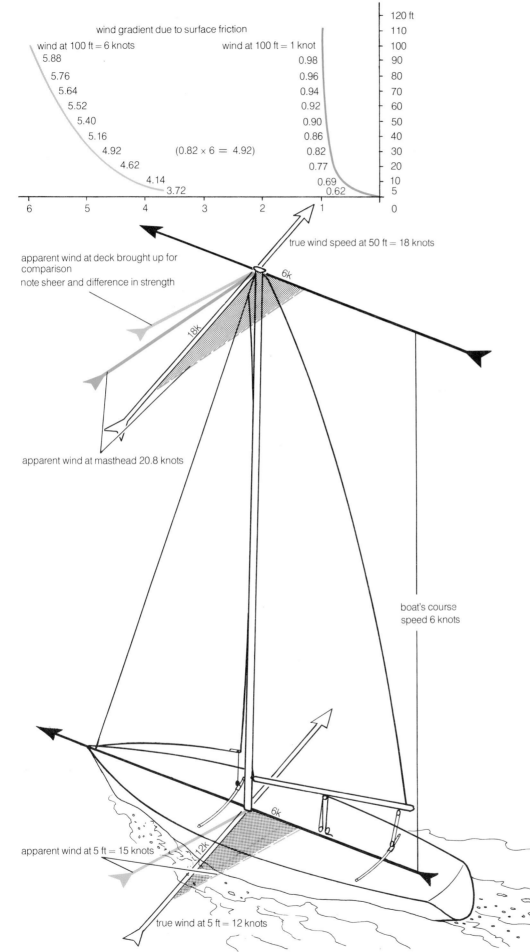

wind gradient due to surface friction

wind at 100 ft = 6 knots	wind at 100 ft = 1 knot
5.88	0.98
5.76	0.96
5.64	0.94
5.52	0.92
5.40	0.90
5.16	0.86
4.92 (0.82 × 6 = 4.92)	0.82
4.62	0.77
4.14	0.69
3.72	0.62

120 ft
110
100
90
80
70
60
50
40
30
20
10
5
0

6   5   4   3   2   1   0

true wind speed at 50 ft = 18 knots

apparent wind at deck brought up for comparison
note sheer and difference in strength

6k

18k

apparent wind at masthead 20.8 knots

boat's course
speed 6 knots

6k

apparent wind at 5 ft = 15 knots

12k

true wind at 5 ft = 12 knots

WIND GRADIENT

This graph shows the frictional effect of the sea surface over the first 100 feet. It is approximate since the effect of waves and the density of the air will vary. For a wind blowing over a smooth surface, including a calm sea, the wind velocity is roughly proportional to $h^{0.16}$.

So if the wind strength at 100 ft is denoted by W100, the wind W at any height is given by $W/W100 = (h/100)^{1.16}$. This gives the graph on the right with the wind of one knot at 100 ft. These figures can then be scaled as desired. The graph on the left shows a wind of 6 knots at 100 ft, therefore the velocity at
50 ft=0.90×6=5.4 knots
30 ft=0.82×6=4.92 knots
10 ft=0.69×6=4.14 knots.
If the wind were 20 knots at 100 ft that at 5 ft would be 0.62×20=12.4 knots and that at
50 ft=0.9×20=18 knots.

APPARENT WIND SHEER

is due to the wind moving slower near the surface than at the mast head, coupled with the boat's speed at an angle to the wind which is constant throughout the mast height.

In the example illustrated the boat has a 50 foot mast and is making six knots to windward in a breeze that is blowing at 20 knots at 100 feet. Using the graph above the true wind at deck level (5 ft) will be 12.4 knots while the wind at the mast head will be 18 knots. Using the boat's course and speed we can construct triangles of velocity for deck level and mast head. These reveal that the apparent wind at the deck will be 15 knots, while the apparent wind at the top of the mast will be some 20.8 knots. Also the apparent wind at the top of the mast will be sheered slightly aft of the apparent wind on deck. It is to allow for this that the sails need some twist. The practical way to establish the amount of twist necessary is to examine the luff telltales, which should go to the top part of the sails.

puts on considerable helm to keep it on track. Instantly the spinnaker trimmer should ease the spinnaker sheet further to relieve the pressure on the helm. Almost half the spinnaker can lift without the sail collapsing and the good crew will know just how far he can allow it to go without losing it altogether. Keeping the pole as far aft as possible does help in broaching conditions. It is imperative to stop the boat from broaching as more ground is lost this way than if the spinnaker is allowed to flap. Nevertheless, in some circumstances a flapping spinnaker can undo snap shackles and patent clips on the ends of the sheets, which can be more disastrous than broaching in terms of loss of ground.

One of the critical factors in getting the best from a spinnaker on a reach is correct pole height. Easy adjustment of this from within the boat is essential. A frequent fault is to have the pole end too low and thereby starve the flow across the sail. The shoulders should be allowed to open up; the sail will then be flatter with a better exit for the air from an uncurled leech.

The middleman, or even the helmsman, should have control of the kicking strap and shy reaches in gusty conditions. By freeing the kicker, the top half of the mainsail can be spilled whilst keeping forward power in the lower half of the sail. The release of considerable heeling moment will help keep the boat upright and prevent a tendency to broach.

Often on a reach the leeward sheet comes above the boom and curls the leech of the mainsail. This is nothing to worry about as it frees the leech of the spinnaker. It must, however, be cleared before gybing.

While running the helmsman must keep the boat moving at its fastest. He will have to follow the wind shifts and it is up to one of the crew to watch the compass headings and to advise the skipper when to gybe to take advantage of these shifts. Just as much ground can be gained and lost on the run as is possible on the windward legs if the shifts are missed.

Boat Preparation and Maintenance

The worst possible place to keep a racing boat is in the water. It should be dry sailed whenever possible. Keeping it in the water will only encourage water soakage into the hull, making it heavy and uncompetitive. It will also necessitate the use of an antifouling paint on the hull. It is impossible to keep a perfect racing finish on a hull subjected to this treatment.

The keel and rudder are the two areas where extra care should be taken. They should be examined each time the boat comes out of the water. Any nicks or dents should be filled in with plastic putty and then sanded back into the finish. The keel and rudder make up a large percentage of the wetted area of the underwater surface and must therefore be as smooth as the hull itself and cared for with a similar affection.

RUNNING AND REACHING TRIM

On a reach the middle crewman who controls the spinnaker will call for course changes so that he can set his sail properly. As the wind increases and the helm becomes heavier to handle he will have to reach some compromise of trim with the helmsman so that the boat does not broach. The middleman controls the sheet and guy of the spinnaker and calls for changes in pole height. The pole should be kept aft with the guy so that the spinnaker and main together present the greatest area to the wind, but not so far aft that the crossflow between spinnaker and main is throttled. The pole should be high enough to allow the spinnaker shoulders to open up properly, with the leech uncurled so that the air can flow out of the sail unhindered. The spinnaker sheet will often ride up on the leech of the mainsail when reaching. This does not matter, so long as it is cleared before gybing. The mast is straight to give a full mainsail, and raked forward slightly to reduce weather helm. On shy reaches in gusty weather some wind can be dumped from the top of the mainsail by slackening the kicking strap and allowing the boom to rise. This keeps the power in the lower part of the sail while reducing the heeling moment. The middleman or even the helmsman will have control of the kicker and it is a useful adjustment in the all important business of preventing a broach. The main help to the helmsman though is for the middleman to ease the spinnaker sheet the moment he feels the boat stagger under the helm. This takes the pressure off the weather helm, provided it is done in time – that is before the boat is heeling so much that the rudder is lifting the stern rather than turning it. When running the helmsman must keep the boat moving as fast as possible, and this means using the wind shifts. One of the crew, usually the forward member, should watch the compass and the wind for shifts and advise the helmsman when to gybe.

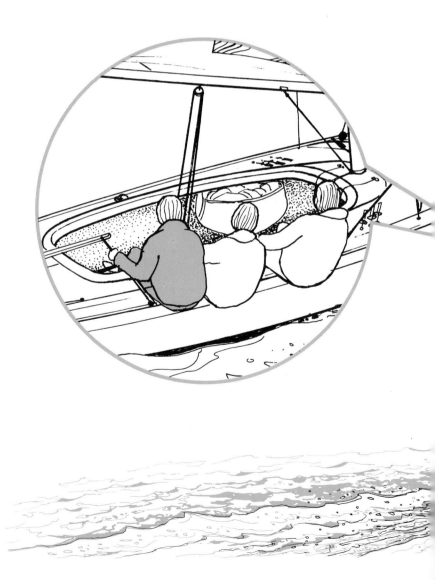

Offshore Boats Sailing Inshore

Teamwork is the keynote of success in racing any offshore boat around the buoys.

All the world's major series for offshore boats include inshore, round-the-buoys races. Each of the Ton Cups and the Admiral's Cup have three such events out of a total of five, while the Onion Patch and Southern Cross have two out of four. Day-racing of offshore boats has become extremely popular and the standard of racing has soared accordingly. Offshore boats are treated like any closed-course racing craft but with more people on board the sophistication of boat and sail handling is of the highest order. There is a place for one man to deal solely with navigation, strategy and tactics. He is a constant source of reliable information to the helmsman, who may make the final decision concerned with close-quarter tactics on other boats. Quite often the skipper takes this role, a helmsman being employed to concentrate exclusively on driving the boat through the water at the maximum speed.

The helmsman will have to work in conjunction with the sail trimmer, or the principal sail trimmer in the case of a biggish boat when more than one main is needed to trim the sails. The two of them will work together to point the boat in the direction called to them by the navigator-tactician and the rest of the crew will provide the muscle power. Each of them, however, will have a specialist role in every manoeuvre and will fit into a pattern of activity dictated by previous practice and rehearsals.

Teamwork is the keynote of success in racing any offshore boat around the buoys. Crew limitations in the level rating classes have imposed greater loads on individual crew members. In classes where these limitations are not imposed, the numbers on board are a matter of personal preference, and this varies from country to country. The Australians, for example, favour small numbers in their crews while the Americans seem to have one more than Europeans in similar sized boats. This could arise from historical causes; the Australians tend to start racing in small boats and, in the past, American yachtsmen have had the opportunity to begin their offshore racing in larger yachts.

Whatever the size of the crew each man must know exactly what is expected of him at each manoeuvre and coordinate with the rest of the people on board. Orders must be incisive so that they are readily understood and confusion is cut to a minimum. Pre-race training is of paramount importance and no skipper should seriously think of racing with a crew that are not familiar with each other. That is not to say that he cannot do well with a pick-up crew, as long as they are all highly experienced and are able to allot their duties before the race begins; but the skipper stands at risk in the close-quarter manoeuvres where

DIP POLE GYBE
The dip pole gybe is used by the majority of the fleet in inshore and offshore racing. Pole gybing as in the keelboats, such as the Soling, is only practicable up to Half-Ton Cup sized boats (22 ft waterline). Larger boats of more than about 50 ft generally use a twin pole system (see page 70) in order to retain greater control in heavy weather.

The sequence of events in a dip pole gybe are as follows:

Boat 1: Spinnaker set and pulling correctly, crew in the cockpit trimming. Skipper gives order to gybe onto the other tack.

One crew goes forward by the mast, ready to release the pole from the spinnaker guy as the boat starts to turn downwind. Meanwhile the crew in the cockpit adjust the spinnaker guy and sheet to bring the pole forward close to the forestay.

Boat 2: Running dead downwind. The helmsman centres the mainsail with the sheet to give the spinnaker clear air and to prevent it collapsing or flogging at the wrong moment. The foredeck crew releases the spinnaker from the pole by pulling the lanyard that exits from the pole near

the mast. One of the crew in the cockpit lowers the pole by its topping lift so that it can sweep down across the deck inside the forestay, guided by the foredeck crew.

Boat 3: Still running dead downwind the helmsman lets the mainsail gybe across and the crew in the cockpit hoist up the spinnaker pole on the other side. The foredeck crew then attaches the pole to the new guy of the spinnaker (the old sheet) and moves back into the cockpit. The helmsman takes up the new course while the crew adjust the sheet and guy and height of the pole to taste.

OFFSHORE RACING
Previous page The Australian boat *Bumblebee* flying a spinnaker during a round-the-buoys event.

THREE TYPICAL
OFFSHORE RACES

a. The Palmelia Race
Plymouth to Capetown,
Capetown to
Freemantle.
Approximately 11,500
miles.

b. Middle Sea Race
From Malta around
Sicily and back to
Malta.
Approximately 611
miles.

c. Channel Race
First offshore race of
Admiral's Cup series.
Approximately   217
miles.

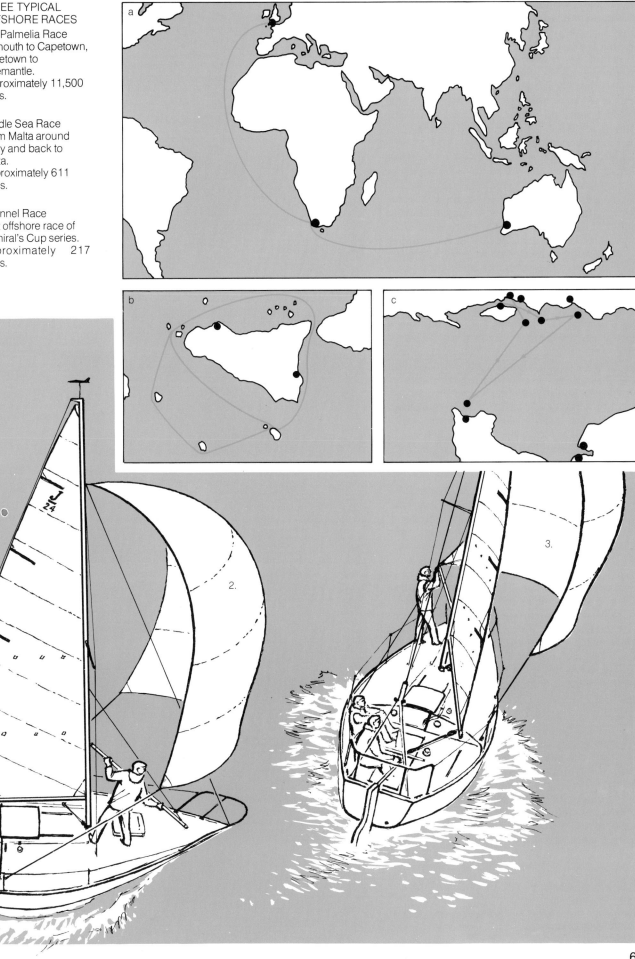

familiarity with the boat and its gear can make certain actions on the part of the crew instinctive and therefore faster and more certain. Watching any well-drilled crew will bear this out.

Racing offshore boats in inshore races differs from one-design keelboat racing in that the speed of the boats, even on level rating classes, does vary and, apart from the level raters, there will be a handicap correction to make at the end. One tenth of a foot makes little difference, even half a foot of rating makes less than half a minute an hour difference, and in the narrow bands of handicap that are used for this type of racing the allowances are therefore quite small for, say, 1 30-mile race. They are, however, significant and there is much the lower-rated boats can do to improve their chances, particularly in slightly restricted waters rather than around an Olympic track. This accounts for the majority of inshore races for offshore boats.

These races are perhaps more interesting than the regularity imposed by the discipline of the Olympic course. The purist will always maintain that the Olympic course is perfection, and in tideless waters perhaps it is; but other courses around established marks in restricted waters are likely to give greater variation in sailing conditions. The triangular course only gives close reaching without a spinnaker when the wind has shifted considerably or the tidal effect is extremely strong, yet this is as testing a point of sailing technique as any other. And is there any greater test of windward ability of both boat and helmsman as a one-legged beat where the requirement is simply to lay the mark without having to put in a short hitch to it and lose ground by tacking twice? That is not a feature of the Olympic course.

With the wind aft there are points of sailing, and manoeuvres, that are never needed around the Olympic triangle. Such contests are rather like offshore races but with different strategy and tactics that are often determined solely by the proximity of shorelines or shallows and the current. There may be a choice of which way to go but it is more likely that success will only come by sailing in a narrow 'corridor'. The skipper and crew must therefore adapt to these peculiar conditions and sail the boat within the limitations imposed.

There are new areas of importance and different techniques to be employed and perfected. There are new hazards to deal with – like a bigger boat going slower ahead – and a constantly changing challenge that makes this type of racing so popular throughout the world. The evening club races in Sydney Har-

RACING TONNERS
Full out on a One Ton Cup Race with Florida in the background.

Waverider (inset) is a constant winner in the One Ton Cup events.

bour, summer Saturdays in the Solent or the weekends in Long Island Sound are all of this type and everywhere sailors strive to improve. Breakthroughs in technique are rare, but in spinnaker-handling improvement has been swift. Pole gybing, similar to that used in the Soling, has increased in popularity with fractionally rigged boats up to half-ton size but it is unlikely that it will go further. With larger spinnakers the now-familiar dip-pole gybe is almost universal although the larger yachts, of 50 ft (15.24 m) or more overall, still use twin pole gybes when the wind is blowing hard and there is a big sea running in order to have greater control of the boat. Eliminating the second pole has given greater freedom on the foredeck and faster gybing as a result.

Starting

When not starting dead to windward in an area where the current must be taken into account, new techniques have to be employed. Starts may be from fixed lines on the shore or from committee vessels, and each one will need to be individually assessed. The navigator-tactician will be faced on occasion with reaching and running starts, and with a situation where every contestant will be trying to start at one end of the line aiming to stay close to shore so that they can beat along it and avoid an adverse current. His problem is to assess which of the available options is the best. He then instructs the helmsman where he wants to be when the gun fires, which direction he should be pointing and, most important of all, why. He will use all the data at his disposal – charts, instruments, tidal atlas and weather forecast – but above all he must check that all the factors agree with actuality. Weather forecasts can be wildly astray and personal prediction based on cloud formation are often better than stereotyped radio forecasts, even those specially complied for coastal areas and prepared for use at sea, which tend to deal with conditions far out at sea rather than the immediate coastal strip. It is a good idea to check out the latest weather predictions with the local airfield. Airfield data will be the most up to date for the area. There is the chance of tides running late on the flood, when long-term winds have forced the surface water. In this case the strength of the ebb may be greater than that predicted in the atlas.

Tidal gradients along a shoreline are all-important to the tactician. He needs to know just how far he can stand offshore without detriment against a foul tide; or, conversely, how close in he can go to cut a corner when the tide is favourable without losing too much of its assistance. The tidal gradient is all important at the start.

Should the start be against a tide close to a shoreline starting tactics must be biased towards that side. Just how far from the shore the start is made depends on the angle of the wind – the more it blows on to the shore, the further offshore it is better to start. It also

TWIN POLE GYBE
Larger racing yachts use a twin pole spinnaker gybe, particularly when conditions are rough. This method gives greater control throughout the gybe since the spinnaker is always attached to a pole. Larger yachts need this additional control because with the other methods the spinnaker always needs some man-handling to get the pole reattached to the sail just at the time it is most likely flog with a mind of its own. With the bigger sail areas the power of a man is proportionally less and a dip pole gybe could be risky for men and gear.

The sequence of actions for a twin pole gybe are as follows:
Boat 1: The spinnaker is pulling well and the crew are in the cockpit, except for the spinnaker trimmer who is on deck by the mast to get the best view, from where he directs the trim. The order is given to gybe.

Boat 2: The boat maintains the same course. At least two crewmen go onto the foredeck to prepare the second pole on the port side. They attach the second uphaul to the outer end of the pole and the downhaul which runs to a block right forward on the deck. They fit the inner end of the pole to the port cup fitting on the mast. *(see inset lower left).*

Boat 3: The helmsman steers downwind and the mainsheet is centred so that the sail does not spoil the flow of wind over the spinnaker. The second pole is hoisted on its uphaul by a crewman in the cockpit and one of the foredeck crew attaches the outboard end to the lazy guy on the port side.

Boat 4: Still heading downwind the mainsail is allowed to cross over. The cockpit crew haul in on the lazy guy on the port side bringing the new pole up to the spinnaker, and ease the sheet which now becomes the lazy sheet. They haul in on the starboard sheet while the foredeck team release the original pole from the spinnaker, unhooking it from what is now the lazy guy.

The boat then takes up its new course as the cockpit crew trim the sheet and guy and adjust the pole height. The foredeck crew releases the original pole from its mast cup and stows it on deck.

depends on whether the shoreline is to the right or left of the course. With the shoreline on the right the boats coming away from it will have right of way as they will be on starboard tack, and an advantage of control can easily be established even as early as this in the race. With a bunch of boats coming in on port there is bound to be some confusion. The most inshore boat can hail for water to tack and put all those outside her about. The only danger is posed by a boat that can just duck under her stern and gain a fraction by being out of the tide for a few seconds less. If the leading boat at this stage is one of the lower-handicapped in the race, her control of the situation benefits her more than it would a bigger boat, although the bigger boat would probably be able to sail clear of her rivals while the smaller one is able only just to stay ahead of the fleet.

With the shoreline on the left of the course the right of way advantage is with the boat going inshore and therefore the skill is in arriving at the shoreline last among the boats who can force the boats coming away from the shore to duck one's stern. Ideally when making the first tack after the start, there should be no boat on starboard to give way to. Much will depend on tidal gradient, wind direction and relative rating (viz. speed).

With the wind free at the start, much will depend on just how free the wind is and its strength. With a close reach to the first mark it may pay in light to moderate breezes to start to leeward, using to advantage the extra speed of sailing slightly higher. In heavier winds this may be negated by the windward boats having greater control, and more disturbance of the wind to leeward. Tide, too, will need to be considered.

With the spinnaker set at the start the prime considerations must be the fastest course and clear air. The second of these is the greater and it may pay to sail for some time in an adverse tide to avoid blanketing from other boats in order to sail away from the fleet. Boats in a bunch will always sail at the speed of the slowest, and that will never be the maximum speed of that boat. Try before the start to see where the gaps in the line are likely to be – against a foul current there is sure to be one just offshore of the bunch. Go for it and be prepared to protect it, but not by luffing to excess. If you are going to luff at this stage of a race it must be early and serve more as a warning to an overtaker that you mean business and that he has all the room in the world to pass to leeward if he thinks he is faster.

Sailing to Windward

The only really useful instrument for sailing to windward, as far as the helmsman is concerned, is a digital read-out speedometer. To windward in daylight the rest of the instruments, apart from the compass, are of little value. The helmsman can see the effect of the wind on the sails and its angle by the tell-tales on the headsail; he needs to concern himself

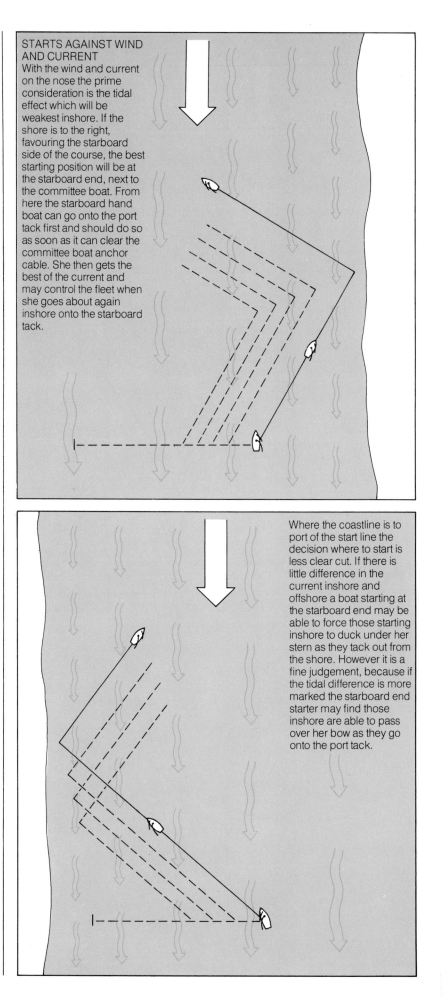

STARTS AGAINST WIND AND CURRENT
With the wind and current on the nose the prime consideration is the tidal effect which will be weakest inshore. If the shore is to the right, favouring the starboard side of the course, the best starting position will be at the starboard end, next to the committee boat. From here the starboard hand boat can go onto the port tack first and should do so as soon as it can clear the committee boat anchor cable. She then gets the best of the current and may control the fleet when she goes about again inshore onto the starboard tack.

Where the coastline is to port of the start line the decision where to start is less clear cut. If there is little difference in the current inshore and offshore a boat starting at the starboard end may be able to force those starting inshore to duck under her stern as they tack out from the shore. However it is a fine judgement, because if the tidal difference is more marked the starboard end starter may find those inshore are able to pass over her bow as they go onto the port tack.

TIDAL INFORMATION
The quality of information on tides varies greatly from one inshore racing area to another. For the Solent, illustrated here, the detail is fairly good. It shows the direction and rates of flow at hourly intervals. Be sure you know whether it is neaps or springs and that you make the right correction for local time. Mark up the hourly sections for the day of the race.

Mean Rate of the Stream at Neaps and Springs is shown in tenths of a Knot. Thus 05.13 indicates mean neap rate 0.5 knots, mean spring rate 1.3 knots.

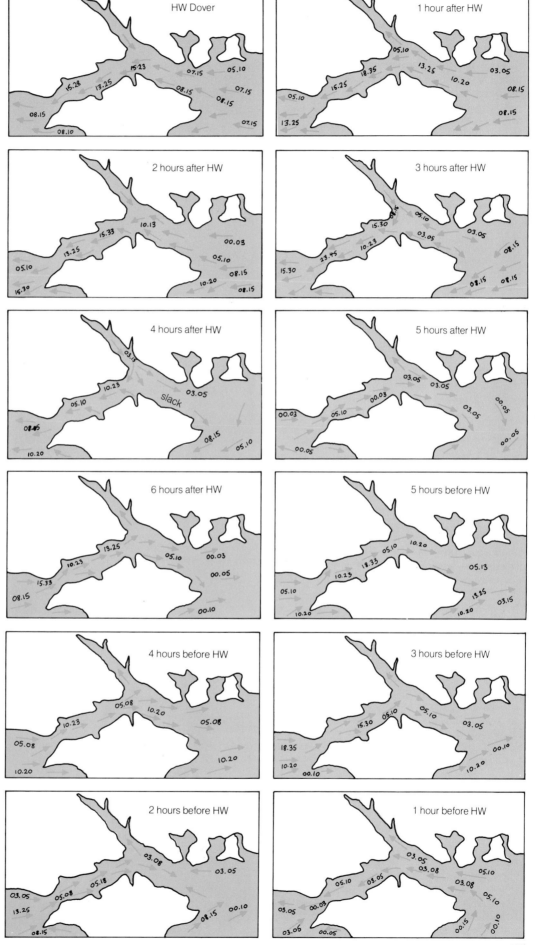

more with the waves. He needs to know whether he is headed or lifted on a tack, but most of all he wants to know that he is driving the boat at its maximum speed. He can try freeing off the sails to see if he can gain speed; if he does he will certainly reduce the leeway angle. Or he can try to pinch a little higher if he can do it without loss of speed. You have only to watch one of these manoeuvres when a wave is badly hit to understand the importance of riding each wave correctly. The helmsman must be to windward, therefore, except in flat water and light airs, where he can see the waves and the gusts of wind marking the water in front and his forward view is not obstructed.

Sail trimming is a team effort and one man's hand should always be on the genoa sheet. In heavier winds he will have to lead the sheet to the weather winch and trim the genoa from there. He must be prepared to ease it as the wind lightens or the boat is slowed by a wave. He has the 'acceleration pedal' of the boat, and the mainsail is trimmed to match. The trimmer's eyes should be on the sail, the waves ahead and the speedometer.

The navigator-tactician must always be aware of the boat's course relative to the next mark and know the most economical way of getting there. If a windward leg is biased so that it becomes almost a fetch, it is important to sail on the tack that takes the boat nearest to the mark first. If the wind frees, the boat will be lifted up to the mark and beat all the others to windward; if the wind heads, the leeward boat has the advantage to cross the windward boats on the shift. The only time when one should consider deviating from this is when it is possible to get out of a strong tide and into a very much weaker one by tacking.

The navigator-tactician must also know what is the course made good in a tideway in order that his call to the mark for the final tack does not over or under stand the buoy. Use of a hand bearing compass against marks on the shore or other navigational marks can give the navigator-tactician this information, or he can calculate the angle knowing the tidal strength and direction and the boat's heading and speed. Then he can call the layline tack to the mark from a hand bearing compass. It is then the helmsman's duty to sail as high and as fast as he can without looking at the mark, particularly with a weather bow tide. The first 100 yards (90 m) of the tack should tell the tactician whether or not he has got it right; if he thinks that the boat should go back on the old tack for a while he must make that decision immediately.

Light Airs

Sail trim on an offshore boat is exactly the same as that on a one-design keelboat around the buoys. The I.O.R. configuration of sail does place considerable importance on the headsail, particularly with masthead rigs, but the whole sail plan must work as a unit. Wind shear and strength are as important as direc-

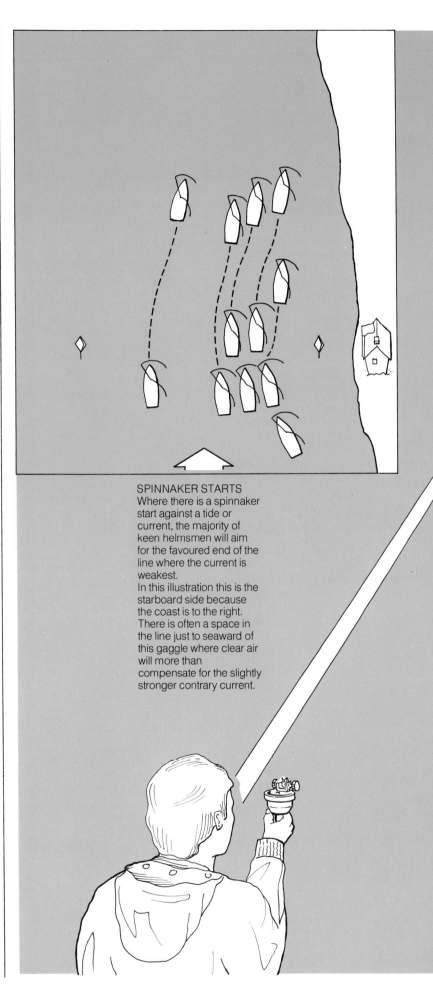

SPINNAKER STARTS
Where there is a spinnaker start against a tide or current, the majority of keen helmsmen will aim for the favoured end of the line where the current is weakest.
In this illustration this is the starboard side because the coast is to the right. There is often a space in the line just to seaward of this gaggle where clear air will more than compensate for the slightly stronger contrary current.

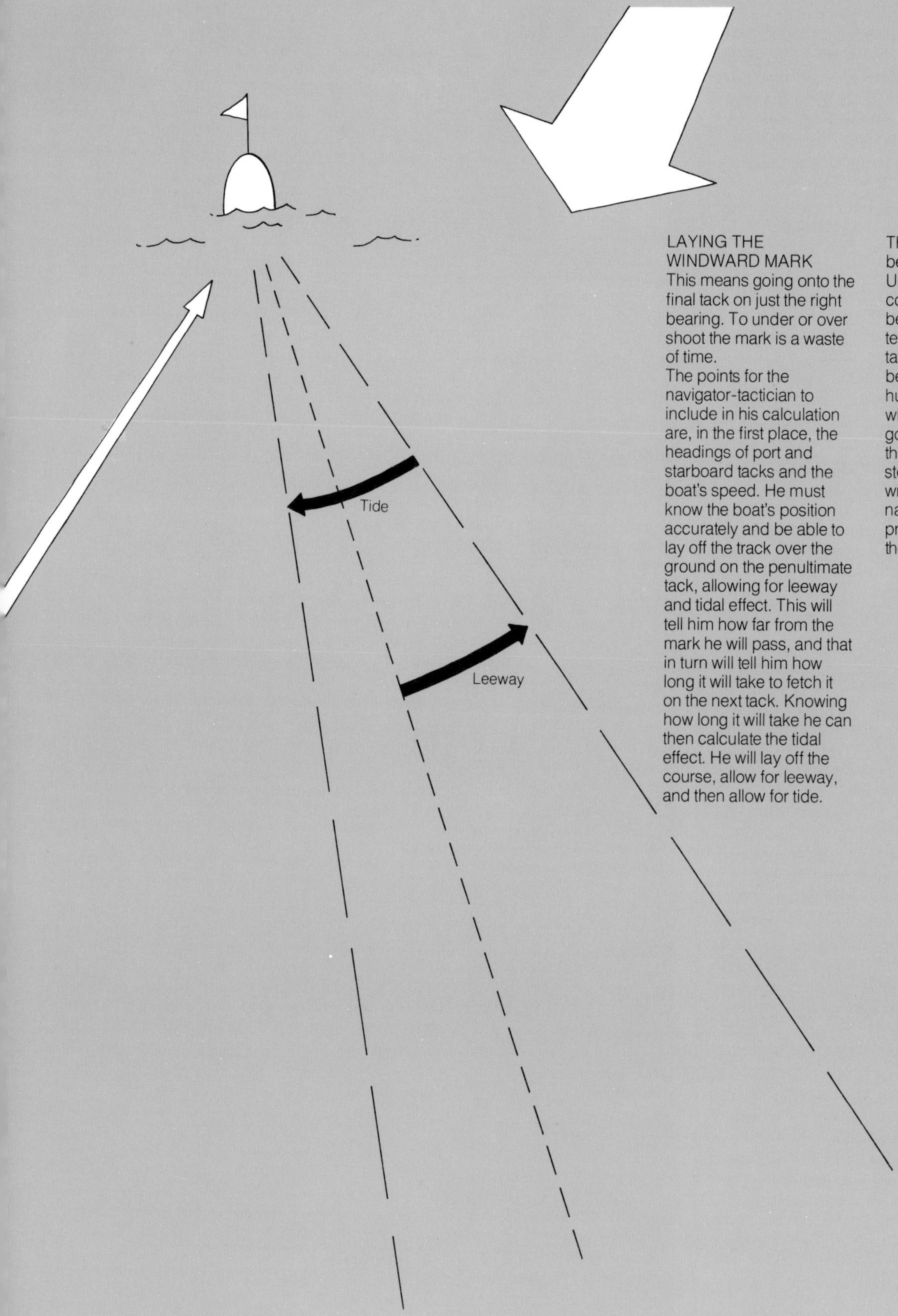

Tide

Leeway

LAYING THE WINDWARD MARK

This means going onto the final tack on just the right bearing. To under or over shoot the mark is a waste of time.

The points for the navigator-tactician to include in his calculation are, in the first place, the headings of port and starboard tacks and the boat's speed. He must know the boat's position accurately and be able to lay off the track over the ground on the penultimate tack, allowing for leeway and tidal effect. This will tell him how far from the mark he will pass, and that in turn will tell him how long it will take to fetch it on the next tack. Knowing how long it will take he can then calculate the tidal effect. He will lay off the course, allow for leeway, and then allow for tide.

This will give him the bearing on which to tack. Using a hand bearing compass he will watch the bearing of the mark and tell the helmsman when to tack. After tacking it should be obvious within a hundred yards or so whether you are in fact going to lay the mark, for the bearing will remain steady. If he has got it wrong the tactician-navigator must decide promptly to go back onto the old tack.

tion and the entire rig must be set up to derive maximum efficiency from the sail plan. The controls for the rig are more sophisticated and better calibrated than on one-design keelboats. Hydraulic backstays, babystays and vangs (kicking straps) are now almost universal in boats of half-ton size and over, each with a pressure read-out dial. The value of a solid kicking strap in light weather cannot be too highly stressed: it allows the boom to be set where the trimmer wants it, independent of the sail, as the weight of the boom is absorbed in the kicker and not in the sail.

Plenty of twist is essential in light weather and this may mean barber-hauling the clew of the jib to weather in order to induce the correct shape. This is equivalent to hauling the mainsheet traveller to windward and easing the sheet to induce twist in the sail. With the long foot of an I.O.R. genoa the clew can be hauled up to weather quite considerably without causing the leech to curl back just above it. Leech-line tension can be eased to help in obtaining correct shape.

A lightweight genoa for winds of up to 10 knots apparent is all but essential for success. With a different shaping and lighter cloth than standard, this sail is better able to set in the light airs but it should not be pressed above the top end of the range that is recommended by the sailmaker or else it will become permanently distorted. It is worth remembering that the effect of wind is proportional to its velocity as well as its density. Cold and damp make the wind heavier whilst dry, hot winds are less dense. On a wet day of 40°F (4°C) in the English Channel a 7-knot wind will have the same effect as a dry offshore wind of 12 knots in Florida when the temperature is 80°F (26°C).

Succcess in light weather windward work requires that the boat is kept moving as fast as possible. Considerable energy from the sails is expended in getting a boat moving from rest, and the skill of the helmsman is tested in 'bridging' the flat areas between patches of wind. In these wind patches it is possible to point quite high and carry one's way into the next breeze, but exactly how it is done depends on the way the next puff is blowing. You should never tack in the flat patches as the boat will be difficult to manoeuvre and almost impossible to get underway again. If you must tack, aim to do so as the boat begins to run out of wind in order to stay in the wind area. Tacking loses many boat-lengths in light airs and the successful boats are the ones which tack least.

Medium Airs

With a breeze of around 12–15 knots an offshore boat can be made to sing around the buoys to windward. The craft becomes alive

RUNNING IN LIGHT AND MEDIUM WINDS
With more crew to handle it, an offshore racing yacht offers more sophistication in trim and handling than keelboats or dinghies.

and skill of helmsmanship can put the rest of the fleet way behind just so long as the boat is complete with good sail trim and the tactics are right. When waves begin to make their presence felt the helmsman must choose his course through them carefully.

One of the real skills is to make the boat beat up to windward by judicious luffing once it is up to full speed and choosing the exact time when the seas are flattest. It is a rhythmic art practised by the best helmsman who seem to have an innate sense of when to slice up to windward and gain half a length without apparently losing any boat speed. It needs years of practice to perfect, but gains can be made whilst practising.

First settle into a good rhythm of steering through the waves with the boat losing little each time one is met. It will be noticed that after every five waves or so there is a longer flat period than normal before the next wave. This is the place for the slight luff and it must be done smoothly yet quickly so that the boat is on her normal course to meet the next wave correctly. Judging when to do it and keeping the speed up are the two key considerations. The sails do not need to be trimmed as the whole movement takes but a couple of seconds. No-one sitting on the weather deck facing outboard should be aware of what is going on for if they are it means the action is being overdone.

The regular-weight genoa will be trimmed without the barber hauler being used and the sheet will be trimmed to give just a slight twist to allow for wind sheer. The angle of attack of the luff must be at the same angle to the wind throughout. As the breeze increases and the boat becomes overpowered, the jib fairlead should be moved aft to tension the foot of the sail and free the leech thereby opening the slot and reducing the keeling movement. With fractional rigs the head of the main will be allowed to twist off first and then the jib flattened.

As the wind increases further it may be necessary to reef or to change headsails. In inshore racing these two manoeuvres should be attempted on starboard tack whenever possible. A close rival can create great difficulties for you by calling you to give way when he is on starboard tack and you are in the middle of reefing the mainsail. With slab reefing, taking a reef in or shaking one out should occupy only a few seconds.

One of the best ways to change a headsail is on a tack. For this reason the genoa is hoisted on the port halyard, in the port groove of the head foil and tacked to the port horn. The second headsail is then hoisted to lay on the weather side of the existing genoa with only the starboard sheet attached. As the boat goes through the tack the new genoa is sheeted in and the port halyard let go, the old sail is gathered in and then the port sheet taken on to the new sail. Next time of course things are not ideal and a similar change would have to be made from port tack to starboard – and a

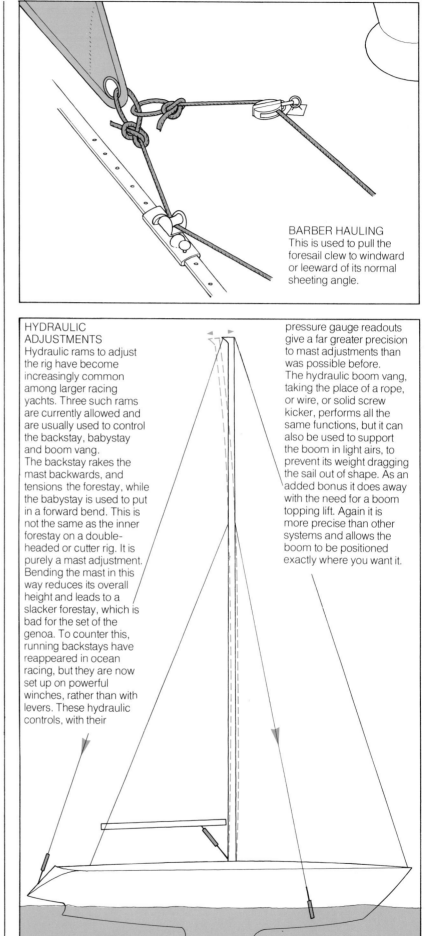

BARBER HAULING
This is used to pull the foresail clew to windward or leeward of its normal sheeting angle.

HYDRAULIC ADJUSTMENTS
Hydraulic rams to adjust the rig have become increasingly common among larger racing yachts. Three such rams are currently allowed and are usually used to control the backstay, babystay and boom vang.
The backstay rakes the mast backwards, and tensions the forestay, while the babystay is used to put in a forward bend. This is not the same as the inner forestay on a double-headed or cutter rig. It is purely a mast adjustment. Bending the mast in this way reduces its overall height and leads to a slacker forestay, which is bad for the set of the genoa. To counter this, running backstays have reappeared in ocean racing, but they are now set up on powerful winches, rather than with levers. These hydraulic controls, with their

pressure gauge readouts give a far greater precision to mast adjustments than was possible before.
The hydraulic boom vang, taking the place of a rope, or wire, or solid screw kicker, performs all the same functions, but it can also be used to support the boom in light airs, to prevent its weight dragging the sail out of shape. As an added bonus it does away with the need for a boom topping lift. Again it is more precise than other systems and allows the boom to be positioned exactly where you want it.

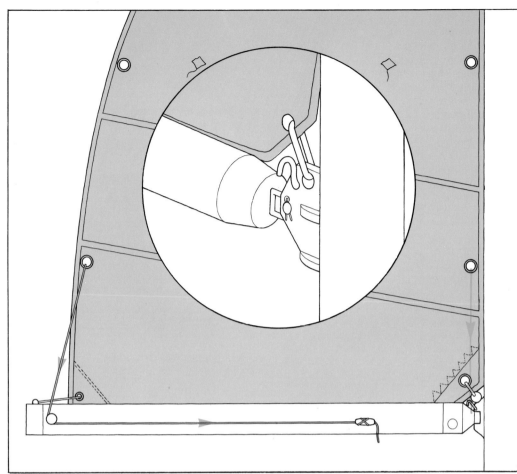

SLAB REEFING

This has improved the old fashioned points reefing system, making it simpler and faster to reef. The halyard is eased and a slab line, or reefing pannant, hauls a cringle on the leech of the mainsail down onto the boom. This forms the new clew. At the same height on the luff another cringle is hauled down and placed on a hook by the gooseneck, thus removing a slab of sail area. The reefing points may be tied up for tidiness sake, but are not essential to the reef. The slab lines are usually led inside the boom and into stoppers in the inboard end-fitting of the boom. These lock the lines once they have been winched down. The slab reef should not be confused with the jiffy reef, which although working on the same principle is merely used to flatten the foot area of the sail rather than to reduce its area.

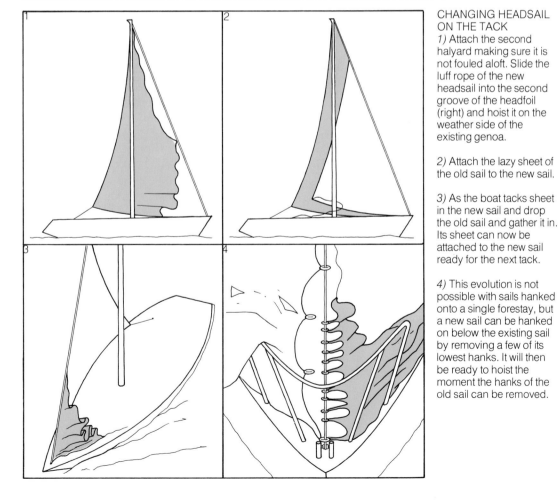

CHANGING HEADSAIL ON THE TACK

1) Attach the second halyard making sure it is not fouled aloft. Slide the luff rope of the new headsail into the second groove of the headfoil (right) and hoist it on the weather side of the existing genoa.

2) Attach the lazy sheet of the old sail to the new sail.

3) As the boat tacks sheet in the new sail and drop the old sail and gather it in. Its sheet can now be attached to the new sail ready for the next tack.

4) This evolution is not possible with sails hanked onto a single forestay, but a new sail can be hanked on below the existing sail by removing a few of its lowest hanks. It will then be ready to hoist the moment the hanks of the old sail can be removed.

great deal more care taken by the tactician to see exactly when it can be done safely.

Heavy Airs

The important thing is to keep the boat upright and this may mean considerable reefing. It is far better to be sailing comfortably with reduced canvas than staggering along with too much, on pressed down and making lots of leeway. With a masthead rig it is the mainsail that is reefed first and always remains, as far as possible, one step ahead of headsail reduction. With fractional rigs the reverse is true. This is because the 'major sail' role is reversed. With a masthead rig the genoa is by far the larger sail and provides the principal force; the mainsail acts as a trim tab to it. With a modern fractional rig the power force comes from the mainsail, the genoa giving it an encouraged entry of faster air over the leeward side.

Mast controls with a fractional rig allow the mainsail to be twisted off and the power lost from the top of the sail without altering the balance of the boat. If one reefs the mainsail before the headsails there is danger of the boat developing lee helm and this makes it incredibly difficult to steer. Some skippers persist in reefing the main first to give them a 'mini-masthead' rig, but it has rarely been known to pay. The fractional rig is perhaps best understood by dinghy sailors and their techniques are the ones that are being applied to greatest advantage in heavy airs by the sailors of offshore boats.

Downwind

Much of the complexity of downwind sailing revolves around the choice of sail combination. It varies for each boat and is one of the things which can be sorted out early in the season by the crew in pre-race training. They must try all the combinations of sails under all types of weather conditions and sail the boat in all possible directions downwind to record all available data. The navigator-tactician should note the wind speed, the temperature, sea state, boat speed and the course against each combination used. In this way a polar diagram can be prepared for each combination of sails. The optimum headings for them at various wind speeds and an analysis of each combination will produce a chart showing which is best for every heading at each apparent wind speed. The tactician can keep these calculations in tabular form pinned above the chart table. He will know which combination to call for before the start of each downwind leg as he will be able to calculate the heading and strength of the apparent wind before the boat is on course. These tables should be used only as a guide; in practice it may be found that other combinations can be made to work almost as well, and for tactical reasons such as a combination that would not require a change for the following leg they may be better in the long run. With headsails other than spinnakers, the data in the tables should

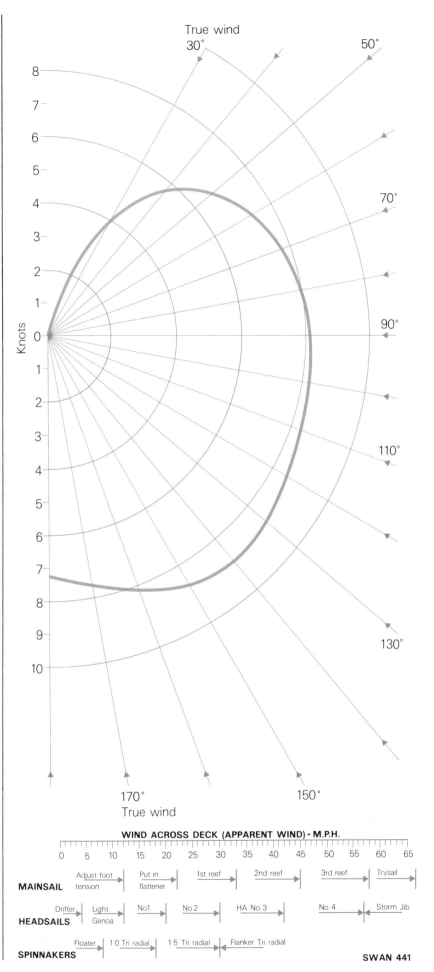

POLAR DIAGRAM OF BOAT SPEED

In racing it is vital to obtain the greatest boat speed on any course for any given wind velocity. It is equally important to know if, or by how much speed the boat will gain or lose by altering course.

The Polar Diagram *(above)* shows boat speed on the various angles of sail from close hauled to a dead run for one wind speed. Further curves can be constructed for other wind strengths. However, in practice, the difficulties in getting accurate readings in conditions which are never constant makes it impractical to construct such curves. This diagram is included to illustrate the rapid drop in speed when the boat is pinched too close to the wind, and also the increase in speed obtained by altering course to bring the wind from dead astern to a broad reach. The height and length of the sea will obviously have a great effect on real performance, but it is useful to know the best points of sailing for any particular boat.

With planing dinghies the increase in speed on a broad reach would be even more marked, creating a greater outward bulge in the curve around 130° to the true wind.

There are several ways the information on sail-setting might be tabulated, the table *(below)* shows the information for sail changes for various wind speeds for a Swan 441, a 44.42 ft. (13.5 metre) ocean racer. Such a table could be elaborated to show sheet settings, lock positions and mast adjustment. A heavy or awkward sea may require; quite considerable changes to obtain the necessary power, but constructing such a table will help greatly in getting the rig set up approximately right to start with.

WINDWARD IN HEAVY WEATHER

In heavy winds it needs considerable reefing to keep a boat upright. Masthead boats reef the main first because the foresail is the source of real power. With fractional rigs the reverse is true and the headsail will usually be changed or reefed first so that it is always a step ahead of the main. Keeping the boat upright also means getting the weight of the crew to windward. The sails will be flatter with the genoa sheeted well aft, flattening the lower part of the sail and allowing the top part to twist off. Note that the genoa sheet has been led across the cockpit so that the trimmer's weight is in the best place.

include sheeting position data. If this is all written down it avoids the mistakes caused by relying on memory. As an extra aid, positions on sheet lead tracks should be marked in paint so that crewmen can find them instantly instead of having to search for a punched-in number on the track.

The sail limitations imposed by the I.O.R. have sounded the death knell to many of the fancy headsails that were once carried under spinnakers. In their place are now multipurpose stay sails which cope with a wide range of downwind situations.

These same sail limitations have restricted the number of spinnakers that the boat is allowed to carry. While these limits are not seriously restrictive, they have encouraged sailmakers to build spinnakers that cover a wider range of wind speeds and directions than before. To some extent this has reduced the number of spinnaker peels seen in races. It is, however, an essential manoeuvre when there are big changes in wind speeds and directions.

One of the most challenging points of sailing for the crew is when the sheets have just been cracked off. The first thing is to barber haul the genoa sheet out to the lee rail, getting it as far outboard as possible. The lead will need to be further forward than the windward going position to take the twist out of the sail by keeping more tension on the leech. This in turn will encourage more fullness in the genoa. There may be, in the boat's wardrobe, a special reaching headsail with the clew cut very high, but with the same L.P.G. as the number one genoa, and which can be sheeted right aft near the stern. This should be used whenever possible. In its absence, the lightweight number one genoa, which is invariably cut with a higher clew than its regular-weight counterpart, can be used effectively in a higher wind range when reaching than it can be when beating to windward.

Matters become more complex as the wind frees and there is an option to use a double head rig. One can forget the double head rig in fractionally rigged boats up to one ton size. The effect of trying to use it is generally to close the slots and reduce boat speed rather than increasing it. The double head rig is efficient only over a narrow band of wind range. It is as well for the tactician to check the boat speed against the wind speed regularly when it is in use, and the crew must be prepared to douse the staysail with the minimum fuss as quickly as possible. The trimmers must have tell-tales on all the headsails to get them working efficiently.

In stronger breezes reaching may have to be done with smaller headsails; and whilst those boats allowed large wardrobes may find room for a blast reacher among the sails they carry there will be no space for one in smaller boats – at least not as a single-purpose sail. Instead a highly effective one can be made by having a second clew fitted some way up the leech of the number two genoa. It might even

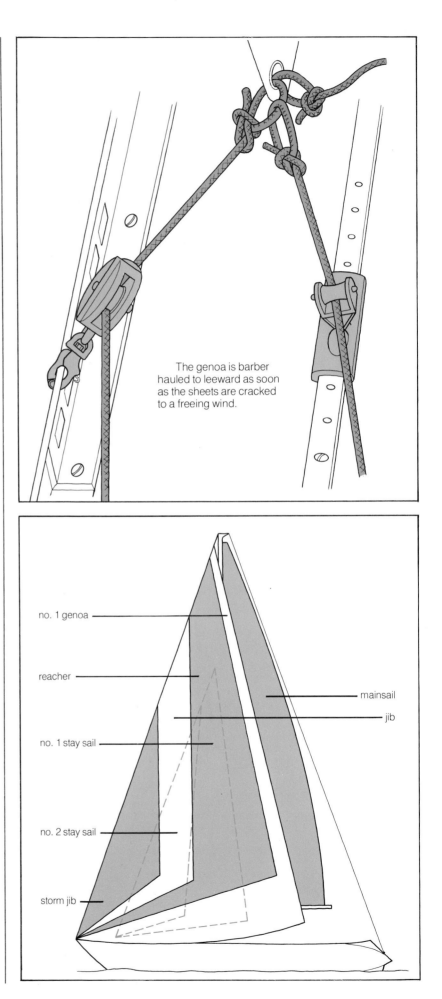

The genoa is barber hauled to leeward as soon as the sheets are cracked to a freeing wind.

no. 1 genoa

reacher

mainsail

jib

no. 1 stay sail

no. 2 stay sail

storm jib

SAIL WARDROBES
These vary according to the class and size of a yacht, the sails permitted under the rules, and the owner's pocket.

DOUBLE HEADED RIG
This rig *(lower left)* works best in larger yachts. It has an inner forestay on which staysails can be set in conjunction with higher cut jibs or jib topsails on the forestay. Used correctly these enhance the slot effect on a reach. The genoas carried for close hauled work will be the same as for the single headed rig.

SINGLE HEADED RIG
The rig *(top right)* sails will vary in cut and weight, as well as in size. A No. 1 and a No. 2 genoa may have the same area, but be of different cloths, the No. 2 being heavier and with a higher cut. A reacher generally comes as far aft as the No. 1 genoa, but is fuller and cut high so that it sheets right aft. A drifter, as its name suggests, is very lightweight and generally cut only slightly higher than the genoa. Spinnakers too, come in differing sizes and cuts to serve various purposes. For downwind work there are in addition special staysails, as well as the blooper – otherwise known as the shooter, streaker and big-boy.

lower right – a No. 2 genoa fitted with a second clew on the luff. Used with the normal tack it makes a good high-cut blast reacher. Used with a matching cringle on the luff it can be reefed.

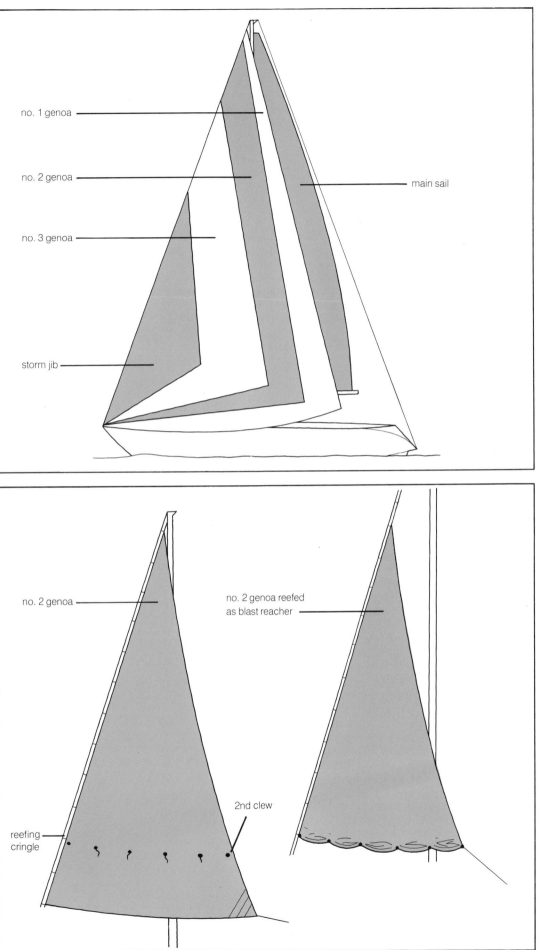

no. 1 genoa

no. 2 genoa

no. 3 genoa

main sail

storm jib

no. 2 genoa

no. 2 genoa reefed as blast reacher

2nd clew

reefing cringle

be used with a matching one in the luff as a reef. This higher clew, when used in combination with the regular tack, will give a very effective blast reaching sail.

In very strong winds it may pay to reach with a very much reefed mainsail and a bigger headsail to reduce weather helm to a minimum. This is another combination that can only be assessed by trial and error, and this is one of the reasons why the crew must try to get practice in extreme conditions away from the race course.

As soon as the wind is far enough aft for the boat to carry it, a spinnaker must go up. The order of hoisting will have been practised by the crew but some steps are fundamental. The halyard and the weather sheet (guy) must be hauled together, particularly when the spinnaker is not set in stops, and the leeward sheet must be free. In this way the spinnaker will not fill and pull the boat over and encourage a broach. Instead, it will fly like a flag until the leeward sheet is trimmed in, providing the pole is properly guyed in position with both lift and foreguy cleated off so that the pole will not sky.

Spinnaker trim

The spinnaker trimmer now takes control of the boat. When reaching, his best position for seeing the luff of the spinnaker is up by the weather shrouds, and standing up. Whoever is working the winch for him (if this should be necessary) must watch his every move and listen for his every word. On the shout of 'trim' the winch men must spring into action, but they can anticipate the call by watching the curl of the luff of the spinnaker.

The trimmer must also consider the problems of the helmsman on shy reach. It may be that he is fighting to stop the boat from broaching, in which case the trimmer must take care never to oversheet and at all times to give more sheet out when the boat begins to head up. The mainsheet trimmer should also anticipate this by dumping the sheet as fast as he can. It might pay to tuck a reef in the mainsail under these conditions, and it is worth remembering when coming on to a reach with one or more reefs in for the windward leg. Then it is best to settle down on the reach before shaking the reefs out, to see whether or not the boat can stand the extra power from the mainsail. Boats with fractional rigs do not have quite as many problems in this area because of the reduced proportion of the spinnaker.

The pole should be trimmed as far aft as possible at all times; the more spinnaker there is to weather of the centreline of the boat, the more resultant force there is from it in the forward direction. The sheet trimmer is the arbiter of how far aft it should be but he may often show a reluctance to bring it far enough aft as it makes the spinnaker difficult to set.

As the wind comes further aft there is the option of setting staysails under the spinnaker, or even keeping the genoa hoisted

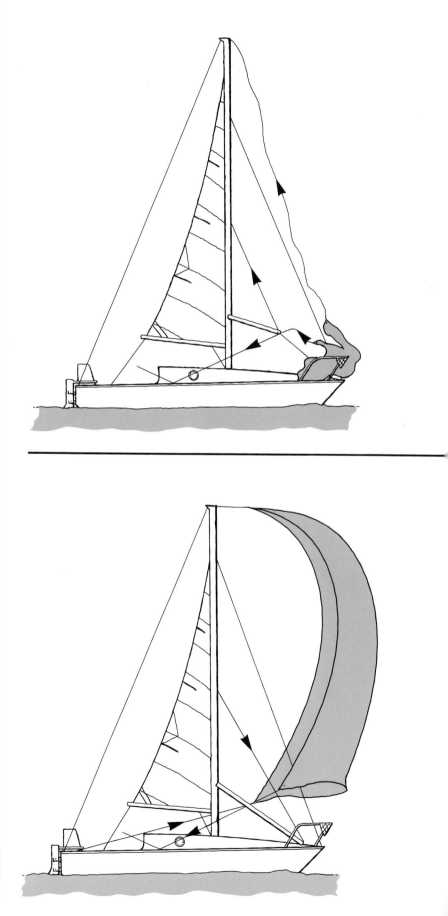

HOISTING THE
SPINNAKER
The halyard and the guy
are hauled in together and
the sheet let fly. Make sure
the pole is in the right
place with both the uphaul
and the foreguy cleated
off. The sail will fly like a
flag until the sheet is
hauled in.

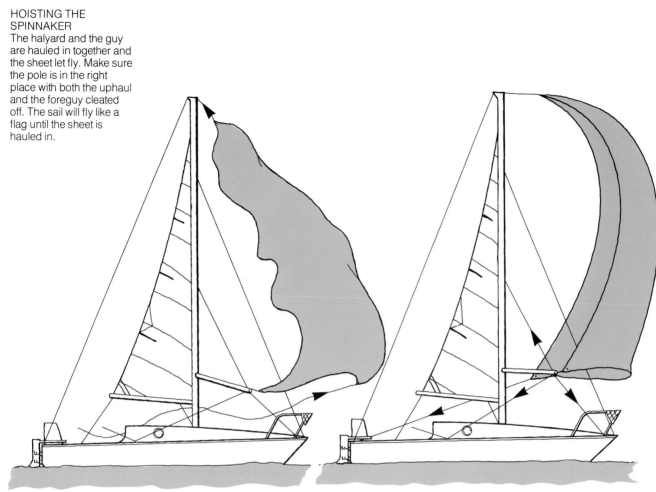

THE WINDWARD DROP
Remove the pole and dip it
onto the foredeck. Haul in
on the lazy sheet on the
weather side where the sail
is held by the guy. As
soon as you have the tack
of the sail within reach
cleat the sheet off tight so
that the sail cannot take off
with you. Haul in the sail as
the leeward sheet and the
halyard are checked out.

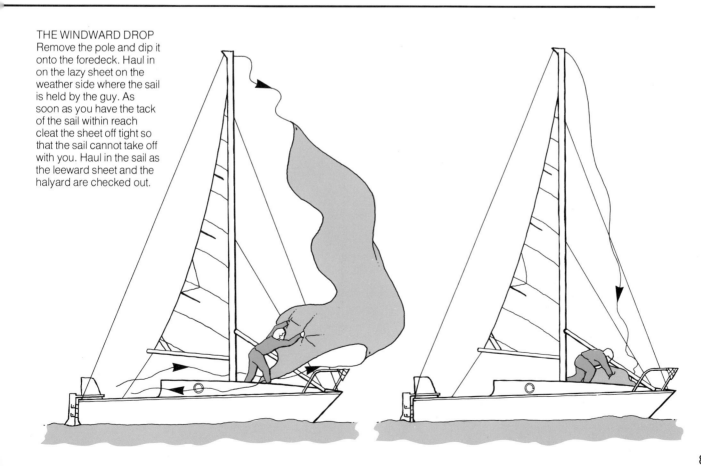

when the wind is sufficiently strong. The temptation to hoist staysails should be resisted in light airs and even in medium breezes as they will serve no other purpose than disturb the air in which the spinnaker is setting. Their purpose is to provide another venturi and thus increase the speed on the wind going across the mainsail and spinnaker. To do so they need sufficient initial wind speed. Staysails tend to be of little use in smaller boats because of their proximity to the other sails; the interference that results outweighs any potential benefit that they might otherwise have provided.

In lighter weather it will pay to reach high of the course on a run to gain boat speed. Just how high is a matter for the tactician who will be interested in any shift in the direction of the wind that he can use to advantage.

Spinnaker Peel

With different spinnakers for different purposes it will certainly become necessary at times to change spinnakers underway. This must be accomplished with the minimum of fuss with one of the spinnakers drawing all the time. The new spinnaker is prepared for a set inside the one in use. The second halyard is carefully attached so that it does not twist around any of the others, or the forestay, aloft. This is where the foredeck boss comes into his own. The tack is snap shackled to an eye close to the outboard end of the pole on a very short strop. The lazy guy or spare sheet are used as the leeward sheet. The new spinnaker is now hoisted and quickly trimmed inside the first spinnaker.

The peel is accomplished by tripping the snap shackle on the guy of the old sail and hauling it in on the old sheet from over the stern as it comes free; the halyard is checked out in sympathy with the crew men dousing the old sail. The guy is then connected into the clew of the new spinnaker and when the load is taken on to the guy, the temporary strop holding it to the end of the pole is released. After that the leeward sheet and a lazy guy can be attached if they are needed.

Dropping the spinnaker can be done either to windward or, more usually, to leeward. The leeward drop is the safer but may be impractical if a gybe is the best manoeuvre before hardening up on a close reach or to windward. Then the weather drop is a must. It involves removing the pole and dipping it onto the foredeck, hauling in on the lazy sheet (the weather side is held by the guy) as the leeward sheet is freed and the halyard checked out in sympathy. To drop to leeward, the sail is tripped from the snap shackle on the guy and the sail brought in by the lazy guy over the stern. Smaller boats where through pole gybing is employed will have only single sheets on each clew of the spinnaker but as the sails are smaller these can be used to douse the sail. In addition it is unnecessary to free the guy from the sail on a leeward drop as the guy is allowed to run free.

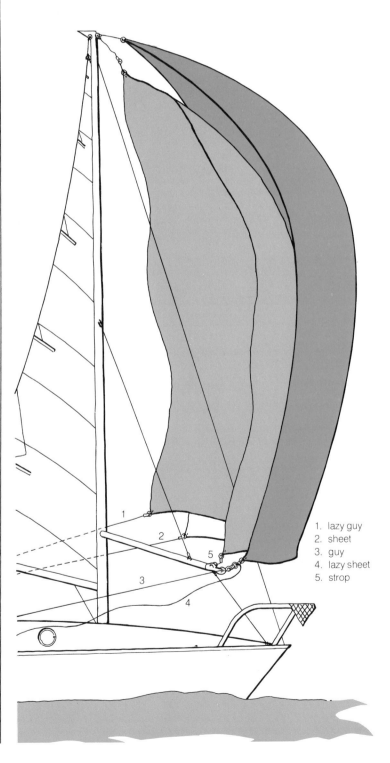

1. lazy guy
2. sheet
3. guy
4. lazy sheet
5. strop

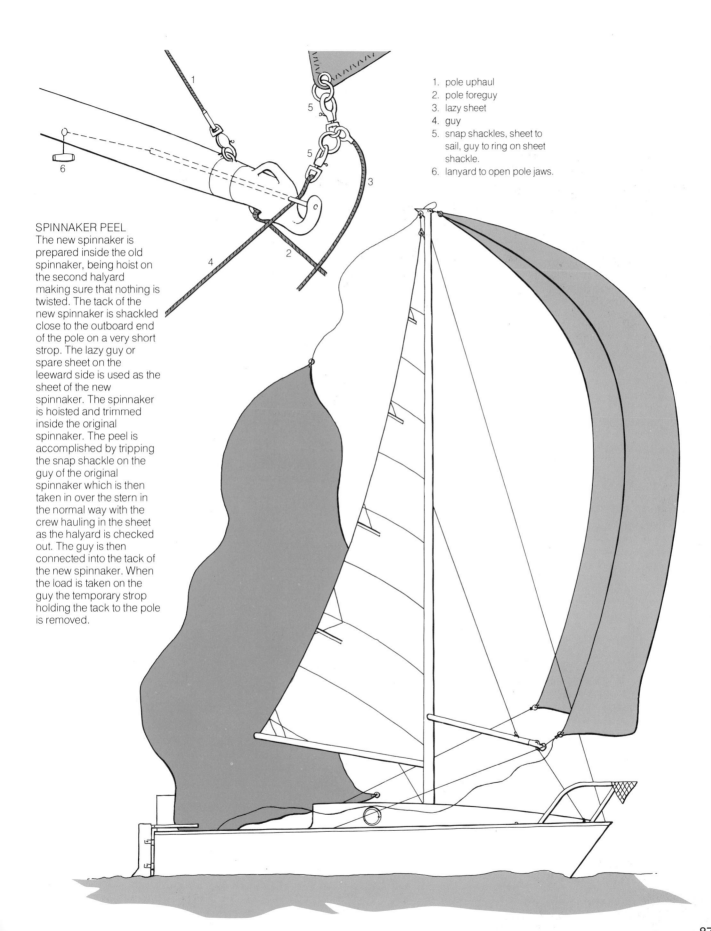

1. pole uphaul
2. pole foreguy
3. lazy sheet
4. guy
5. snap shackles, sheet to sail, guy to ring on sheet shackle.
6. lanyard to open pole jaws.

SPINNAKER PEEL

The new spinnaker is prepared inside the old spinnaker, being hoist on the second halyard making sure that nothing is twisted. The tack of the new spinnaker is shackled close to the outboard end of the pole on a very short strop. The lazy guy or spare sheet on the leeward side is used as the sheet of the new spinnaker. The spinnaker is hoisted and trimmed inside the original spinnaker. The peel is accomplished by tripping the snap shackle on the guy of the original spinnaker which is then taken in over the stern in the normal way with the crew hauling in the sheet as the halyard is checked out. The guy is then connected into the tack of the new spinnaker. When the load is taken on the guy the temporary strop holding the tack to the pole is removed.

Ocean Racing

Strategy must be decisively planned as there are the additional problems associated with racing for a long time.

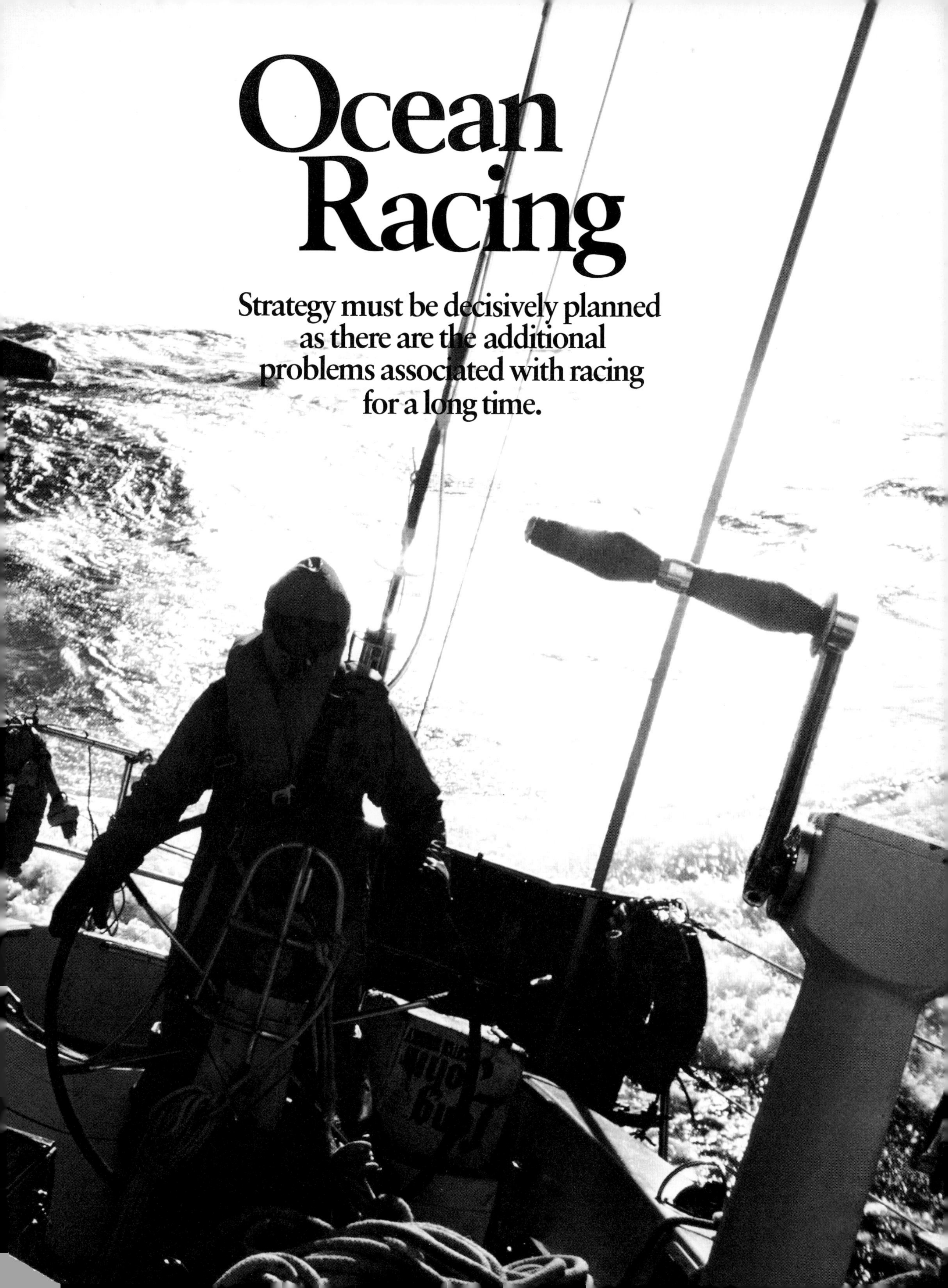

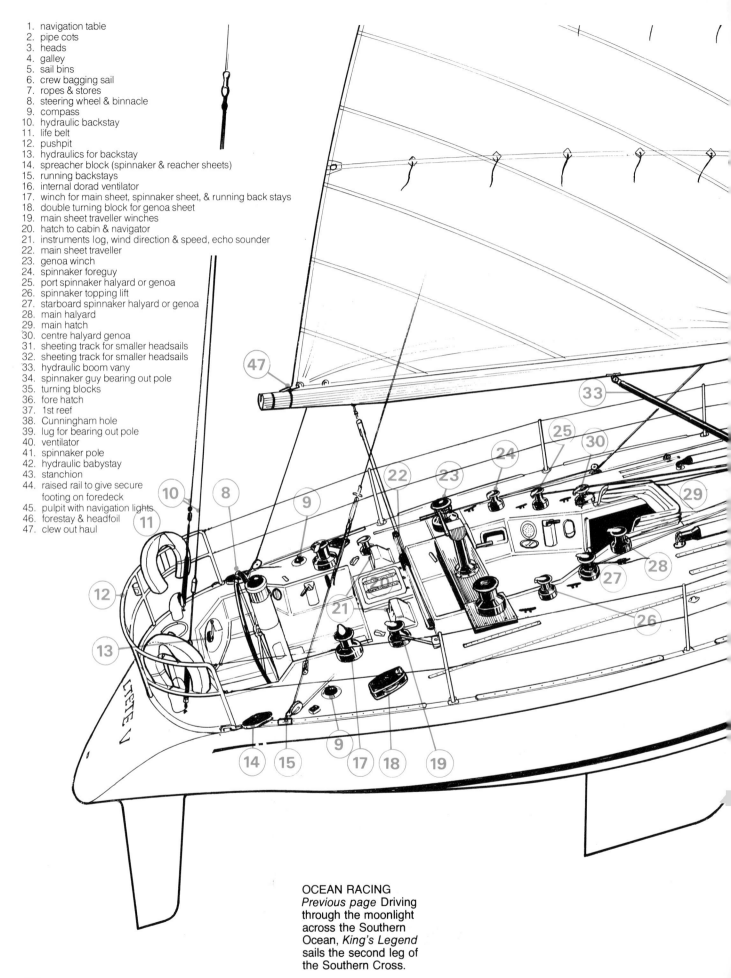

1. navigation table
2. pipe cots
3. heads
4. galley
5. sail bins
6. crew bagging sail
7. ropes & stores
8. steering wheel & binnacle
9. compass
10. hydraulic backstay
11. life belt
12. pushpit
13. hydraulics for backstay
14. spreacher block (spinnaker & reacher sheets)
15. running backstays
16. internal dorad ventilator
17. winch for main sheet, spinnaker sheet, & running back stays
18. double turning block for genoa sheet
19. main sheet traveller winches
20. hatch to cabin & navigator
21. instruments log, wind direction & speed, echo sounder
22. main sheet traveller
23. genoa winch
24. spinnaker foreguy
25. port spinnaker halyard or genoa
26. spinnaker topping lift
27. starboard spinnaker halyard or genoa
28. main halyard
29. main hatch
30. centre halyard genoa
31. sheeting track for smaller headsails
32. sheeting track for smaller headsails
33. hydraulic boom vany
34. spinnaker guy bearing out pole
35. turning blocks
36. fore hatch
37. 1st reef
38. Cunningham hole
39. lug for bearing out pole
40. ventilator
41. spinnaker pole
42. hydraulic babystay
43. stanchion
44. raised rail to give secure footing on foredeck
45. pulpit with navigation lights
46. forestay & headfoil
47. clew out haul

OCEAN RACING
Previous page Driving through the moonlight across the Southern Ocean, *King's Legend* sails the second leg of the Southern Cross.

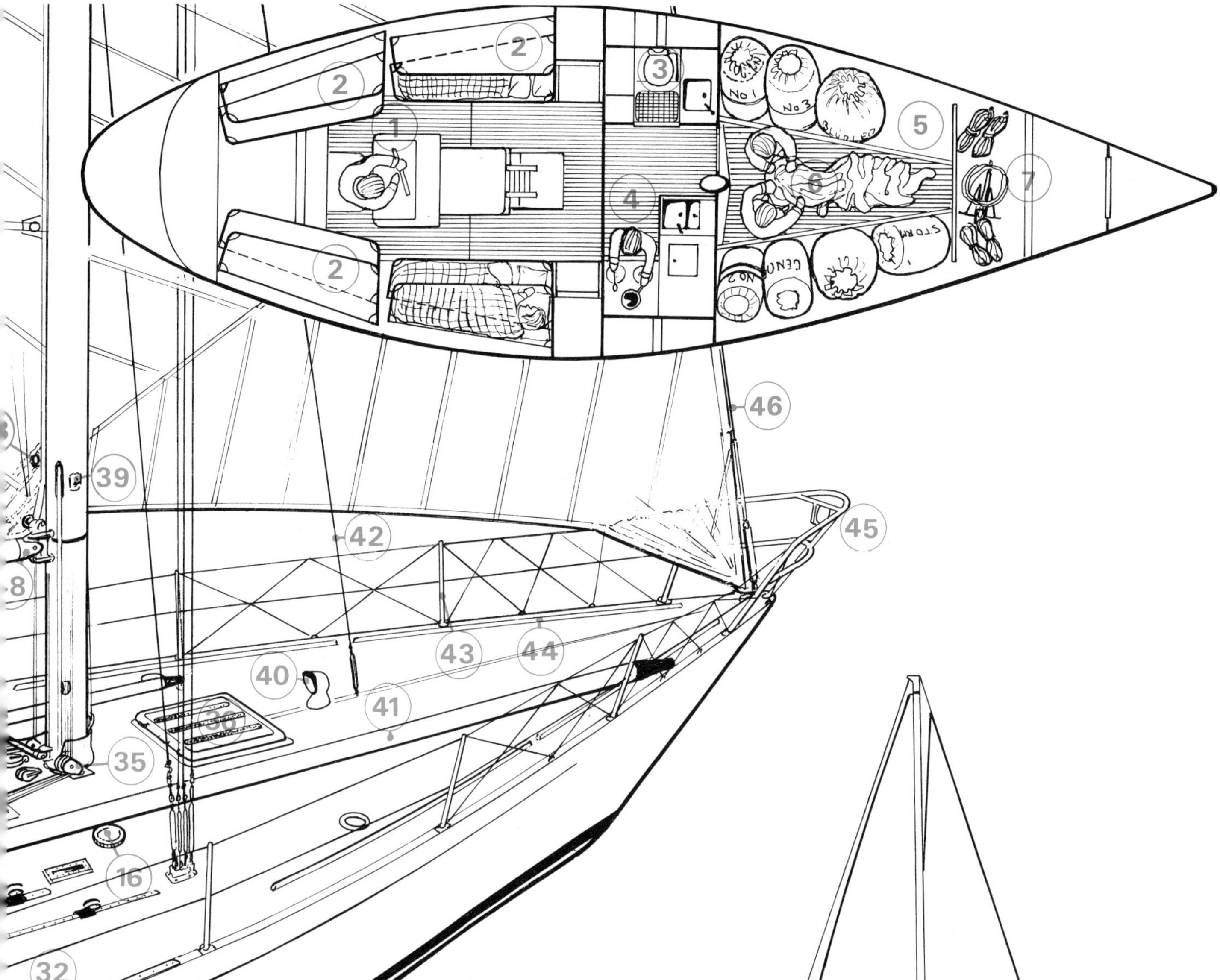

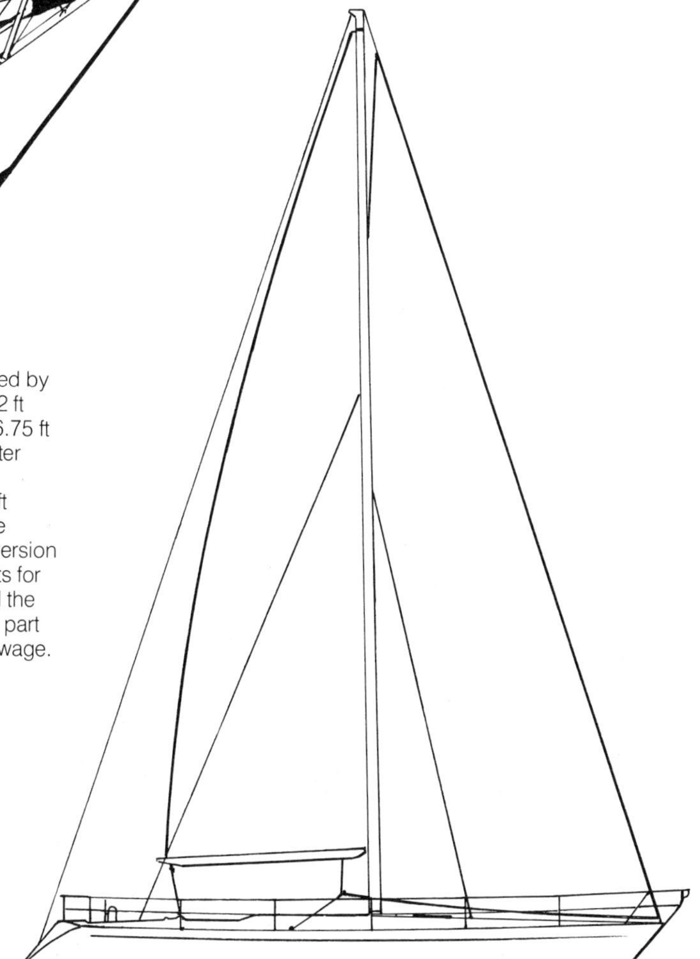

A Swan 441 Designed by Ron Holland is 42.42 ft (13.54 m) overall, 36.75 ft (11.20 m) on the water line, with a rating of approximately 35.8 ft (10.90 m). This is the stripped out racing version with sample pipe cots for the watch below and the whole of the forward part given over to sail stowage.

Whilst needing all the fundamental skills of closed-course racing, ocean racing is a totally different concept. Almost all the tactics of racing around buoys are irrelevant as yachts are no longer in close contention, even in level rating regattas. Strategy must be planned to a far greater degree and there are the additional problems associated with racing for a long period of time. There is an even greater need for crew harmony and for the skipper to exercise the control that keeps morale high. The crew must blend as a team and be prepared to work towards the common goal of winning; they need to be prepared to cope with the frustrations and set backs that the sport can all too often deal out.

Sleeping and feeding properly play a large part in successful ocean racing. Crew members must learn to pace themselves correctly or the value of their individual skills is nullified. Old systems of watch keeping are giving place to new as ocean racing becomes more competitive. An influx of dinghy sailors in the early 1970s revolutionized the sport when they introduced extensions of their round-the-buoys racing into the longer events. They were prepared to treat them in the same way as they did the shorter races, going flat out the entire time. It put great demands on the other crews, who had to find ways of changing half a century's traditional methods. The old four-on, four-off alternating watch system became an anachronism as specialist upwind and downwind helmsmen emerged. The afterguard became separate from the rest of the crew and rotating watches evolved.

One-night races are treated much more like round-the-buoys events with only the helmsmen allotted specific rest periods (the rest will grab what they can and some will even catnap on the weather rail when going to windward). It is more of an all-out effort. It is preferable that some should get a couple of hours' undisturbed sleep but when a major sail change is required or there is a buoy to round, all hands must turn out. With a rotating crew watch, it is best to aim for one fresh man to come on deck every hour. This will infect new vitality at regular intervals. Helmsmen, too, should change frequently. This need not be regularly, but will depend on circumstances. A helmsman can maintain maximum concentration and optimum performance rather longer when the boat is, say, going to windward in medium airs than if it is charging before a big sea with the spinnaker and blooper set and 25–30 knots of apparent wind astern. In such testing conditions he is likely to tire quite quickly and will need to be relieved far sooner than usual.

Longer races require greater regimen and a watch pattern must be established soon after the start if it is to be effective. The pattern will vary between boats depending on their size. The smaller the boat, the smaller the number in the crew and the greater the problem of maintaining a watch system. Quite different

Eleven Man System

Time	Dave	Bob	John	Simon	Paul George Alastair	Stephen Jim Peter
midnight	STEER	TRIM	OFF		ON	OFF
01.00	STEER	TRIM		OFF	ON	OFF
02.00	OFF	STEER	TRIM	OFF	ON	OFF
03.00	OFF	STEER	STEER	TRIM	ON	OFF
04.00	TRIM	OFF	STEER	STEER	ON	OFF
05.00	TRIM	OFF	OFF	STEER	ON	OFF
06.00	STEER	TRIM	OFF	OFF	OFF	ON
07.00	STEER	TRIM	OFF	OFF	OFF	ON
08.00	OFF	STEER	TRIM		OFF	ON
09.00	OFF	STEER	STEER	TRIM	ON	OFF
10.00	TRIM	OFF	STEER	TRIM	ON	OFF
11.00	TRIM	OFF	OFF	STEER	ON	OFF
12.00	STEER	TRIM	OFF		ON	OFF
13.00	STEER	TRIM		OFF	OFF	ON
14.00	OFF	STEER	TRIM		OFF	ON
15.00	OFF	STEER	STEER	TRIM	OFF	ON
16.00	TRIM	OFF	STEER	TRIM	OFF	ON
17.00	TRIM	OFF	OFF	STEER	ON	OFF
18.00	STEER	TRIM	OFF		ON	OFF
19.00	STEER	TRIM		OFF	ON	OFF
20.00	OFF	STEER	TRIM		ON	OFF
21.00	OFF	STEER	STEER	TRIM	OFF	ON
22.00	TRIM	OFF	STEER	TRIM	OFF	ON
23.00	TRIM	OFF	OFF	STEER	OFF	ON
24.00	STEER			OFF	OFF	ON

Four Man System

Time	Bob*	Hugo	Hugh*	David
midnight	OFF	TRIM	STEER	OFF
01.00	OFF	TRIM	STEER	OFF
02.00	OFF	TRIM	STEER	OFF
03.00	OFF	OFF	STEER	TRIM
04.00	OFF	OFF	OFF	TRIM
05.00	STEER	OFF	OFF	TRIM
06.00	STEER	OFF	OFF	TRIM
07.00	STEER	TRIM	OFF	OFF
08.00	STEER	TRIM	OFF	OFF
09.00	OFF	TRIM	STEER	OFF
10.00	OFF	TRIM	STEER	OFF
11.00	OFF	OFF	STEER	TRIM
12.00	OFF	OFF	STEER	TRIM
13.00	STEER	OFF	OFF	TRIM
14.00	STEER	OFF	OFF	TRIM
15.00	STEER	TRIM	OFF	OFF
16.00	STEER	TRIM	OFF	OFF
17.00	OFF	TRIM	STEER	OFF
18.00	OFF	TRIM	STEER	OFF
19.00	OFF	OFF	STEER	TRIM
20.00	OFF	OFF	STEER	TRIM
21.00	OFF	OFF	OFF	TRIM
22.00	OFF	OFF	OFF	TRIM
23.00	OFF	OFF	OFF	OFF
24.00	OFF	OFF	OFF	OFF

* Helmsman

WATCH ROTAS

There are many ways of organizing a watch rota and various factors to consider when choosing the best for any particular race. Most boats evolve a system best suited to their needs. In recent years, this has meant splitting the helmsmen from the rest of the crew

In the 11 man crew rota, the four helmsmen are rotated under one system while the rest of the crew work and sleep to the more traditional four on, four off routine. In the case of the helmsmen, they will each come on watch for the first hour and a half, when they act as sail trimmers, getting the feel of the boat, the wind and the sea. Then they will steer for another hour-and-a-half before going off watch for three hours. Thus there is a new man on every hour-and-a-half and nobody takes over the wheel cold. The other six men rotate in two watches, four hours on an four hours off. The navigator is on call at all times, but is not included in the rota.

With a four man crew, such as that on a quarter-tonner, there is not the same flexibility for specialist watches. In the rota shown, Bob and Hugh are the helmsmen. They interchange every four hours. The two parts are staggered, so that there is someone fresh on deck every two hours.

Where there are five men, as in a half-tonner, the navigator will usually remain out of the watch system but will always be available to work on deck if necessary.

thought must be given to the matter of how to achieve the best use of the four-man crew of a Quarter-tonner and the 10 aboard a 45-foot Admiral's Cup contender. Some factors are common to both whilst others are strictly individual.

The basic essentials of an ocean racing boat are that she should be driven at the optimum speed in the right direction at all times. This requires good helmsmanship, sail trim and navigation. Whenever the number on board allows, the navigator's job should be confined to navigation alone. With a short-numbered crew he will get other jobs to do as well, but the more time he can devote to navigation the greater the chances of winning. Someone must trim sails constantly as the wind is for ever changing, and the helmsman must be fresh. With a four-man crew in a Quarter-tonner the demands on the crew are therefore high and only one can be 'off watch' at any one time and all must be capable of any tasks demanded. With five on a Half-tonner the navigator's role can be doubled with that of cook and utility man and a more equable rotation of tasks among the other four. Greater specialization can be obtained with the larger numbered crews. With three helmsmen rotating, the steering of the boat can be kept at an optimum level with the addition

perhaps of the skipper, leaving four men in the crew to rotate as sail trimmers on the Admiral's Cup boat during racing.

Food is more important than most ocean racers will admit. A little taken often is a good maxim for sustenance and morale. The food must be sufficiently substantial, easy to eat but never boring. The crew that races on pre-packed cheese sandwiches and vacuum flasks of coffee will never have the impact of a crew with variety in their diet and which includes hot food.

I have a vivid memory of a grey windy day in Sajuna Bay, Japan, during the long offshore race in the Quarter Ton World Championship. We had been out for 24 hours in strong winds and knew that it would be at least another 20 hours before we would finish. At the time we had full mainsail and a spinnaker set running in biggish seas and surfing down the faces of the waves. It had been a tough night of power two-sail reaching and beating. The three of us on deck were at a low psychologically, a low relieved only by the thrills of the surfing. The off-watch crewman suddenly brought a pan full of hot scrambled egg into the cockpit. Within minutes it had been devoured, morale was at a new high and the boat was going faster than it had been before–power to food.

CREW OF 11   250 MILE RACE STARTING 20.00 HRS. FRIDAY

Friday supper (eaten at dock or on way to start) & prepared on shore	Beef casserole with potatoes and fresh green vegetables Apple pie and cream Coffee 1 cut loaf	**Reserves** 6 tins 'main meal' soups 3 tins potatoes 2 lbs rice 2 doz rashers bacon 2 cut loaves
Overnight	1 dozen cup mix soups/Oxo Coffee and tea	**Check:** Salt and pepper Gas bottle
Saturday		Matches (1 box sealed in polythene bag) 36 Mars-bars, 36 Kit Kats
Breakfast	2 dozen eggs-scrambled 24 rashers bacon 2 cut loaves coffee and tea	36 Small Chocolate bars 72 Assorted soft drinks (cans) 24 Oxo cubes, Tea, Coffee Cocoa, 3 lbs Butter, Jam
Lunch	Sliced beef/ham/salami for sandwiches Bowl of lettuce hearts (12) and tomatoes (24) Apples (12) Oranges (12) 2 cut loaves Large quiche-cooked ashore	Marmalade, Marmite (Meat extract) Cakes (fruit slab etc) 2 bottles squash Dry Ice-if available for ice a box
Dinner	8 oz steaks Tinned potatoes and peas/beans carrots Individual fruit pies with cream coffee 1 cut loaf	
Overnight	1 doz cup mix soup/Oxo Coffee and tea	
Sunday		
breakfast	2 doz eggs 2 doz sausages 2 cut loaves coffee and tea	
Lunch	Large quiche Sliced meats for sandwiches 2 cucumbers, tomatoes (24) apples (12) Oranges (12) 2 cut loaves	
Race should end here.		

Breakfast and dinner are the two important meals when ocean racing. Something hot at each end of the day is essential while sandwiches can carry you through at lunchtime. Hot drinks on cold days and cold drinks on hot days should always be readily available. Nothing stimulates a crew more during the night watches than regular hot drinks and surprise snacks. Ocean racing is physically demanding and energy sources should be constantly available. Most crews carry candy bars, chocolate or dried fruit and nuts but few bother to indulge in pre-race diets that would prepare them properly.

In the week prior to a race crews should go on to a high-protein diet, eschewing carbohydrates completely. This will help to burn off the stores of carbohydrate energy in the body in the form of glycogen and prepare the system to release readily the energy from carbohydrates. A high carbohydrate diet can then begin on the day before the race and continue throughout to obtain top performance by the crew. It is a small point but it does work very effectively. You become tired less easily and can give more effort to racing the boat.

If you are selecting a man, or woman, to cook on board an ocean-racing boat, it is essential that they can in fact fill that role. All too often those who claim they can fall down on the job. It is not easy to cook in a tiny galley with the boat heaving in the sea, and above all do it with good grace. Sea cooks are born, not made, and not surprisingly the good ones find their way on to the bigger and best boats in the fleet. If there are to be restrictions in the diet, it is as well for the crew to know about them well in advance. One half-tonner I knew, whose crew were a bunch of bon viveurs, lasted a whole season of ocean races on bacon sandwiches and hot meat-extract drinks without complaint!

For most ocean races the cook can pre-prepare most of the meals ashore. These can be deep frozen and taken aboard in an ice chest. The ice will melt in about a day but it gives the deep-frozen food 24 hours more before it begins to thaw. Stews and casseroles, vegetables and roasts can all be taken on board in plastic bags once they have been deep frozen. Some sea cooks might even plan their season's culinary delights for the crew during the preceding winter and store them in the freezer. Plain food is kinder on the stomach that is likely to be upset by the sea than fancy food. Highly spiced food is not the best thing to go with force 7 if you wish to avoid seasickness.

Racing Navigation

This is not a black art or some mysterious mumbo jumbo; race navigation is a skill which anyone capable of logical thought can master. Like a computer, the navigator can produce better results with more information at his disposal. Some of the input is fundamentally basic while the rest helps to refine

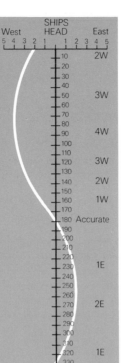

SHIPS HEAD

West	East
5 4 3 2 1	1 2 3 4 5

10 — 2W
20
30
40
50 — 3W
60
70
80
90 — 4W
100
110
120 — 3W
130
140 — 2W
150
160 — 1W
170
180 — Accurate
190
200
210
220
230 — 1E
240
250
260
270 — 2E
280
290
300
310
320 — 1E
330
340
350
360 — 2W

COMPASS DEVIATION
The compass is normally swung and corrected by a professional compass adjuster. It is usually possible for him to correct the compass so that deviation amounts to only a few degrees east or west. He will then produce a deviation chart. Common sense dictates that you do not stow metal objects near the compass. A chart showing the deviation curve in graphic form (left) is easiest to use and should be fixed where it is visible from the chart table. At sea the navigator can and should check the compass deviation at sunrise and sunset, if it is possible to get a bearing from the steering compass to the sun as it touches the horizon. The calculation is very simple, quite accurate.

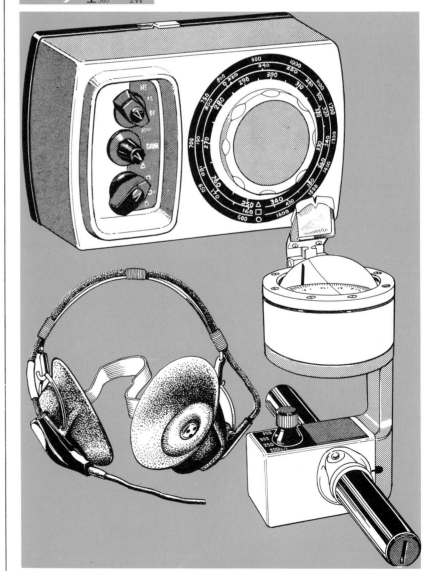

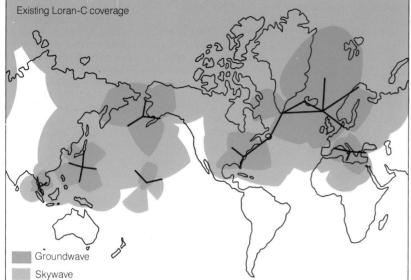

Existing Loran-C coverage

Groundwave
Skywave

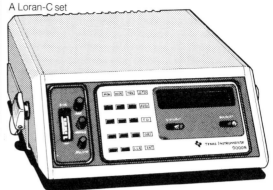

A Loran-C set

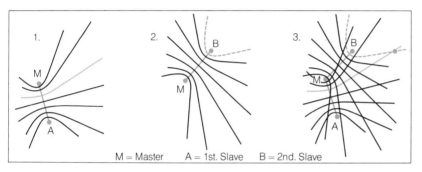

M = Master   A = 1st. Slave   B = 2nd. Slave

LORAN, OMEGA AND DECCA
position finding systems are only allowed in some racing areas. They are complex, expensive and very accurate. Loran, Omega and Decca use land based transmitting stations, operating in chains, that put out a pattern of radio waves that are identified more or less automatically by the receiver on board. Special charts printed with the patterns of each station are used, and these give something akin to a circle of distance-off from the stations received. Two or more such circles from different stations provide the fix. The diagrams lower left illustrate the Loran C system.

1) Shows the pattern put out by the master and first Slave Station (A). The Slave responds to the Master's signal after a predetermined period. After a slightly longer period
2) the second slave (B) responds giving a second pattern.
3) Shows the two patterns superimposed. The receiver recognises which line of each pattern the boat is on, giving a fix. Satellite navigation uses an on-board computer linked by radio to satellites and shore stations. Loran and Decca coverage is somewhat localised, being designed for the busiest shipping areas in the world. Omega and Sat-nav are more or less worldwide.

DECK LOG							
Date	Time	Log reading	Course steered since last entry	Course required	Wind	Barograph	Remarks
June 10	0435	024	—	—	NW 3	1001	Depart Bridge buoy
	0500	026	135 C	135 C	NW 4	999	Baro dropping rapidly. Cloud thicker and lower.
	0600	033	135 C	135 C	NNW 5	998	Gusting. No 2. Spinnaker.
	0735	033					Log stopped
	0750	034					Log working again.
	0800	035	140 C	135 C	N 6	997	Main reefed. Run off to get faster ride. Wind veering.
	0810	035·5					Bearing Flame Hd. Light 224°C. Depth 42 m. Crossed wake of Daphny-H'Bory Ferry 0805.
	0900	044	145	135	N 6	997	Fishing boats 3 miles S'board beam. Rain, heavy gusts.
	0930	048	145				Flame Hd. Lt. 245°C

DECK LOG
A major part of the navigator's information comes from the deck log kept by the crew. First he needs to know the course steered in the past hour – not the course you were given or would like to have steered. He needs the log read accurately and noted together with the time. Keep an eye on the log, for they get fouled with weed and run out of powers from the batteries without notice. The navigator needs regular observations of the wind, sea, sky and barometer so that he may keep abreast of the ever developing weather pattern on which tactical decisions are based.
Remember it is the speed of the weather development that is most often wrongly forecast, and it is this timing that is critical in racing.
The most irrelevant seeming things may help a navigator confirm his DR plot. Suddenly running into weed, fishing boats that are probably working an offshore bank, or a ferry crossing your path. Note them with the time and the log reading and the bearing.

the answers. Most of it will be based on observation but some of it will be guesswork and intuition, yet the strategy of the boat is decided on the results. Therefore wherever possible the navigator should be freed of all other duties; he will have more than enough to do in order to navigate properly, without having to worry about the washing up.

The good navigator is a meticulous person who records all his observations in a notebook and tabulates them so that any anomaly will stand out clearly. Regular observations are essential for his Dead Reckoning – the basis of his navigation. Without a regular DR plot the rest of his observations, be they celestial, radio, electronic or simply eyesight fixes, will be more difficult. From a good DR the navigator at least knows fairly accurately *where* to look for his next observation and this can save him a great deal of time. Anyone who has groped his way across the English Channel in search of the CH1 buoy off Cherbourg in a thick fog with an electrical storm in the offing will know the value of good DR plots. When the navigator comes on deck in conditions like that and says 'sailing in this direction, at this speed, should bring the buoy up on the port bow in 18 minutes' and it does appear there, give or take a minute or two, the crew know he has been hard at work since the last mark was left, checking compass headings of the boat and the figures from the yacht's log.

Extra input comes from tidal atlases and tables and a small amount from intuition like the estimated leeway angle, and the whole adds up to the individual's skill. The crew can be grateful he gets it right. Conversely, all their hard work in sailing the boat at its fastest with expert helmsmanship and sail trim will be wasted if they have been led the wrong way by incorrect information from the navigator.

One can obtain a fix in any number of ways. Checking the DR against a depth sounding is one and this is often used by racing navigators to verify the accuracy of the DR. But it is only a check. More accuracy can be obtained from a line position. This comes by taking a bearing on an object, either by sighting it with a hand bearing compass or from a bearing taken on a radio transmitter whose position is known. A line of position can then be drawn on the chart.

A boat's location is the point at which two or more lines of position meet. Its accuracy depends entirely on the accuracy of the lines of position. Although a visual sight may be within 2° it is unlikely that a radio plot can be less than 5° out. At best a 'cocked hat' plot is made on the chart. The smaller the 'hat' the more accurate the bearings. Shallow lines of position will give a more inaccurate fix. Ideally, two lines of position should cross at 90° while three should cross each other at 60°.

In longer offshore races the navigator must be familiar with the use of a sextant for celestial navigation when he cannot obtain bear-

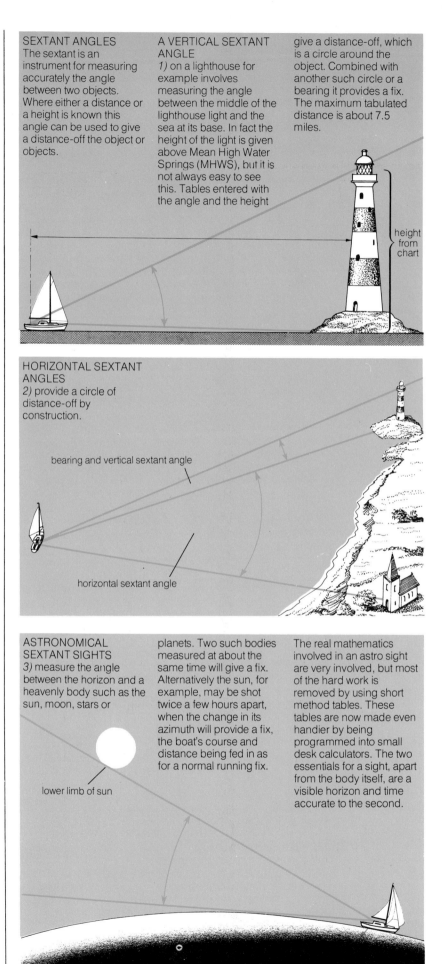

SEXTANT ANGLES
The sextant is an instrument for measuring accurately the angle between two objects. Where either a distance or a height is known this angle can be used to give a distance-off the object or objects.

A VERTICAL SEXTANT ANGLE
1) on a lighthouse for example involves measuring the angle between the middle of the lighthouse light and the sea at its base. In fact the height of the light is given above Mean High Water Springs (MHWS), but it is not always easy to see this. Tables entered with the angle and the height

give a distance-off, which is a circle around the object. Combined with another such circle or a bearing it provides a fix. The maximum tabulated distance is about 7.5 miles.

height from chart

HORIZONTAL SEXTANT ANGLES
2) provide a circle of distance-off by construction.

bearing and vertical sextant angle

horizontal sextant angle

ASTRONOMICAL SEXTANT SIGHTS
3) measure the angle between the horizon and a heavenly body such as the sun, moon, stars or

planets. Two such bodies measured at about the same time will give a fix. Alternatively the sun, for example, may be shot twice a few hours apart, when the change in its azimuth will provide a fix, the boat's course and distance being fed in as for a normal running fix.

The real mathematics involved in an astro sight are very involved, but most of the hard work is removed by using short method tables. These tables are now made even handier by being programmed into small desk calculators. The two essentials for a sight, apart from the body itself, are a visible horizon and time accurate to the second.

lower limb of sun

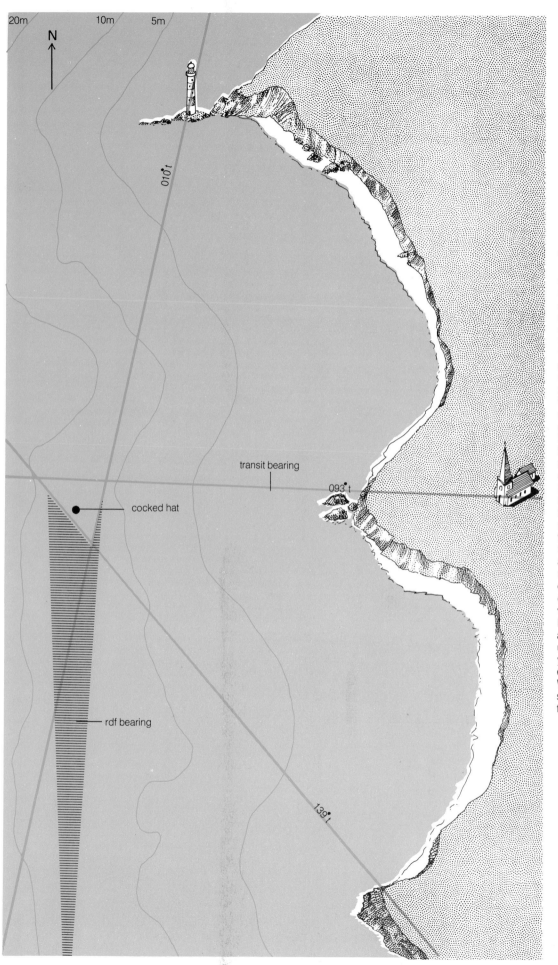

20m   10m   5m

N

010°t

transit bearing

093°t

cocked hat

rdf bearing

139°t

BEARINGS

Almost anything visible can be used for a bearing provided you can identify it on your chart. Lighthouses, churches, rocks, headlands, landmarks and buoys all provide good bearings. A transit bearing where two objects are in line provides perhaps the most accurate bearing. Two bearings are best when they cross at ninety degrees and the fix become progressively less good the narrower the angle becomes. Three bearings give you a triangle called a cocked hat, except in the rare cases where they actually meet at the same point. Any compass bearing may be combined with other information, such as the depth under the keel from the echo sounder or a radio bearing. Remember that it is mathematically unlikely that you will be inside your cocked hat, so if approaching some danger lay your course to be on the safe side. Always double check your chartwork. Even the finest navigators make silly mistakes. The difference is that they know they can make them and are ever watchful. Also one should not be ashamed to put up a crib, for example to remind you which way to correct for compass deviation and magnetic variation. After 24 hours of bashing to windward it is all too easy to find you are unsure about something you thought you had etched into your brain. When taking bearings you should automatically note the log reading and time.

ings from land or radio transmitters and the soundings cannot be pinpointed. Sun, moon and star sights are now computed with a small electronic calculator. There are only a few times in the day when a navigator can use his sextant. These are at dusk and dawn, when both the stars and the horizon can be seen; at noon, to obtain a line of latitude and other times for sun and moon shots for lines of position. Because of this the DR plot following an accurate celestial fix is of the greatest importance.

In this modern age the navigator's tools are becoming more complex. In addition to the log and depth-sounder and Direction Finding radio he may have the use of OMNI, LORAN and OMEGA. These are automatic direction-finding radios which are allowed only in some ocean-racing areas of the world. They are expensive and accurate and take a great deal of guesswork out of the racing navigator's calculations.

The biggest source of information to the navigator is the crew itself, particularly the helmsman. His honesty will contribute much to the accuracy of navigation. The navigator needs to know, as nearly as possible, the accurate course sailed. It is no use the man at the helm repeating to the navigator the course he was given when he has not been able to follow it accurately. It may be that he has gone further off wind down the face of the waves to get the best speed from the surf, but he has come back up above course when climbing up the backs of the waves. The helmsman must then know what course he has averaged during the period.

Strategy

Racing strategy is determined by the wind and current, rarely by the position of the other competitors; although in the later stages of races and in level rating they will upset the ideal strategy and a compromise might have to be made.

In closed-course racing, where it is the same throughout the course, the current does not figure as a calculation in the strategy of a race; but in offshore racing, where the strength and direction of the current is likely to vary throughout, it forms a major consideration. Tidal flow will reverse every six hours and if one is crossing this current to ignore it will prove diasastrous. The objective is to use the tidal current to the maximum effect. It can be used to give a direct gain in speed or direction or it may be used to increase the apparent wind over the sails and thereby increase the speed of the boat.

Permanent ocean currents, like the Gulf Stream in the Atlantic or the Coro Nero in the Pacific, must also enter the calculations of strategy. They can be used to advantage as I found out once to my cost in a Bermuda Race and once to my advantage in the Quarter Ton Cup in Japan. Together with the other two boats in the British Onion Patch team, we watched the other competitors climb out to

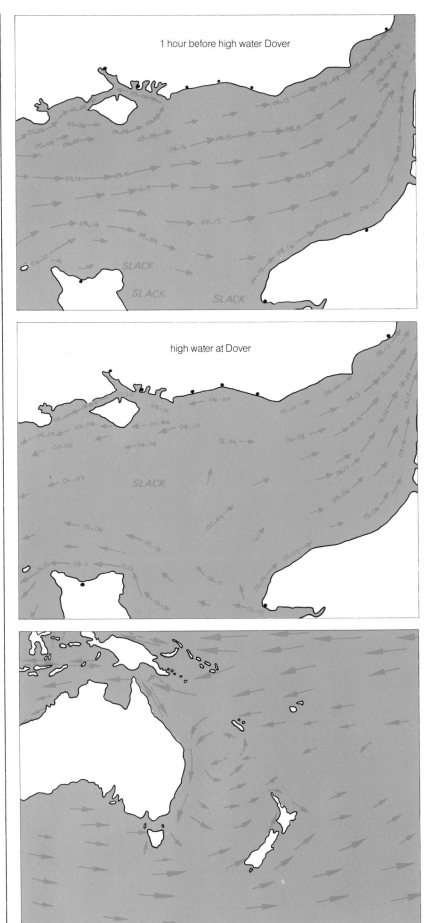

1 hour before high water Dover

high water at Dover

section from general surface current distribution of the world

TIDES AND CURRENTS
There are many sources of information on tides and currents. Generally, the more important the shipping area the better the data. Illustrated above are two hourly pages from the British Admiralty tidal atlas for the English Channel, and (lower) a section from the ocean current chart published with Ocean Passages For The World. The tidal atlas arrows show the direction for that hour and the rate of flow at neaps and springs. —17.30 means 1.7 knots neaps, 3.0 knots springs, and you interpolate accordingly.

CHART TABLE
The chart table is an important part of the racing yacht. A sensible and practical layout will not only ease the navigator's task, but probably make his work more accurate. As with other things, order breeds order.

The electronic instruments, depth sounder, log, RDF set and wind indicators should be readily to hand, as should the compass repeater if fitted, and a clock and barometer. Navigating instruments such as dividers, compasses, parallel ruler, pencils and rubber should have a secure stowage within arms reach. Either in a book, or stuck on the bulkhead, the navigator will have cards prepared before the race showing the course complete with directions and distances, instructions for the race with the signals to be used, and the necessary tidal information tabulated ready for use. Some navigators prefer to have most of this on one sheet as in the example on the next page. Also visible should be the steering compass deviation curve, and the frequencies, times and call signs of the RDF beacons likely to be useful. Charts are usually stowed in a drawer under the table, and it is a great help if both table and drawer are big enough to take a folded chart. Almanacs and books should again be within easy reach.

Finally, navigation usually requires concentration and two hands. Therefore everything should have its own stowage place and the navigator should have a decent seat and something solid to brace his feet against.

a rdf set
b wind speed
c log
d compass deviation
e race course
f pre-computed data
g radio transmitter
h instrument stowage
i chart drawer

windward as we left Newport at the start of the Bermuda Race. We went further east in search of the warm water of the Gulf Stream whose meander would help us go south. In the event we picked up the wrong side of the meander, which was going north, and in consequence we sailed an extra hundred miles and finished way down the fleet. In Japan proper use of the Coro Nero took us from 13th to 5th on the beat from Mikimoto Island to Oshima light tower and put us back in contention with the leaders. We sailed on what appeared to be the tack furthest from the rhumb line immediately after rounding Mikimoto Island but it was the tack that took us quickest into the favourable current. All our rivals went the other way and paid the penalty.

Strategy must be planned by the navigator and the skipper. They will back their hunches on what the wind will do, having first obtained the best weather forecast information. It matters greatly to them the time any changes in wind strength or direction take place. Their planning is on a much larger scale than that of a closed-course skipper and some of it will be a gamble – but of the short-odds variety. They must have at their disposal as much information as possible and the ability to interpret that information so that it can provide useful data for the race.

Navigation Pre-planning

Much of the navigator's work should be done before he ever gets on board the boat for the race. He can take the charts, tidal atlases, almanack and sailing instructions home with him and produce the essential working cards to pin up on the wall. Set out for quick reference should be the rhumb line courses between the marks; high water times at major points of the course, and the strength and direction of the tides at hourly intervals at as many positions as possible. These should also be transferred to the charts in local time. As an aide memoire the starting time and relative signals together with details of the starting line should be on another pinned-up card so it can be easily seen.

Extracts from various sources are then in one place for easy reference. With them will be the latest weather predictions. The navigator will have taken the radio weather forecasts for the past 24 hours and have prepared a synoptic chart. He will check out with local aerodromes and weather stations for the latest meteorological details before going afloat and will have made his own observations of cloud formations, wind direction and change.

Thoroughly familiarized the navigator will hold a conference with the skipper and crew and put them in the picture. Questions at this time save a lot of unnecessarily wasted time during a race and each member of the crew should be aware of the overall plan. If there is any subsequent change all the crew must be informed.

Navigator's Log

Pre-computed Navigational Data

Date.......7TH JULY

B.S.T.	LOG	DIST. RUN	COURSE REQD. (C)
1500	13.9	5.4	
1531	16.4		
1600	19.2	5.3	
1607	19.8		
1610	20.1	0.9	264
1700	24.4	4.3	

FROM	TO	RHUMB LINE
BERRY HEAD	E. BLACKSTONE	199(
E. BLACKSTONE	START	215(

RADIO BEACONS

STATION	C/S	FREQ.	RANGE	TRANSM
BERRY HD.	BHD	318	25	AIR BEACON - CC
START	SP	} 298.8 {	70	01 - 07 - 13 - 19 - 2:
EDDYSTONE	DY		20	FOG ONLY 00 - 06 - 1:
LIZARD	LZ		70	05 - 11 - 17 - 23 - 29 - 3!
ROUND ISLAND	RR	308		03 - 09 - 15 - 21 - 27
ST. MAWGAN	SM	356.8		AIR BEACON - CC

LIGHTS

NAME	CHARACTERISTIC	RANGE	FOG SIGNAL	
BERRY HD.	2 Fl – 15s	18		W
START	3 Fl – 10s	21	SIREN – 60s	W
EDDYSTONE	2 Fl – 10s	18	TYFON 3 – 60s	G.
P/MOUTH B/W	Fl – 10s Sectors	W13 R12	BELL – 15s	G.
ST. ANTHONY	Occ 20s W.R. Sectors	14	HORN – 20s	W
LIZARD	Fl – 3s	22	SIREN 2 – 60s	W
TATER - DU	3 Fl – 15s	16	EFH 2 – 30s	W
LONGSHIPS	Iso – 10s W.R. Sectors	17	TYFON – 15s	G.
WOLF ROCK	Alt Fl W.R. – 30s	16	DIA – 30s	G.
SEVEN STONES	3 Fl – 30s	12	DIA 3 – 60s	R
ROUND ISLAND	Fl R – 10s	20	SIREN – 60s	C
PENNINNIS HD.	Fl 15s	17		C

Day SATURDAY   **Variation** 8° W

(DEV)	(M)	(T)	L/WAY P/S	WAKE C/RSE	TIDAL STREAM °/KNOTS	BARO.	WIND	OBSERVATION
2E	202	194	3P	191	040/0.4	1003	SW/4	
								RDF Start Pt. 305(M) 103(Rel) 297(T) Loop Corr. -3 : 294(T)
2E	207	199	3P	196	260/0.3	1004	SW/4	Baro. rising
								RDF Start 341(M) 134(Rel) 333(T) Loop Corr. -5 : 328(T)
2E	207	199	3P	196				Tacked - Start abaft beam — A/C 310 (C)
1W	302	294	3S	297	226/0.4	1005	WSW/4	Wind veering.

DIST.	FROM	TO	RHUMB LINE	DIST.
4.2	START	LIZARD	255(T)	63
?.4	LIZARD	ST. MARY'S SOUND	266(T)	43

B.ST.   EXTRACTS FROM TIDE TABLES   METRES

TIMES	DATE DAY DOVER RANGE	DOVER		DEVONPORT	
...UOUS	SAT 7TH JULY (4.4)	0459	5.8	0526	1.4
?1-37-43-49-55		1203	1.5	1141	4.7
?-24-30-36-42-48-54		1715	5.9	1744	1.6
				2353	4.7
?-47-53-59	SUN 8TH JULY (4.0)	0035	1.4	0612	1.6
?-39-45-51-57		0553	5.5	1225	4.5
...UOUS		1252	1.8	1836	1.9
		1812	5.7		
	MON 9TH JULY (3.6)	0125	1.7	0042	4.5
		0653	5.4	0708	1.8
		1351	2.0	1323	4.4
		1916	5.5	1942	2.0

DESCRIPTION OF TOWER

?5' High on H/Land
Circular
?ranite R. Lantern
?rcular granite
octagonal
octagonal

?granite
?ranite
L/V
? White tower
W. metal tower

TIDAL NOTES

Start Point — W. going stream 1615/2115 — 7TH.
Lizard — W going stream 0353/0853 } — 8TH.
1612/2112 }
0453/0953 } —9TH.
1716/2116 }

ST MARY'S Differences on Devonport.
HW (1323)   LW (0708)
-00.40 +0.2   -00.50 -0

EXTRACTS FROM ALMANAC

DAWN	0415	MOONS PHASE	D
SUNRISE	0500	MOON RISE	1503
SUNSET	2110	MOON SET	0028/9TH.
DUSK	2153		

NAVIGATOR'S LOG

NAVIGATOR'S LOG
The navigator's log will record everything he needs to work up his dead reckoning (DR) hour by hour. Printed log books as shown here are readily available. Some navigators prefer more or less detailed information and will draw up a book to suit their own needs. Whether the arithmetical work is done in a book or on loose sheets it should always be entered carefully with plus and minus signs for the corrections and each step labelled. In this way the DR can be checked and re-checked if there is any doubt. Kept up meticulously DR can take you hundreds of miles with considerable accuracy, and in bad weather it frequently has to.

PRE-COMPUTED DATA
This can be entered on cards and displayed on a convenient bulkhead, or it may be entered on a printed sheet as illustrated. It is a great help to have looked up all the information you are going to need while in the comfort of your home, not only because you will then know where to find it again, but because this data forms the basis of many tactical decisions and the longer you have mulled it over and visualised the possibilities the better.

The Crew

The crew on deck are not just a bunch of string pullers during an ocean race – they have a major role to play in the boat's success. They are fewer in number than for round-the-buoys racing but they have to complete similar tasks just as efficiently. Sails have to be set and trimmed and this is a full-time operation day and night. Let-ups lose valuable ground. Members of the crew must develop a working pattern which suits them and the helmsman. It is the helmsman's decision as to which sails should be set in order to sail from one mark to another in the shortest possible time. He may want to bear off more than the desired course to take full advantage of the waves when surfing, but then he will have to come back further and with every change of direction he will need to have the sails trimmed. The good crewman will derive satisfaction from knowing that the sails have been trimmed to the best of his ability all the time, and he will appreciate the need for the constant attention they must have. He can be stimulated. A regular hourly log-reading from the navigator on a long leg will indicate an improvement or falling off in speed and this can goad both helmsman and crew into activity.

The crew have a number of routine manoeuvres to accomplish during most races. Wind changes will necessitate spinnaker hoists, peels and takedowns; staysail hoists and drops; reefing and headsail changes. Many can be effectively done short-handed but some may require one or more of the off-watch crew to help. Crews will learn not to call off-watch members unnecessarily, for resting is important.

Sailing to Windward

There has been much argument in the past as to whether an ocean-racing yacht need ever be hard on the wind. Some thought that major wind shifts eliminated the need for a boat to be sailed close hauled, and that the boat should instead be sailed faster slightly free. This was a theory based on lucky breaks by people who had employed it. Ever since the keen small-boat sailors have entered the sport and reduced the effect of luck to a minimum the theory has been exploded. Modern interpretation of weather forecasts and patterns have been largely responsible for this as they can reduce the element of chance in wind shifts.

They might, however, lead to a boat sailing free into a wind change in order to derive the most benefit from it. That is where the strategy of ocean racing takes over from the tactics of round-the-buoys events. It is conceivable that one might do the same thing on an Olympic course, if you could see boats lifted a long way on the other tack ahead of you, but that is a rarity rather than a normally planned strategic move in ocean racing.

More often than not the windward way is the only way and it can be a long slog in which few get any rest. It is not very easy to sleep in

TO WINDWARD IN HEAVY WEATHER

The increased size of the seas in open water require more power to punch through them. In a high wind the drive should be kept low in the sails so that the maximum forward power is obtained. Both sails need some twist, but they also need to be flattened low down. The mainsail will be flattened with the leech Cunningham which works like a small slab reef near the bottom of the leech. The term jiffy reef is perhaps misleading because the purpose is only to tension the sail out and down, not to reduce the area. The luff Cunningham is then used to flatten out the wrinkles and get the flow right in the lower part of the sail. The mainsail will need to be further out on its sheet traveller, and to match this and prevent the slot being choked the genoa needs to be sheeted out too. However it also needs to be well flattened in its lower area. The usual way of achieving this is to put a snatch block on the lee rail and attach a second sheet through it. The two sheets are then trimmed together, but the precise position of the sail clew can be varied. The more it blows the more the tension is put onto the leeward sheet. One crew will trim the genoa, and where available another man will play the mainsheet traveller, both of them easing out when the boat is stopped by a wave. The technique for handling big waves is to sail around them, luffing up on the crests and bearing away on the backs of the waves to pick up speed. If a rhythm can be established and the boat is not stopped there is no need to alter the sheets, for the apparent wind will move aft as the boat slows and luffs at the crest of the wave, and move forward as it speeds down the back. If the boat does hit a wave badly the trimmers must ease the sheets to get her moving again quickly.

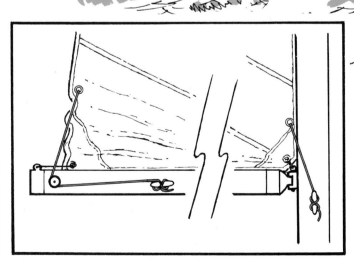

an ocean racer pounding to windward, although life below has improved in lighter displacement boats. They seem to ride over the tops of the waves instead of bucking through with the resultant heavy pitching motion.

The shortening of the crew will leave one or two people to trim the sails. Someone must always be on the genoa sheet and this has to be trimmed to match boat and wind speeds. When the boat speed drops it can be the result of hitting a wave, and the helmsman will want to bear off to get the boat going faster again. The genoa must then be eased slightly and, as the boat comes back on-course with the speed improved, the genoa must be sheeted in again. Should the wind lighten the helmsman will want the headsail to be fuller, so the sheet is eased. When the wind strengthens it is more efficient to sail with a flatter genoa and the sheet will therefore be hardened in. The trimmer will know his job and will need very few orders from the helmsman. With a man available the mainsail will be trimmed in sympathy with the genoa, otherwise the trimmer will follow genoa trimming by trimming the mainsail.

Out at sea the waves will be larger and the helmsman will be required to take greater avoiding action. The technique is to steer round them. The boat slows when it is climbing up the face of the waves and is luffed as the apparent wind comes aft; then it is borne off as the bow goes through the crest and uses the back wave to gain speed again. The apparent wind will then come forward and the sheets will not need to be trimmed.

Going to windward in heavy weather provides more problems out at sea than it does on inshore courses because of the size of the waves. More power will be needed to drive through the seas yet it is still important to hold a high course. The effect of leeway must be reduced to a minimum by keeping the boat moving as fast as possible. Sail trim will endeavour to keep drive low down in the sails so that maximum forward power is generated, increasing boat speed.

To do this, twist is needed in both sails but it must be appreciated that the mainsail and the genoa are no longer in anything near regular wind. The pitching motion of the boat will accelerate the flow of air across the craft as the mast swings forward and slow it down as the mast swings aft, so that at times the sails are both over- and under-trimmed. Since the most powerful part of the pitching cycle is when the mast comes forward, the sails should be trimmed for the less powerful part of the cycle. The the head of the sails need some fullness to help drive the boat and the amount of twist should be slightly less than for the same average wind on an inshore windward leg.

To flatten the sails the genoa lead must come aft, which will free the leech and allow for some twist. At the same time the sheet lead should be further outward to open the slot

TO WINDWARD IN LIGHT AIRS
Keep the sails as full as possible if there are any waves to dive through. Sail further off the wind than in flat seas. Trim the main boom close to the centre line with the traveller well to windward and the sheet eased. Barber haul the genoa to windward. As the boat picks up speed, the apparent wind will move forward and the sail will be trimmed in. As the boat slows, the wind will move aft. Do not luff up but maintain the course with the sheet eased.

slightly. The mainsail will be further outboard on the traveller and so the genoa must go further out too. This is best accomplished by using a second sheet set through a snatch block on the lee rail. The two sheets must be trimmed together but the angle of the sail to the midline can be varied. The harder it blows the more tension there is on the outer sheet and less on the inner. Choking the slot in heavy air is one of the quickest ways to slow the boat.

The mainsail will need to be flattened and careful adjustment must be made using the leech Cunningham in conjunction with the luff Cunningham. These should be used together but not hauled down completely to form the much misnomered Jiffy reef. It is not a reefing action, as such, that one is looking for but a draft control of the sail. Most of this draft control comes from hauling out and down on the leech Cunningham and the luff Cunningham is only tensioned to clean up the flow air in the lower forward part of the mainsail.

Jib Cunninghams are not used until the maximum tension has been obtained on the halyard, at least with stretchy luff genoas. There has been a move in some smaller ocean racers towards wire-luffed genoas set without a headfoil, and these of course must be trimmed for shape by the Cunningham. These genoas allow quicker changes to be made, and they can often be made without a man having to go on the foredeck, which is a positive bonus in smaller boats.

In light airs there is often a left over swell from earlier wind and the sails will then need to be full to drive through. The helmsman will have to sail the boat further off the wind than he would otherwise point it. The main boom will be trimmed close to the centreline of the boat with the mainsheet traveller up to windward and the genoa barber-hauled to windward. With the main outhaul eased, this will ensure that the sails are at their fullest.

In the very lightest airs an ultra-light windseeker headsail will be needed. It is cut high on the clew and the boat is sailed further off the wind with it than normal. It will need constant trimming. At first the sheet is well freed but the boat will begin to gain speed and the apparent wind will move forward quite dramatically; the sheet must therefore be trimmed in as the boat gains way. Conversely, as the wind drops the boat will slow and the apparent wind move aft. The helmsman should not luff as this happens but maintain a course with the sheet eased. Most helmsmen have too little practice with this specialist sail and in ultra-light airs in major events it is those sailors from predominantly light-air regions that score highly. Every effort must be made to practise with the windseeker genoa. The opportunity often occurs while waiting for a race to start on a summer's day when the sea breeze is about to fill in. In the period of calm between the land and sea breezes practice with the windseeker can provide some

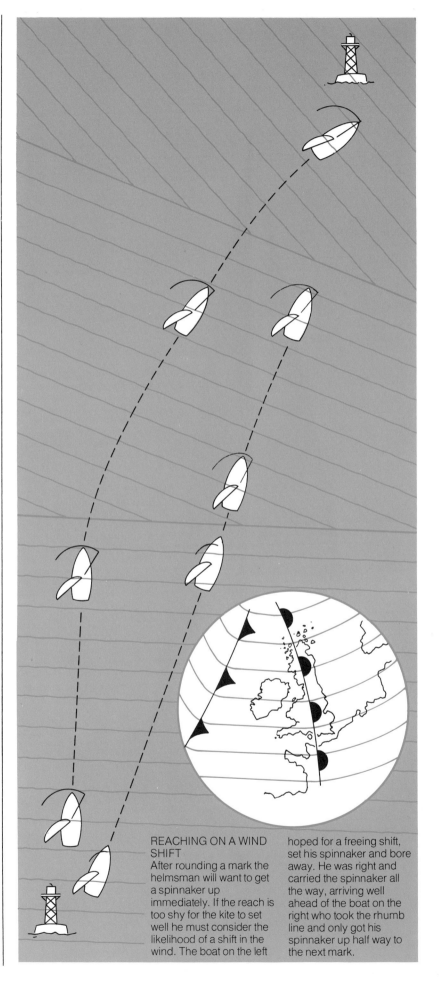

REACHING ON A WIND SHIFT
After rounding a mark the helmsman will want to get a spinnaker up immediately. If the reach is too shy for the kite to set well he must consider the likelihood of a shift in the wind. The boat on the left hoped for a freeing shift, set his spinnaker and bore away. He was right and carried the spinnaker all the way, arriving well ahead of the boat on the right who took the rhumb line and only got his spinnaker up half way to the next mark.

WIND SHIFTS
Using the wind shifts on a dead run makes an important difference to the overall speed. A look at the Polar Diagram on page 80 shows immediately the difference in speed between having the wind on the quarter or dead astern. Use each little wind shift to get the wind on the quarter, gybing as necessary to keep close to the rhumb line. In this example the boat on the right has not bothered to gybe to the small shifts and has lost considerable ground against the left hand boat which used each shift as it came.

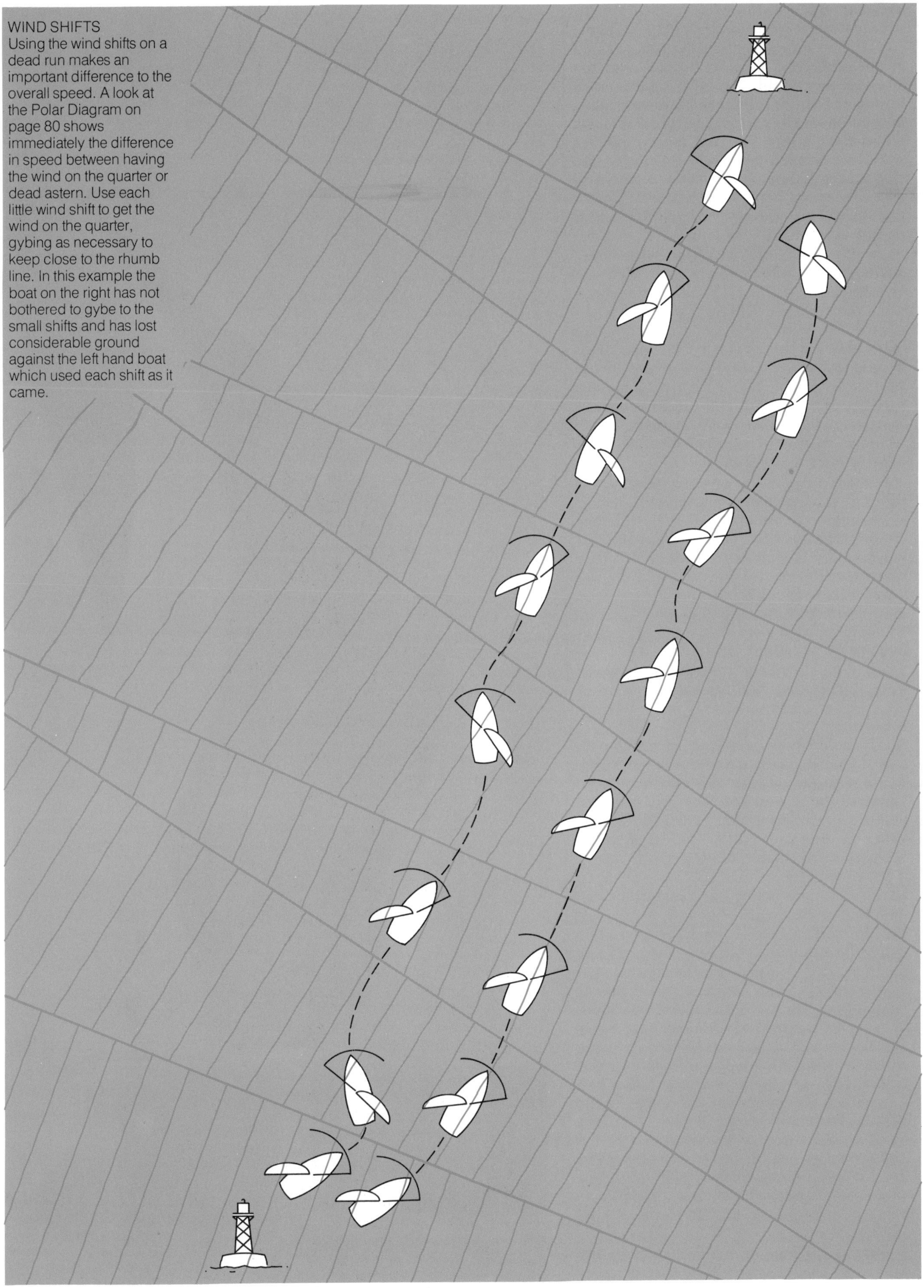

useful insight into its habits which will be needed when it is employed offshore in anger.

Reaching

The reaching leg strategy is no longer one of setting a course for the next mark and sailing the rhumb line to it. It may be that this is still the fastest and in that case the rhumb line would be sailed, but the helmsman may find that a few degrees alteration in course will give him much better speed. The navigator and skipper will have a fair idea as to whether or not they can tolerate this deviation, or make it work, in their strategy and so, once again, the choice of course is made from several options.

The most difficult choice is with sheets just started. There is always a reluctance to go to leeward of the rhumb line in these conditions in case the wind heads and the boat has to bear back up to the mark. This, of course, can spell disaster unless the shift is great enough to make all the boats beat to the mark. Much will depend on the weather forecast as to what strategy is employed.

There is less worry when a spinnaker can be flown. The helmsman will want it set as soon as possible, even if it does mean sailing below the prescribed course. He will argue that the wind is bound to free and allow him to sail up to the mark. Even if it does not, nothing will have been lost, but if it is not set and the wind does free a considerable amount of ground will have been lost over the boats that set their kites early and went off to leeward. Once again, it is a matter of consultation between navigator, skipper and helmsman.

Running

All the tactical considerations of running on closed-course races apply in ocean racing. The navigator will plot the boat course to allow for the tide and the boat will be sailed on the gybe closest to that. Other factors will have to be considered, particularly an expected wind change, but it is worth watching for the minor shifts and using them to advantage. I can remember sailing this way back across the English Channel in a fleet of Half-tonners; all but a few hung on to one long gybe and then came back into the buoy on the other. Those of us who had bothered to play the wind shifts came out more than 7 miles ahead of the leader from the other bunch. Our group would not have been badly affected by any major shift but the only one which would have suited the others to our disadvantage was a 120° backing, as they had gone out on the right-hand side of the course. We may have been helped by some 8° of veer but it would not have accounted for all the ground we gained on the main body of the fleet. Gybing to each wind shift does not make the navigator's job easy. He has to make a correction for his DR plot each time and he always needs to be kept informed.

Spinnaker trimming is the essence of fast downwind sailing and it needs constant atten-

OFFSHORE RACING
Offshore racing is an unrelenting effort to keep the boat sailing at top speed. While those off watch try to grab some sleep, the deck watch drive the boat as hard by night as by day. Combating fatigue and low moral is very important. Ensure that there is someone fresh on deck every hour to join those who already have the feel of the boat and make hourly log readings. Above all, supply regular hot food of the kind that settles the stomach.

tion. A torch shone on the luff at night helps both trimmer and helmsman but those who can adapt to seeing without it are at an advantage. Then only on the blackest nights, without a moon, is the torch essential. Since one is going to contrive manoeuvres at night like gybing, it is essential that the crew are totally familiarized with the routine so that they do not run into difficulties.

Safety
The I.O.R. regulations are quite specific: a life jacket and a safety harness shall be carried for each person on board whilst racing. They should be worn in strong winds, particularly at night. The regulations state that each life jacket shall be equipped with a whistle, which is used to attract attention to a man in the water. It is often difficult to see a man in the water but he can be located by sound.

When Chris Bouzaid went over the side in the 1973 One Ton Cup in Sardinia, he was grateful that he had a strong pair of lungs and vocal chords. The boat had both spinnaker and blooper set and these had to come down before the boat could be turned around to pick Bouzaid up. By the time they were down the yacht was nearly half a mile from the man in the water. As he saw the boat returning Bouzaid started to shout loudly and it was his voice that enabled the crew to find him.

Safety harnesses, equipped with a long and a short reach hook, are a definite aid to working on deck in rough conditions. They allow a man to devote two hands to the job rather than having to use one hand to keep himself from going overboard. Almost all the fatalities of men lost overboard have occurred to people not hooked on properly. There are danger moments, such as when changing helmsmen or coming up from down below. On both occasions an unhooked man can be washed overboard.

In addition to a whistle there are some other safety devices that may be carried by crew members. There are on the market personalized high intensity strobe lights that make it easier to pin point a man gone overboard in the dark. On one ocean racer that I sailed each man was issued with a pack of 10 mini-flares. The pack was no bigger than a cigarette pack and each flare was effective.

One-designs and Level Raters
Racing offshore in either of these highly popular types will bring extra problems in that the strategy has to be highly modified to cope with the necessary covering of the boats nearby. At the front of the fleet most will want to go the same way in any case but a split can cause strategic headaches. Most races are part of a series and one should play percentages and go the way you have analysed as being correct.

As a series is terminating however care must be taken to cover one's closest rivals just as long as doing so doesn't take one too far from the rest of the fleet. Compromises have to be made to survive.

1) Throw lifebelt, dan-buoy and light. Shout "Man Overboard!"

2) One man keeps his eyes on the person in the water.

3) Throw trail of floating objects.

4) Maintain course and note bearing of man. Start engine.

5) Take down reaching/running sails.

6) Make short tacks back along your track to the man.

7) Turn up to the wind with the man on the lee side.

MAN OVERBOARD

This chilling call should not freeze your reactions. Like most emergency procedures, people respond better if they have had some practice. This is true of fires as well, and a drill should be held periodically so that everybody knows the procedure and is familiar with the equipment – where it is, how it works and why it is used. Perhaps the worst time to go over the side is when the boat is surfing along on a black night under spinnaker, blooper and all the rest, with a sea big enough to hide the man in the water every time he or the boat is in a trough. The actions following a man falling over are as follows:

1) Throw the life belt with dan-buoy attached. It should have an automatic light on it. Shout "Man overboard!"
2) Detail one crewman to keep his eyes on the man in the water throughout the rest of the emergency.
3) As the boat sails away from the man, throw a trail of floating objects which will give you something to come back on. Although it goes against the grain it makes sense to throw something big first.
4) The helmsman should maintain exactly the same course. Check that the man in the water is on the reciprocal. Start the engine.
5) In a quick and orderly fashion get down the running/reaching sails ready to beat back.
6) Continue to leave a trail of floating objects, cushions, gash bags, half empty lube oil cans and so on. Check there are no ropes trailing into the propeller.

7) As soon as the deck is in order, gybe or harden right up to close hauled. At this point the navigator should write down the course to be made good back to the man, the log and the time, and also estimate the distance the boat has sailed since he fell in the water.
8) The boat then stitches short tacks back along this line, returning to the man in the water.
9) When you have found him bring him up to leeward with the boat pointing nearly into wind. This is much more difficult than doing the same thing in calm water and it is worthwhile practicing this unfamiliar activity at sea. Two other points are worth making. Firstly the man in the water will have a much

better chance of being seen if he carries a small personal strobe light, or a pack of mini-flares. A whistle is also a help. Secondly, if it is not too hazardous, a lookout up the mast at the spreaders will see over the waves very much better than people on deck.
If the man is not found and you are quite sure you have passed the place where he fell in, then a square search must begin. It should be organised methodically so that the whole of the area where he could be is fully covered. It is here that the things you threw overboard at the beginning will provide invaluable reference points. The closer their proportions correspond to a man in the water the more useful they will be as they will drift at the same rate.

Multihulls

The speed, acceleration and manoeuvreability of the multihull requires a different plan of campaign and method of sailing.

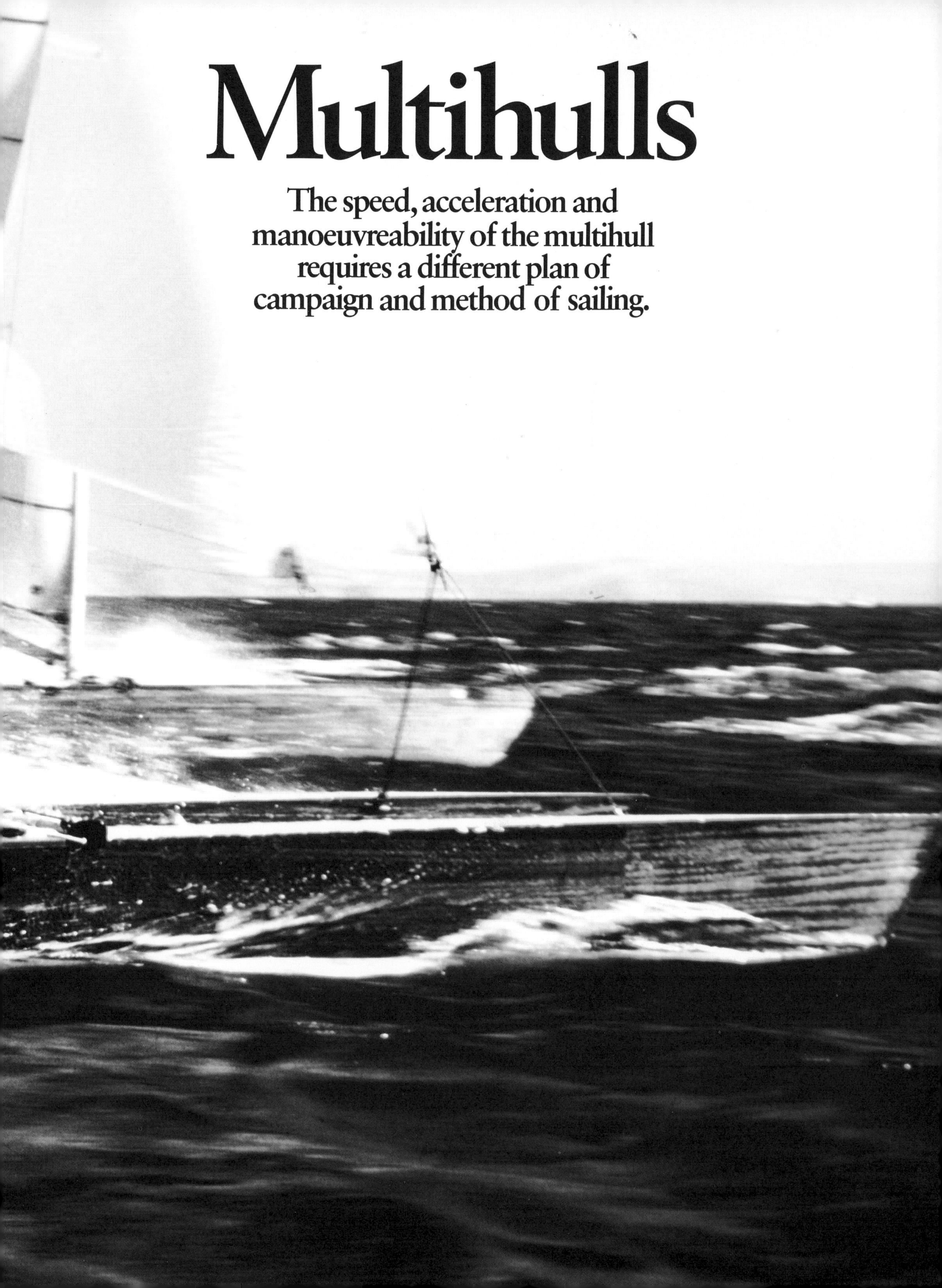

Compared with other types of craft, racing a multihull demands a shift of emphasis which depends on the size of the boat. Boat-speed assumes greater significance but tactics still remain important, though not necessarily to the same extent that they do in monohull racing. The great difference in speed, acceleration and manoeuvrability of the multihull makes it necessary to follow a different plan of campaign and method of sailing. This difference is less marked in the larger offshore multihulls than in day-racing boats.

Boat-speed is of paramount importance. The need still exists for well-determined strategy in a race but, because of manoeuvrability problems, boat-for-boat tactics are not as readily adopted as in more conventional classes. Downwind strategy is more important than upwind, particularly in light, day-racing boats, and there is greater need for sail trim because of the responsiveness and acceleration of the multihull.

Multihull racing

Multihull racing is in its infancy compared with other types of yacht racing. It began as recently as the late 1950s and took some time to overcome considerable antagonism from conservative, traditional yachtsmen. There was less opposition in the United States than in Britain and Europe, and it was the success of the Robert Harris-designed Tigercat at the One of a Kind regatta at Miami in 1959 that gave the green light to catamaran enthusiasts all over the world.

Almost without exception catamaran classes have dominated the day-racing scene but for offshore events both two-hulled and three-hulled craft can be raced effectively. Much of what has been written in earlier chapters of this book applies to offshore boats but for the round-the-buoys catamaran racers things are much more specialized. Initially there were almost as many classes as boats as design development gathered pace, but once the I.Y.R.U. chose classes for international racing this proliferation ceased and development came to concentrate on sophistication of rigs and gear. In the short life of multihull racing many yachtsmen have transferred their allegiance from the top end of monohull racing and this has brought progress in gear design. A great deal of monohull development can be transferred directly, although multihulls do present their own peculiar problems.

Preparation of the boat

The old maxim of Uffa Fox that 'weight has value only in a steam roller' is doubly applicable to a racing catamaran. Every effort must be made to keep the boat as close to the

TORNADO
The Tornado has been an SRI Olympic boat since 1976

which shows the sophistication this young sport has achieved.

1) mast spanner
2) clew outhaul winch
3) clew outhaul
4) diamond stays
5) mast heel swivel
6) trapeze line
7) restraining line
8) jib sheet
9) main sheet
10) luff tell-tales
11) jib luff tension control
12) main luff tension control

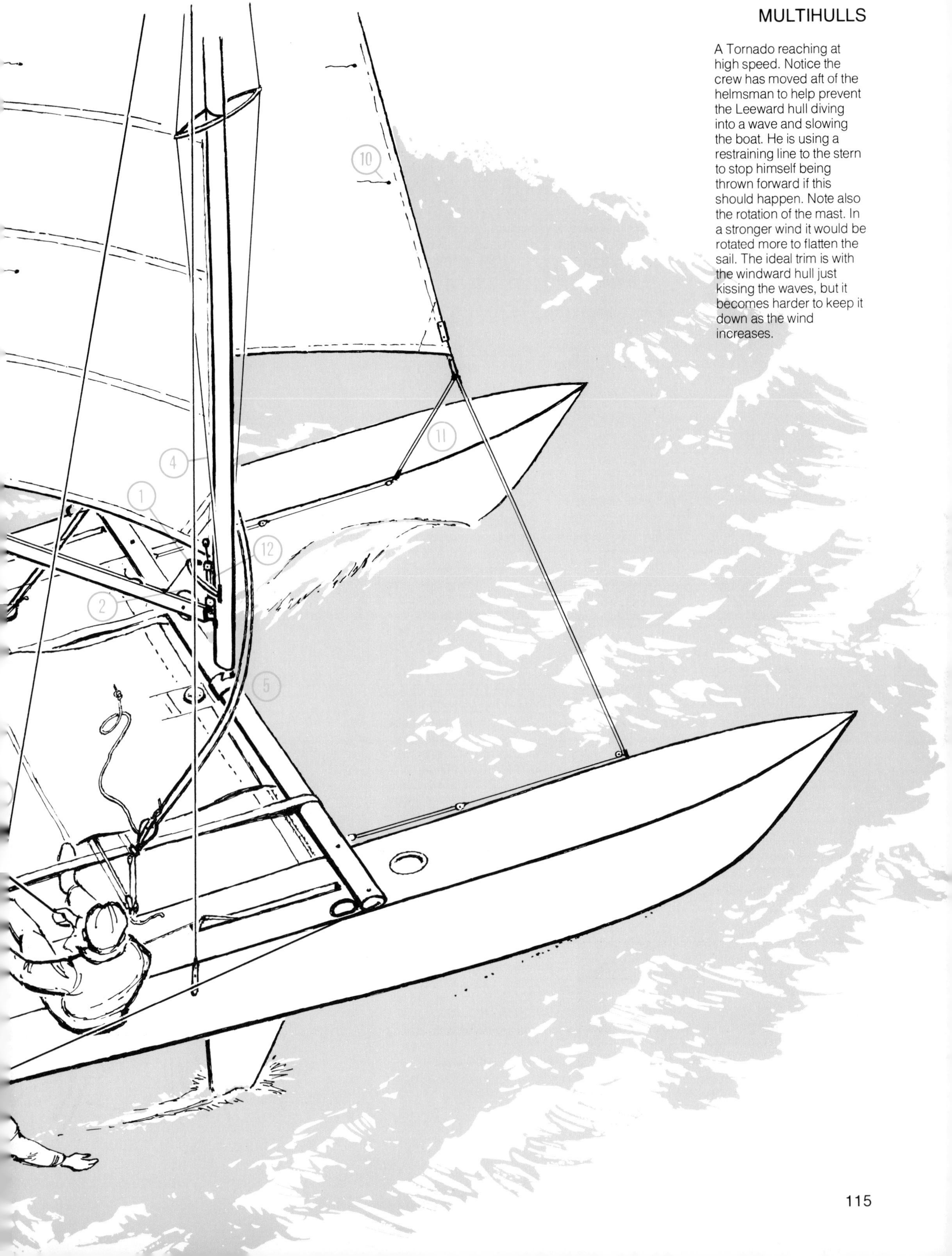

A Tornado reaching at high speed. Notice the crew has moved aft of the helmsman to help prevent the Leeward hull diving into a wave and slowing the boat. He is using a restraining line to the stern to stop himself being thrown forward if this should happen. Note also the rotation of the mast. In a stronger wind it would be rotated more to flatten the sail. The ideal trim is with the windward hull just kissing the waves, but it becomes harder to keep it down as the wind increases.

minimum class-weight as possible, and to keep the weight from the extremities of the hull. Weight reduction must not, however, be done at the expense of reducing the stiffness of the hulls themselves, or of the structure as a whole. Tornado gold medallist Reg White, himself a boatbuilder, is emphatic about the importance of a stiff, light boat and believes that the majority of the races that he has won are due to his pre-race preparation.

Much of the work is in the hands of the boatbuilder initially. It is therefore essential to go to a builder who specializes in a particular class and whose boats have been at the forefront of racing fleets. The builder will know what is needed, having learned from the requirements of the top sailors, but he will lend a sympathetic ear to individual tastes and requirements.

Bad pitching motion is one thing that stops a catamaran better than anything else so all steps should be taken to reduce pitching propensity to a minimum. Concentration of the weight in the centre of the hulls will help considerably as will keeping the centre of gravity of the rig as low as possible. Almost certainly, the mast will have a minimum weight and a minimum height of centre of gravity, but this is likely to be the only restriction. Care taken in keeping down the weight of all gear aloft, including the full-length sail battens, will be rewarded.

More than normal care must be taken of the centreboards and rudders. Rudder-blades, when not in use, should be kept in soft, foam-lined, tailored bags, and so should dagger-boards. Pivoting centreboards must be regularly examined. The foils must be properly profiled and experience points to the NACA 0006 section as being the best.

There are no short cuts in making foils. To prevent warping and distortion by natural causes a board of suitable size is made by glueing up a series of square sections to slightly more than the required thickness of the finished foil. The grain should be reversed alternately in these square strips and epoxy glue used. The strips are then held together with sash cramps until the glue is cured. After cleaning off the surplus adhesive a flat board is surfaced and a profiled foil cut from it. A centreline is then cut carefully into the edge as a working reference when shaping the section. Half templates should be cut for various widths to check sectioning and the surfacing done with a sharp plane. When the board is nearly correct the final surfacing is done with sandpaper over a block. The foil should then be covered with the finest glass cloth and epoxy resin and when that is cured surfacing is carried out with wet-and-dry sandpaper on a block. The foil is then painted with several coats of white epoxy paint, cutting back between each one with wet-and-dry sandpaper and finally finishing with 600-grade and a burnishing paste. It is a time-consuming process, which is reflected in the price of a professionally prepared foil of the correct quality.

MULTIHULL RACING

This is a very young sport in comparison with other types of yacht racing. The initial proliferation of designs in the early 1960s ceased when classes were chosen by the IYRU for international racing. In day-racing catamarans have dominated the scene, but among the larger boats competing in offshore event's, three hulled boats race just as effectively. There is a constant development in both the design of the boats and their gear. Because of the very high speeds attained, the loadings on the hulls and the rigging are much higher. It follows that the boats must be properly constructed and regularly checked for signs of failure. This applies to the rig too where the higher apparent wind speeds mean that sheets and blocks must be increased in size in comparison with other similar sized yachts, and also that fittings must be through-bolted to something substantial. The rigging needs to be checked regularly and carefully for bent pins, frayed rope and wire and other signs of trouble. The higher speeds also put a premium on the finish of the wetted surfaces, particularly the foils, and it is essential that they are free from warping, and are aligned properly. Multihull races are usually held under the international rules for A, B, C and D class cats. These are rated classes and for A, B and C classes the length, beam and sail area are limited. For D class cats only the sail area is restricted, and it must be 500 square feet (46.45 sq m). The A class is a single hander, B and C classes are two man boats, and D class catamarans are three man boats.

Spars, sails and rigging on multihulls need the same attention as on any other boat but it must be remembered that the loadings on these are greater because of higher windspeeds, due to faster boat-speeds, and the increased staying base for the shrouds. Sheets and their purchases are generally increased for similar-sized sails because of the greater loadings. The rigging must be checked for bent clevis pins and shackles and these must be replaced with ones a size larger. Experience in catamarans has shown that fittings must be through-bolted to something substantial if they are to withstand the conditions.

Starting

Because of the sailing characteristics of a twin-huller, starting in a catamaran is quite different from that of any other type of small boat. The fast acceleration of a catamaran allows its crew to position themselves almost on the line with sails flapping, well in advance of the starter's gun. It is not difficult to maintain this position and, with a few seconds to go, harden the sheets to hit the line with the gun. Of course, every other boat will be aiming to get to the best position on the start line, too, and windward boats can be forced over early by those to leeward. So it is best to take up a position well to leeward of where you want to start and to work up to windward, slowly accelerating, to reach maximum speed at gunfire. It is an easy thing to practice against a buoy and this should be done to gauge just how an approach should be made.

Clear wind after the start is essential as the ground lost through tacking twice can be enormous. It is important to start on the tack that pays the greatest dividend, or at least to be in a position to go on to that tack quickly after the start. If the right-hand side of the course is paying then it could be beneficial to start just behind the leader at the committee-boat end of the line and tack just as soon as you can cross the committee-boat's anchor-line. At that end the crew is in control of the situation; even if the line is biased to favour the pin-end slightly, there will be a graduation of ability to tack down the line. The pin-end starters will be the last to get on to the favoured port tack.

The mainsheet of a catamaran is essentially a two-handed operation at the start, so it is vital for the crew to have control of the starting watch – even more so than in monohulls. The countdown, clear and concise, should be for the skipper's ears alone and not so loud that the entire fleet can make their start on it. The helmsman can then concentrate on aiming the boat at the correct position relative to the boats around him without the distraction of having to refer to the watch.

Starting in light airs is perhaps more difficult as it is not beneficial to 'park' close to the line and hope to accelerate away. What wind there is is likely to be badly cut up and it is all too simple to find yourself left behind if

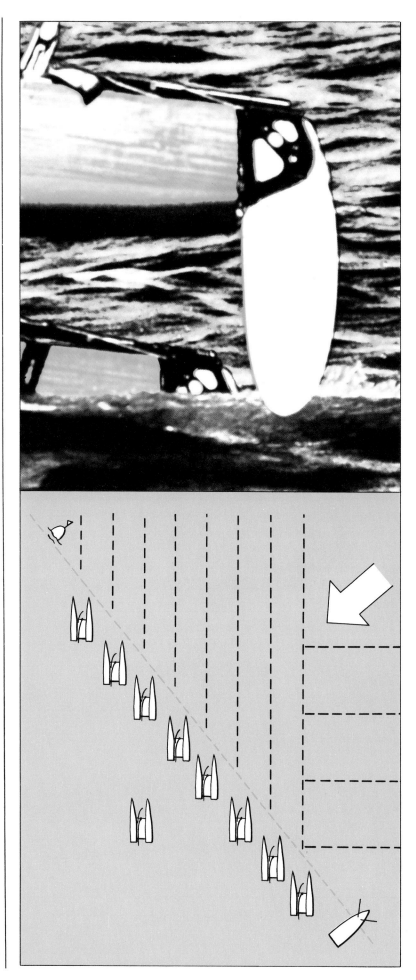

MULTIHULL FOILS

These need special care. Any damage or warping will have a more profound effect on speed than it would have with an ordinary dinghy. They should be properly constructed to prevent natural warping, and profiled correctly. When not in use they should be kept in soft, padded tailored bags and stowed with care so that other gear does not finish up on top of them.

STARTING

In multihull races starting requires a different approach to that used in other kinds of yacht racing. The sparkling acceleration of a catamaran makes it possible to position the boat close to the line with the sails flapping, and then to accelerate up to full speed in the final seconds to hit the line on the gun. When the starboard side of the course is favoured *(right)* it may be best to make your start at the committee boat end, and to tack as soon as you can clear the committee boat's anchor line. Starting at that end enables the crew to control the situation by being able to tack when they like. This holds true even if the line is biased a little towards the pin end *(lower left)*.

In strong winds *(lower right)*, when the starboard side of the line is favoured, it may pay to come in late at the committee boat end at full speed and to power over the top of the boats to leeward.

In light airs the main consideration is to obtain clear air with which to get the boat moving fast.

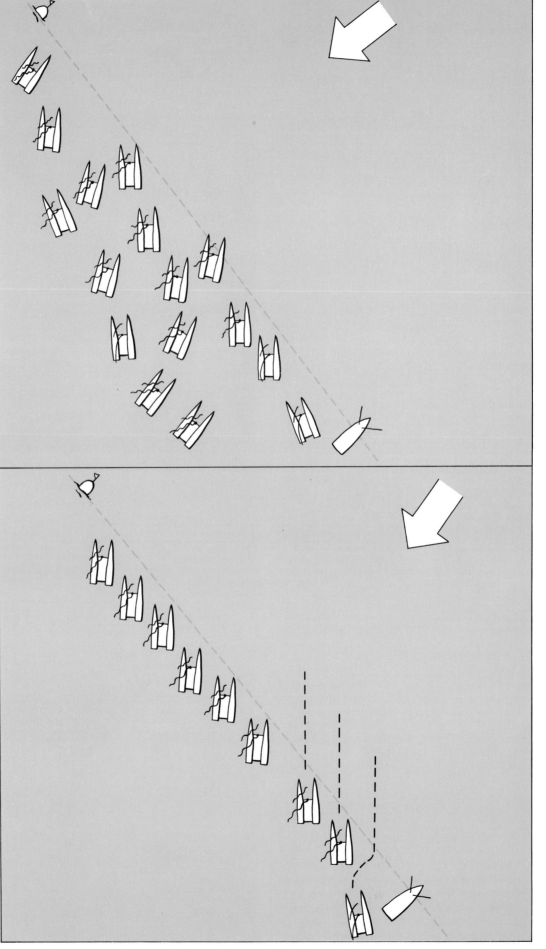

that technique is applied. It is necessary, therefore, to keep way-on and to eschew what appears to be the best position on the line, opting instead for clear air. In no time it will be possible to be in the controlling position, able to tack either way for the favoured side.

In strong airs with a starboard-favoured end it can pay to come in late at the committee-boat end of the line and, with speed on, power over the top of the immediate bunch to leeward. It nccds vcry careful timing and nerve to pull off this manoeuvre properly. It can only be done by one boat successfully and there may be more than one trying for the space.

Sailing to windward

A balance must be struck between good boat-speed and pointing ability, and a helmsman's skill is in understanding how high he can point the boat without losing too much speed. This is further complicated by the effect of leeway, which increases at slower speeds. The balance, therefore, is critical, and judgement can only really be acquired through practice against other catamarans of the same class. Two boats can train very successfully together if one maintains speed and direction while the other experiments alongside with different pointing and footing. When training like this all other features must be as alike as possible, particularly the jib sheeting angle and mast rotation. Calibration is therefore necessary. Much of Reg White's success – he became the first ever catamaran Olympic gold medallist – was due to many hours of training in this fashion against his son Robert.

He describes the situation as one of feeling right and certainly the catamaran sailor will know when it is all working for him, and indeed when it is not, but it is also essential to know how to get into this perfect situation when sailing upwind. Wild angles of heel are merely spectacular; they have no place in the racing man's book, as the boat is slowed considerably by heeling which lowers the leeward hull into the water and totally alters the lines of the hull. In moderate airs it should be possible to keep the boat so that the weather hull is just kissing the water with both the rudder and centreboard fully immersed. In lighter weather this is not possible, although the 'unsticking' – lifting – of the weather hull should be encouraged, and in a strong breeze it becomes increasingly difficult to keep the weather hull down on the surface, although this should be the aim.

Techniques for keeping the boat at the right angle of heel vary but because of the heavy loadings on the sheets it is not efficient to be constantly trimming them upwind. Slight increases in wind strength can be accommodated by the crew stretching further out on the trapeze or a slight luff. The path of a catamaran going to windward often appears as a series of scoops to windward using the extra breeze to keep the speed up whilst point-

SAILING TO WINDWARD

In a multihull sailing to windward is a compromise between pointing as high as possible towards the wind, and maintaining a good speed. Leeway also increases with slower speeds. The ideal angle of heel is with the weather hull just kissing the water, its rudder and centreboard fully immersed. The weather hull should be lifted as soon as the wind permits. In heavier winds the problem is to keep it down, but the ideal position remains the same. The track of a catamaran sailing to windward often appears as a series of scoops. This is caused by gusts which free the wind and enable the helmsman to luff to windward. As soon as the helmsman feels the speed begin to drop he will bear away. The sails will be trimmed for the stronger gusts, easing them out while being careful to keep the weather hull flying. As the gust dies the sheets can be hardened in to maintain the correct angle of heel.

ing the boat slightly higher. The luff cannot be prolonged or else the boat will slow, so the catamaran must be returned to its original course after a few seconds. Exactly when this should be done is a matter of judgement for the helmsman, a judgement that is heightened by experience. He will feel the speed begin to drop and will know then that he must bear away; at the same time he will have the stall registered by the weather tell-tales on the jib.

Naturally the helmsman and crew cannot cleat off the sheets and hope to sail to windward in a series of luffs; the sails will have to be trimmed in the stronger gusts and care must be taken not to overdo the easing for if this happens the weather hull will return to the water with a thump, knocking more wind out of the sails and stopping the boat completely. Conversely, as the gust begins to die down the sheets can be hardened, thereby keeping the boat at the correct angle of heel.

Trim of the sails involves not only the sheets, as almost all catamaran classes allow controlled rotation of the mast and this alters the shape of the mainsail considerably. The more the mast is rotated the more it bends in the fore and aft plane of the boat, thereby flattening the sail. Rotation must be matched with the clew outhaul tension to obtain the best possible sail shape and this means that both will have to be properly calibrated. Diamond-stay tension is another factor in rig set-up because slackening the diamond stays allows the mast to bend further. Care must be taken when experimenting with large amounts of rotation and bend as the diamonds can easily be released too far with the result that the mast collapses. In light weather the mast is kept very much in line with the boom so that the sail is at its fullest with the clew pulled well out; the harder the wind blows the more the mast is rotated.

Waves play an important part in the way a catamaran is sailed upwind. Because the hulls are finer than those of a single-hulled boat they can cut through waves rather more readily, but the resistance of a catamaran to pitch is far less. The helmsman must therefore take care to avoid the worst of the waves at all times. With bigger waves the technique is similar to that of monohulls, luffing up the face and bearing away through the crest and down the back. But when reaching top speed to windward down the back of the wave care must be taken to ensure that the lee-bow does not bury into the face of the next one, which will slow the boat considerably.

In light winds a special technique must be employed. The crew will move to the lee-hull and keep his weight well forward whilst the helmsman moves forward on the weather side. The object is to try to lift the weather hull slightly and for both hulls to come clear at the stern, thereby losing wetted surface area. This also alters the centre of lateral resistance of the catamaran, encouraging the slight weather helm that is necessary for good sailing ability. Mast rotation is kept to a

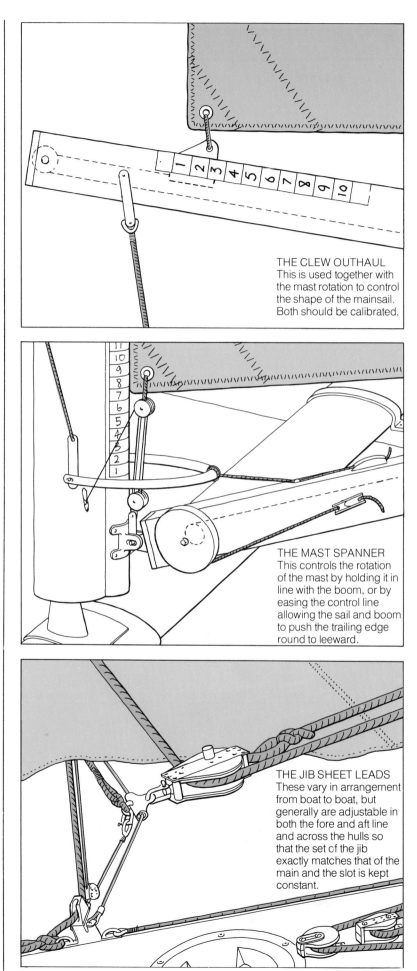

THE CLEW OUTHAUL
This is used together with the mast rotation to control the shape of the mainsail. Both should be calibrated.

THE MAST SPANNER
This controls the rotation of the mast by holding it in line with the boom, or by easing the control line allowing the sail and boom to push the trailing edge round to leeward.

THE JIB SHEET LEADS
These vary in arrangement from boat to boat, but generally are adjustable in both the fore and aft line and across the hulls so that the set of the jib exactly matches that of the main and the slot is kept constant.

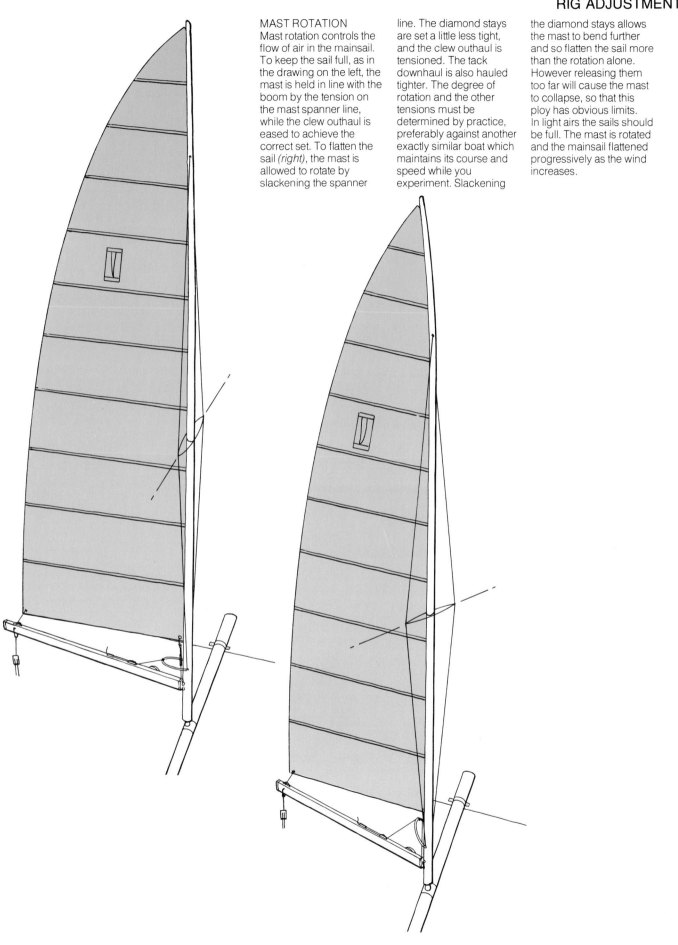

MAST ROTATION

Mast rotation controls the flow of air in the mainsail. To keep the sail full, as in the drawing on the left, the mast is held in line with the boom by the tension on the mast spanner line, while the clew outhaul is eased to achieve the correct set. To flatten the sail *(right)*, the mast is allowed to rotate by slackening the spanner line. The diamond stays are set a little less tight, and the clew outhaul is tensioned. The tack downhaul is also hauled tighter. The degree of rotation and the other tensions must be determined by practice, preferably against another exactly similar boat which maintains its course and speed while you experiment. Slackening the diamond stays allows the mast to bend further and so flatten the sail more than the rotation alone. However releasing them too far will cause the mast to collapse, so that this ploy has obvious limits. In light airs the sails should be full. The mast is rotated and the mainsail flattened progressively as the wind increases.

minimum and the diamond stays are tightened in lighter airs to prevent mast bend. The mainsheet traveller is pulled up to windward and the sheet eased slightly to encourage a moderate amount of twist into the mainsail. The jib must be trimmed in sympathy with the mainsail even to barber-hauling the clew to weather; the 'slot' will then remain constant throughout. The two sails must then be trimmed for every gust and eased against afterwards; a rhythm established between helmsman and crew here will reap dividends.

Sailing upwind
Upwind tactics in a catamaran are of a quite different type than those applicable to a monohull because of the time a twin-hulled boat takes to tack. Early examination of the course before the race for permanent wind bends and forecasted knowledge of shifts are necessary for success, together with the ability to sense a temporary shift of sufficient magnitude to warrant tacking.

Covering an opponent is not easy. It is all too simple for the leeward boat to ship out by reaching off for a very short time. Therefore the blanket cover is generally eschewed and a loose cover is applied on one's closest rival to prevent him from getting into a totally different wind stream and moving ahead that way. Tacking duels, except in match-racing, should not be undertaken as they will allow boats behind to close rapidly. In match-racing, however, a tacking duel can often bring about a quick change of places. It is easy to muff a tack when the pressure is on and as the initiative lies with the boat astern the boat ahead can easily be forced to tack when the wave pattern is quite unfavourable. Dramatic changes in the fortunes of the two boats in the Little America's Cup have occurred during tacking duels of this kind. There is little the defending boat can do. If she breaks off the cover it is possible for the attacker to get into a different wind or better wave conditions; if she continues to cover she will slowly lose ground and can slip badly with a wrongly executed tack.

Reaching
Perhaps the most exciting part of sailing a catamaran is with the wind just free. The boat then comes wildly alive and attains its fastest point of sailing. Keeping it moving smoothly is all-important and once again it is the coordination of helmsman and crew that is the criterion for success. All catamarans will tend to bury the lee-bow on a reach particularly as the wind increases. Trimming the sheets in sympathy is therefore essential; if the jib is not eased with the mainsail the slot is choked and the main does not go off.

The mainsheet traveller is set as far outboard as it is necessary to be when the wind is lightest and the mainsail is sheeted in. The action of the mainsheet becomes more one of a vang and thus the initial easing of it induces twist into the sail, spilling wind mostly from

IN VERY LIGHT AIRS In these conditions the crew will move well forward on the lee hull, and the helmsman sits forward on the weather hull so that the boat is heeled slightly to leeward and the sterns of both hulls are lifted a little out of the water. This not only reduced the wetted surface. But also provided a little necessary weather helm.

The mast will be held in line with the boom, the diamond stays will be tight, and the clew outhaul and tack downhaul eased to give a full sail. The mainsheet traveller is hauled to windward and the sheet eased to allow the top of the sail to twist off. The jib is trimmed to match with the fairleads well inboard and the sheet eased to give a similar twist.

the top. Similarly, the first easing of the jib-sheet produces twist to balance that of the mainsail.

Reaching is one time when physical strength is important in a catamaran. The trimming of the sheets in strong winds is a constant task and it is even possible in certain wind strengths to induce extra speed by pumping both sheets together. I.Y.R.U. rules only allow pumping to induce planing and it may be difficult to prove that the increased speed of a catamaran produced by pumping is indeed a form of planing. The rule will doubtless be tested, and until an adverse decision is made pumping will form an important part of fast reaching in catamarans.

Stopping the lee-bow from burying is brought about by both helmsman and crew moving aft and keeping the sheets eased as the bows go down. The deceleration forces of the boat are immense when the bow does bury, and for this reason all the top crews use a restraining line leading from the stern of the boat to the trapeze harness-hook. In heavy airs the crew is likely to take up a position aft of the helmsman and to cope with this his trapeze wires must have sufficient length adjustment.

In light airs the crew will be well to leeward where he will have an excellent view of the slot and the tell-tales on the leeward side of the mainsail. He must be ready to move to windward at any gust but, more importantly, he must still trim the jib in sympathy with the mainsail.

Running

True running rarely occurs in racing catamarans, which benefit from reaching downwind and gybing, using the wind shifts in the same way as one might do upwind, except that a header is used for assistance while a freeing wind should cause a gybe to be made. The technique is not simple and requires a great deal of practice and coordination between helmsman and crew. A good tactical compass, or better still one on each hull, is essential for downwind sailing.

A catamaran downwind will gybe through approximately 90° – exactly what the angle is will depend on the boat, its rig and the strength of the wind. The boat is sailed as free as possible without the rig stalling out. The crew will know the rhumb-line angle from the weather mark to the leemark (it is the reciprocal of the weather leg) and will have made a note with a chinagraph pencil of the angle expected on each gybe. If he finds the boat is on a bearing worse than the theoretical angle he should inform the helmsman, who will then gybe the boat. The crew will continue to watch the compass and inform his helmsman of the shifts, particularly when these take the boat higher than the theoretical sailing angle. It is the skipper's responsibility to assess whether or not the shift is permanent enough to use it to advantage.

In light winds the crew has to learn that the

REACHING IN A CATAMARAN

An exciting manoeuvre, for it is the fastest point of sailing. It is the time when physical strength counts and co-ordination between crew and helmsman is most necessary to keep the boat moving smoothly. Catamarans tend to bury the lee bow, especially in high winds, which causes an explosion of water and very rapid deceleration. To prevent it, the crew and helmsman move right aft, sometimes with the crew on the trapeze going behind the helmsman. To prevent themselves being thrown forward when the bow does bury all top crews use a restraining line from the stern of the boat to the trapeze hook. The sheets are eased as the bow begins to dip, and they must be eased together or the jib will choke the slot.

boat will head up slightly on each gust and that this is not a course alteration due to wind shift, but otherwise the principle is the same. In almost no wind at all a dead square run may work best of all, and one should be encouraged to experiment in practice to see in what wind speed it does or does not become effective. Slower catamarans that use spinnakers will tend to employ this tactic almost all the time, but they are the exception rather than the rule.

Offshore multihulls

Fashion and personal fancy have been the deciding factors in whether the offshore racing multihull should have two hulls or three. Some people have suggested that the three-hull configuration has greater stability than the catamaran, but as many trimarans have capsized as twin-hulled craft. It does appear to be more dangerous than racing conventional boats offshore, but if reasonable care is exercised these dangers can be minimized greatly.

All too often the cause of mistakes in offshore multihulls – and monohulls, too – results from carrying too much sail. No matter what point of sailing, the offshore multihull does not like to be over-pressed with sail. To windward this will result in the leeward outrigger of the trimaran and the lee-hull of the catamaran being depressed into the water and thereby slowing the boat, making it more susceptible to tripping stern over bow.

Much of the offshore multihull's success stems from good design and building. Weight is a disadvantage but lack of strength spells disaster. A high degree of good engineering in modern boatbuilding materials is therefore required. Moulded plywood, glassfibre-reinforced plastics and aluminium alloy have all been used effectively, either alone or in composite construction with or without the addition of steel and carbon-fibre reinforcement. The stresses on an offshore multihull are enormous and fallibility can cost life. The boat must therefore be examined regularly and carefully at all the major stress points, the most important being where the cross beams join the hulls.

In all other respects the racing of offshore multihulls is similar to that of conventional monohulls. Seamanship and good navigation are essential and there is the added need for more rapid changes of sail because the multihull is much less tolerant of excessive canvas than a single-hulled craft.

MULTIHULLS IN
ACTION
The *British Oxygen*,
close hauled, on her
way round Britain.

Overall Tactics and Strategy

Tactics involve making use of manoeuvres allowed by the rules to attack or defend a position.

Racing tactics can be divided into attacking and defensive. Elemental factors – the strength and direction of the wind, the current, the land effects, the depth of water, the size of the waves and the weather – are best regarded as fundamental considerations in formulating strategy. Tactics in a race involve making use of manoeuvres allowed by the rules to attack or defend a position. It has to do with disturbing another boat's airstream, or positioning yourself in such a way that you are able to make best use of any wind change and preserve your place in the contest. The best attacking policy is to maintain clear wind at all time so that you can sail at the fastest speed, but the tactics of other competitors can never be ignored.

An intimate knowledge of the rules is essential if your tactics are to be effective. Tactics need to be well planned yet capable of adjustment in accordance with developments during the race. A thorough knowledge is needed of all the alternatives that are open to you; and you must grasp every opportunity to better your performance that is provided by the aerodynamics of the rig. There are chances of exploiting the weakness of your opponents or of sailing into a stronger position. These should not be overlooked. Other contestants will be doing likewise so you must be able to counter their moves by taking appropriate action.

The I.Y.R.U. rules provide the definition of right of way. A boat has right of way on starboard tack; if it is the leeward boat; if it has an inside overlap at a mark; and if it is sufficiently clear to windward so that the leeward yacht cannot tack. The action of the wind over the sails provides the effects which can be used for attack and defense. There are four categories here.

1. The blanketing from the sail
2. The deflection of the wind over the sails
3. The draught from the slot
4. The increased propulsion over an opponent's sail.

Tactics are influenced in different ways. Weather and current conditions alter at various points around the course and one must constantly watch for the effects of the change and use them to the best advantage. Clouds or smoke or flags, or the way other boats are pointing, will all give a clue to wind change as will the surface of the water. The state of the race is important as well. Sometimes the situation alters slowly and the changes are then easily recognized. At others, as in mark rounding, things can change rapidly and may be anticipated in part only. The effectiveness of tactics is influenced by the mental attitude

FAILED TACTICS
Previous page How not to do it: spinnaker trouble in the *Selavy*, during the Sardinia Cup Race 1978.

PRECISION MANOEVRES
Quarter tonners racing at Cowes, rounding a starboard hand mark.

of the crews. Adrenalin may run high in the close-quarter excitement of the start or when rounding marks, but on a leg alertness and all-out effort is harder to maintain. Morale can be raised by the experienced sailor; it must not be allowed to sag because of some minor setback. Concentration on all aspects of a race is imperative. It includes keeping an eye on the strategy and tactics of the opposition which will influence your own plan of action. You may be able to predict the tactics of an opponent by previous experience of sailing against him.

Each race must be planned separately but in doing so the experience gained from other races should be put to use. This is particularly pertinent towards the end of a series when a pattern of local conditions have been established and the opponents' tactics are understood. In the early stages of a race take every opportunity to sail your own course. It is foolhardy to indulge in the defensive type of tactical ploys that are more applicable to the later stages of a race. The object at the beginning is to establish a position from which the race can be won. In no circumstances should you allow an opponent to dictate the run of the early stages. It is even prudent to lose a couple of lengths if this enables you to follow your pre-determined plan.

The Start

It is impossible to exaggerate the importance of a good start. To be in clear air and able to go to the preferred side of the course is what every sailor seeks, but few have the ability to command it every time. It is this ability, more than any other, which singles out a regularly successful sailor from the rest. This ability is highlighted in the most serious racing, such as the America's Cup where it is often one person's duty to be the helmsman at the start and then hand over to the principal helmsman once the boat is clear of the starting line.

Starting is a time of aggression. There is one place on the line to be, and it is imperative that you establish your 'right' to it. Just how this is done will vary on almost every occasion although some basic principles apply. One cannot be dogmatic in a general sense as a host of variables determine the exact attitude to adopt for an individual start. The type of boat and its characteristics will play a large part, so too will the strength of the wind, the state of the water and the strength of the current. Experience is the purveyor of guidelines and it is always worthwhile, after a race, to analyse the start of the boats that were successful, particularly those that led in the early stages. From that analysis it should be possible to build a series of examples of how and why certain starts paid under various conditions and this may help you decide on your starting tactics.

Once a starting procedure has been determined – and remember it might have to be varied at the last moment because of a wind shift – all effort must go into its execution. An

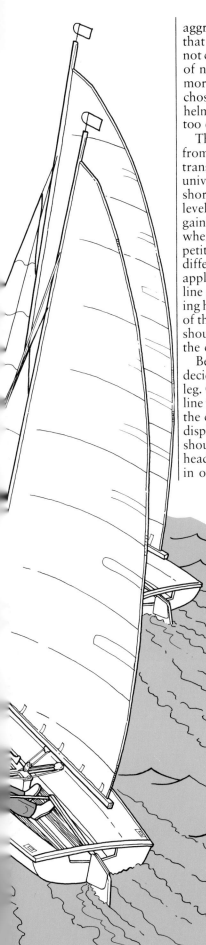

aggressive attitude is necessary, but not one that attracts the attention of competitors. Do not come to the line shouting at the helmsmen of nearby boats – that will only make them more determined to shut you out of your chosen starting place. In a good-class fleet the helmsmen will know the rules and will be all too eager to stay out of trouble.

There are three main types of starting line: from a committee vessel; from a shore-based transit; and a Gate start. The first is almost universal in top-class regattas while the shore-based start is common at club-racing level and in restricted waters; Gate starts are gaining in popularity at championships where there are a great number of competitors. Each type of starting line needs a different technique, but some of the principles apply to each, notably the need to cross the line going as fast as possible and concentrating heavily on boat speed for the first minutes of the race in order to establish clear air. You should also go towards the favoured side of the course as soon as possible.

Before the start many things have to be decided in planning the strategy for the first leg. On a course with a committee vessel start line the first leg is invariably to windward and the course direction to the first mark will be displayed from the committee vessel. This should be noted and a check made of the heading that it is possible to sail on each tack in order to show the favoured tack. It is as

well to check the bearing if the windward mark can be sighted – race committees have been known to make mistakes – for if this is incorrect it will alter the bearings of the gybe and leeward marks from the preceeding buoy.

Current deviations, available from charts or tidal atlases, should be checked to see if one side of the course is favoured. Careful readings should be taken of the wind direction all over the area of the first windward leg to determine the period of oscillation and to find out if there is any wind bend that could help in the choice of a particular route on that leg.

Most important of all is to check the bearing of the line relative to the wind. Rarely is the line set exactly at right angles to the wind, and the difference that this makes is important. For example, if the line were 100 yards (91 m) long and biased at 5°, one end would give an advantage of just over 12 yards (11 m). The greater the bias and the longer the line, the more the advantage of starting at one end.

Race committees have a happy habit of biasing a line away from the favourable side of the course, thereby eliminating any great advantage from the bias. The expert starting helmsman will then make his choice of starting place by endeavouring to find a position that allows him to get to the right side but without losing too much of the bias advantage. It will have to be a compromise, and one chosen with great care.

LUFFING

Before clearing the start line you may only luff slowly. After the gun you may luff as hard and as suddenly as you like, and may even attempt to touch the windward boat, provided you have *luffing rights*. You have luffing rights if you are clear ahead of another boat, or if you are the leeward yacht and are far enough ahead of the windward yacht for your mast to be ahead of her helmsman. When the windward helmsman reaches a position where he is ahead of your mast he hails *"Mast Abeam"*, and you loose your luffing rights. In the drawing on the left, the leeward boat is attempting to luff the windward boat so that she will be astern with no overlap by the time they reach the two-boats-length-circle around the mark. The windward boat will attempt to establish an overlap by getting her bow past the other's stern by the time they enter the imaginary circle. If she can do this then she will almost certainly pass ahead around the mark.

Whichever end is favoured is bound to attract a large proportion of the competitors and among them will be many of the fleet leaders. Inevitably there will be a crush and unless you are absolutely certain of coming clearly away from the bunch it may well pay to eschew this area altogether. There will be a big area of wind disturbance around this bunch but the general trend of wind will be to bend away from the line, lifting starboard-tack boats at the port end and port-tack boats at the starboard end.

One other consideration is likely to cause crushing at the ends of the line. This is the one minute rule, which requires that any boat that crosses the line less than a minute before the start must go around either the committee vessel or the pin end buoy before recrossing the line and starting.

Tactics therefore vary depending on the numbers of starters. With less than 25 boats on the line you can always go for the best starting place every time. In a fleet of this size the correct technique will enable you to claim the best position without trouble. In all races several attempts should be made, before the actual start, to hit the line exactly where you want to at a precise moment. That way, the helmsman has a good idea of where he needs to be on his run at a given time. Practice starts should be done at half speed so that you retain full control of the boat. Easing the sheets will slow the boat and hardening them will accelerate it. It is even possible to apply the brakes by pushing the boom out sharply and luffing the wind coming on to what was the lee side of the main sail and push the boat backwards.

With a championship start for 70 to 100 boats the pole areas are generally too crowded to enable a contestant to get clear away. The place to start in such an event is a quarter of the way up the line from the favoured end. If the other side of the course is favoured then it can pay to start in the middle of the line as there is likely to be a sag in the line at this point and sufficient clear air so that you can get well away and tack soon.

Coming out of the start the main aim is to sail the boat fast and free. For that reason you should make every effort to create a space to leeward so that you can drive out from under the lee of any boats to windward. By sailing just a fraction freer than normal the boat will go faster and make less leeway than her rivals who will almost certainly be trying to out-pinch each other. Windward boats will soon begin to fall off and come in to the deflected wind of boats that have sailed slighty faster to leeward. If there is a slight heading in the wind it will be possible for the good starter to tack and cross the fleet to windward.

With a line heavily biased to port there may be a temptation to start on port tack. This should be firmly resisted unless the line is so biased that starboard-tack boats will have difficulty in crossing the line. Even then the port-tack boat is in danger. Port-tack starts are strictly for the stunt driver.

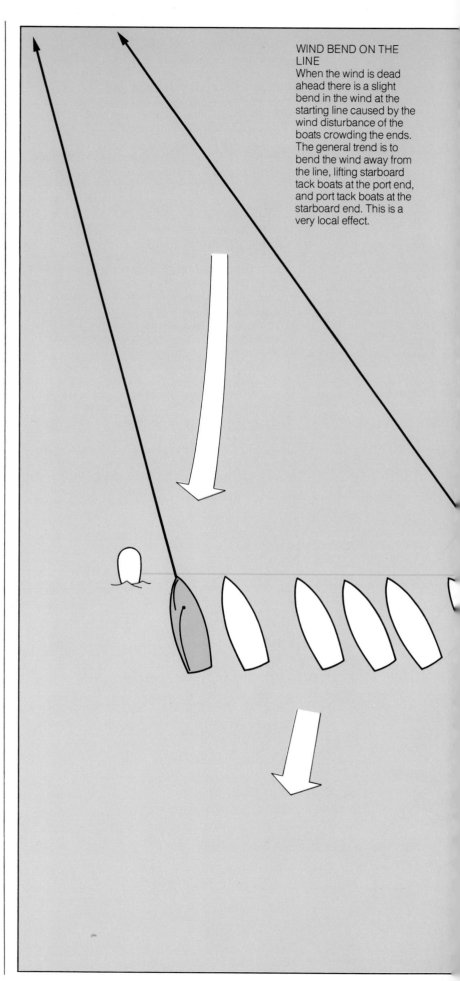

WIND BEND ON THE LINE
When the wind is dead ahead there is a slight bend in the wind at the starting line caused by the wind disturbance of the boats crowding the ends. The general trend is to bend the wind away from the line, lifting starboard tack boats at the port end, and port tack boats at the starboard end. This is a very local effect.

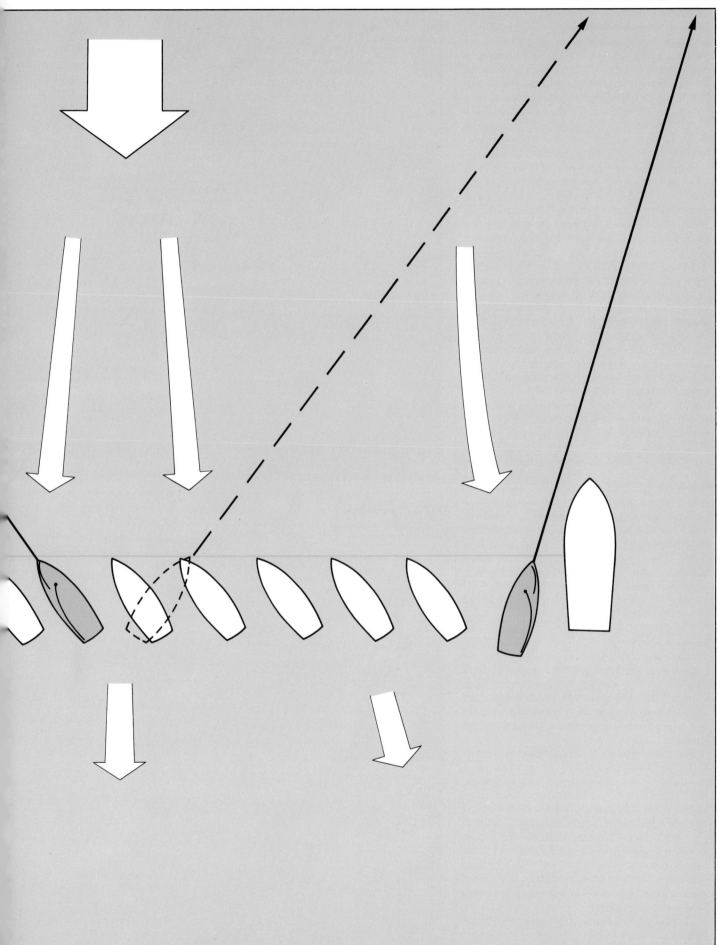

Starting from a shore-based transit line presents individual problems and requires different tactics. It is very rare for this line to be set to windward, and when it is there is bound to be heavy bias. It is more likely to be influenced by tidal factors and there will doubtless be wind-bending influence of the shore line to be considered as well. Shallow water will need to be taken into account as well. All these aspects will have to be evaluated before the choice of position is made.

The shore-based start line may or may not have an inner or an outer limit buoy on the line. It may consist of a single pole ashore to a buoy in the water, or it may be two poles on shore which form the line when in transit. Even in this last case there may be inner and outer limit buoys.

It is unlikely that there will be many starters from a shore-based line and so it will be easier to claim the best starting position. There are notable exceptions to this, such as the annual Round the Isle of Wight Race and the Round Zeeland in Denmark, but for the most part races from these lines will have less than 25 starters. The tactics used are, for the windward starts, the same as those for committee vessel start lines. Starting on a reach or a run, however, does involve new tactics, as discussed in Chapter 3. It is a question generally in such circumstances of one extreme or the other, being either the most windward or the most leeward boat. To windward one will be able to blanket all the boats to leeward and thus have an aerodynamic advantage; to leeward would give a right of way advantage and it might be possible to sail a higher course which would be faster. The determining factor is almost certainly the position of the first mark. The closer it is the more likely a leeward start, but much depends on establishing an inside overlap. Position at the mark is of major importance, particularly if the next leg is to windward.

The Gate start has become the race committee's answer to huge fleets. It eliminates a string of recalls but it does remove some of the excitement of starting. To be properly effective it requires wind that is steady in both strength and direction. The crush at the start then leads to congestion at the weather mark, but a long first boat generally allows the fleet to spread out sufficiently.

Planning strategy for a gate start is simple. It is based on which side of the course is favoured. If it is thought better to go up the port-hand side or the beat, a start is made as soon as possible after the pathfinder boat has opened the gate. If the starboard side is favoured, then the start must be made just before the pathfinder boat rounds up to go behind the gate launch. It is slightly more difficult to hit that end accurately. Care must be taken not to get too far from the pathfinder to discover the gate shut.

If you are chosen to be the pathfinder because of your finishing position in the previous race, you must remember that the race

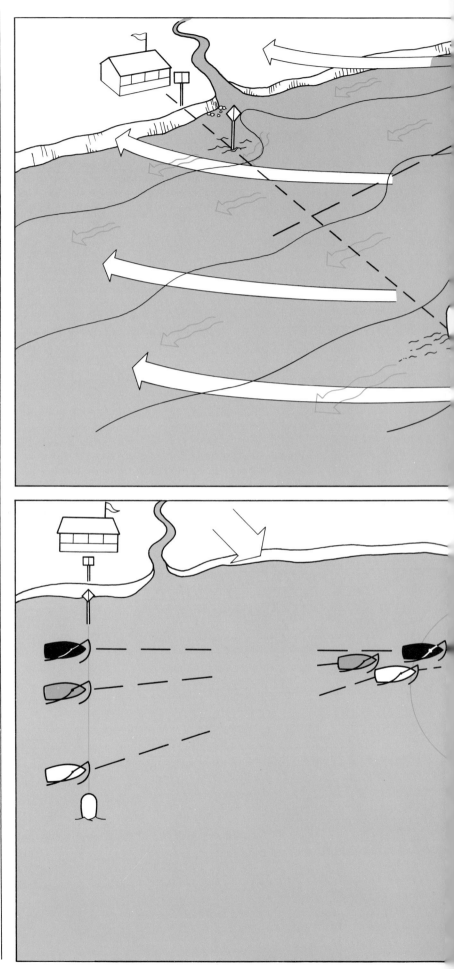

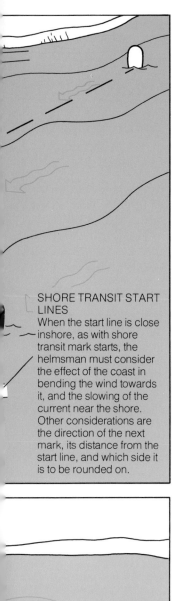

SHORE TRANSIT START LINES
When the start line is close inshore, as with shore transit mark starts, the helmsman must consider the effect of the coast in bending the wind towards it, and the slowing of the current near the shore. Other considerations are the direction of the next mark, its distance from the start line, and which side it is to be rounded on.

A RUNNING START
This is quite common from shore transit marks, the same considerations apply. In this case it may pay to start at the leeward side of the line if this allows you to establish an inside overlap by the time you reach the imaginary two-boats-length circle around the next mark.

begins for you as soon as you start the path-finder run for you are racing each boat that starts. If you sail slowly, all the starters will have an advantage over you.

The Windward Leg

To gain a tactical advantage on the windward leg it is essential to sail extremely hard and fast away from the start in order to be in a position to tack at will. Once in this clear position the objective is to sail the windward leg in the shortest possible time.

Prior checks will have revealed any notable wind bends over the course and where these exist they should be used to advantage. In their absence a first beat is planned by tacking on each of the heading shifts. With a shore line to windward of the course, compass checks are not necessary as the beat's heading can be checked against a feature ashore, but the compass provides an infallible method of locating wind shifts.

The average headings of each tack will have been noted before the start and written down close to the compass. As an extra aid there can also be a note of what bearings are good and which are bad. On starboard tack, when the bearing numbers decrease the boat is headed; when they increase the boat is lifted. On port tack the opposite applies: a decreasing bearing means a lift, and increasing bearing denotes a header. Just how much of a heading shift should be made before the boat is tacked

depends on the type of boat and how long it takes to return to full speed. A Finn, for example, can tack far quicker than a Flying Dutchman and her helmsman is therefore more able to take advantage of the shifts. The extra seconds that it takes to tack a Flying Dutchman make it more necessary for a shift to be of greater proportions. Offshore racing boats have other factors to take into account and whilst using individual shifts is just as important for them, the larger scale of their windward legs may dictate a contrary strategy to what might seem right in the immediate circumstances.

Having used the wind shifts to advantage and taken a lead, you may find that the boat is out to one side of the rest of the fleet. No matter how advantageous this position may appear to be, a tack must be made to get back with the rest. When out on a wing it needs only a small wind shift to reverse the situation. Taking one long tack out to the lay-line for the windward mark is a tactic which should only be employed when weather conditions have proved it to be beneficial or if you are trying to recover from a recalled start when desperate measures are needed to try to get back into contention with the leaders.

The tactics of a windward leg are directed to influencing other boats to do what you want them to do for your ultimate benefit. It is possible to direct them towards the 'wrong', unfavoured side of the course or even to go

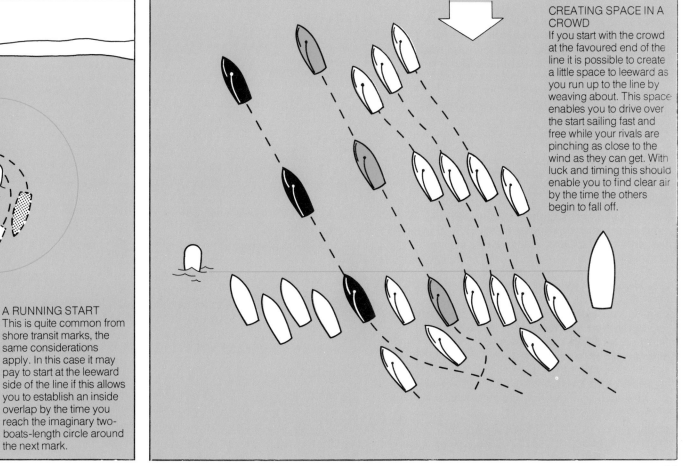

CREATING SPACE IN A CROWD
If you start with the crowd at the favoured end of the line it is possible to create a little space to leeward as you run up to the line by weaving about. This space enables you to drive over the start sailing fast and free while your rivals are pinching as close to the wind as they can get. With luck and timing this should enable you to find clear air by the time the others begin to fall off.

more slowly than necessary. In addition it is almost possible to get your opponent 'wrong-sided' at a turning mark – and it is around the corner that big gains can be made.

Let us consider two boats level on opposite tacks. The starboard-tack boat can go on the offensive in two ways. If the favoured side of the course is to the left she will hold her course and force the port-tack boat to lose a length by dipping her stern. This is a passive attack and is countered by the port-tacker coming about soon after dipping the starboard-tacker's stern so that the original right-of-way boat cannot tack. The port-tack boat's alternative is to carry on for some time and hope to catch the original starboard-tack boat when they meet again.

In the same circumstances but with starboard-tack boat marginally ahead her attacking move would be to tack into a safe leeward position and then apply a squeeze on the port-tacker by sailing fractionally higher and using the disturbed air created by her own sails to push her opponent back. The same tactic can be applied by a port-tack boat marginally ahead. The easiest defence is for the other boat to tack simultaneously. Otherwise it is possible to bear away slightly as the attacker tacks into the lee bow position to try to establish a safe windward position and then by aggressive erosion sail over the top of the attacker's wind. Should the attacker slightly miss a perfect tack, this spells disaster as the roles will quickly become reversed. Failure to get the windward advantage will mean that the defender will have to tack as soon as possible. Again, much depends on which side of the course, or which tack, is favoured at the time. The attacker might use these tactics to herd the other boat with the rest of the fleet.

With both boats level and converging the port-tack boat can launch an attacking move. When some three lengths from the starboard-tacker she should tack on to a parallel course and then endeavour, by sailing slightly higher than her rival, to gain a safe leeward position. The port-tack boat should adopt this tactic when the starboard tack is favoured as the only defences are for the other boat to sail as high and remain the same distance apart, or to try to sail faster by freeing her sheets slightly and endeavouring to overtake to windward.

When the starboard-tacker is a length clear and decides to tack dead ahead, which she should do if the port tack is favoured, the port-tacker has two alternatives. She can tack simultaneously (but that would put her on the non-favoured tack) or she can bear away as soon as the other boat begins to tack and try to sail through to leeward. This can only work when the two boats are close, otherwise the port-tack boat will have to give away too

CLOSE TACKING
Hairsbreadth judgement in action as *Jan Pott* G909 just clears *Sorcery* US 4785 on the starboard tack.

much in order to get sufficient clear air. If the port-tack boat is about two lengths or more down as the starboard-tack boat begins her tack, she must tack immediately.

When two boats are sailing parallel and are close-hauled, either may attack and each has a defence. When the leeward boat is just on the limit of the windward boat's interference zone, the windward craft may wish to ensure that the leeward boat does not escape. She will then bear away slightly to get a proper cover on the leeward boat, which can counter by bearing away at the same time or by tacking away once the windward boat has established her covering position. The windward boat will resort to this tactic only on the last leg of the course or if there is a turning mark nearby, otherwise the slowing-up that it causes will bring the rest of the fleet into close contention.

In order to attack from the same position the leeward boat can try a false tack. All her crew will make their preparations for tacking obvious to the windward boat, encouraging her to tack simultaneously. The leeward boat then begins a tack but returns to her old course when the weather boat has committed herself to the new tack. If the windward boat tries to return to the old tack immediately she will be in danger of having no way-on at all and she can easily be passed by the leeward boat which goes no further in her tack than head to wind before returning.

Modifying this tactic, the leeward boat's crew can be secretive in their preparations for the tack and catch their rivals to windward by surprise when they tack. The windward boat's tack will then be slower because it is hurried. The leeward boat will be able to tack again and either gain considerable ground with the windward boat tacks to cover, or manage to split tacks and shake off the cover altogether. The windward boat's crew should be aware of this tactic and should watch the leeward boat's crew closely when it is vitally important to keep the close cover, for example, on a beat to the finish or nearing a windward mark.

A windward boat with her rival two lengths abeam to leeward might investigate a move to put herself upwind of the leeward boat by bearing off slightly and thereby sailing fuller and faster to such a position that the leeward boat is in her cone of wind interference. The leeward boat can either bear away on to a parallel course as a means of passive defence or it can counter-attack by sailing slightly higher to get a safe leeward position.

Nearing the windward mark position becomes all important, and the boat to leeward and astern can often control the order of rounding the buoy. It is not prudent to have a long lay-line to the weather mark because a freeing shift can allow leeward boats to make up to the lay-line and squeeze out the boats to weather. In addition the boat on a close lay-line is in danger from a boat ahead that tacks dead upwind and pours on sufficient dis-

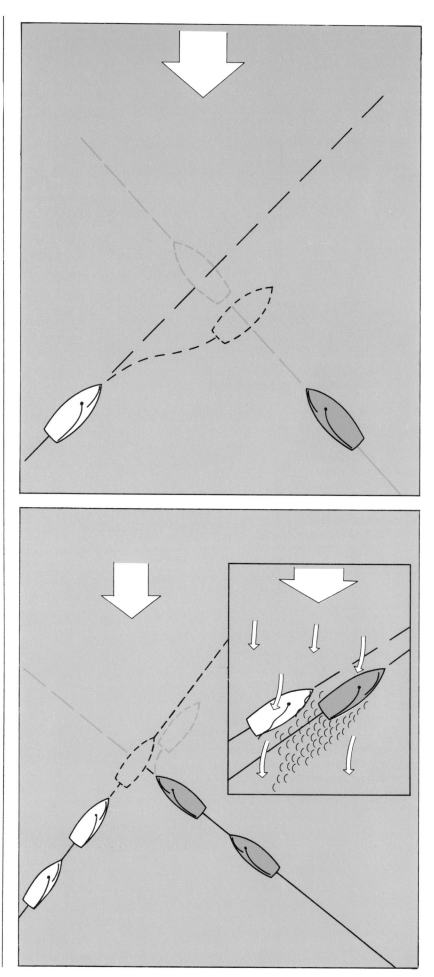

PORT AND STARBOARD

Boats on port tack keep clear of boats on starboard tack. However they have a choice in how to keep clear. They may tack, or they may dip under the stern of the starboard tack boat. Whichever course is chosen it should be planned as part of the tactics of the race, taking into consideration the other boats, the mark to be rounded, and the wind and current. A good lookout is therefore essential if a sudden hail of "Starboard!" from under the jib is not going to send you crash-tacking in confusion. Assuming that you were on port tack for a good reason, it usually pays to dip under the other boat's stern *(top left)*, rather than tack.

Having dipped under the stern of the starboard tack boat he may then continue and hope to reverse the roles at the next meeting, or he may tack almost immediately and by following astern and a little to windward prevent the opponent from tacking when he wishes *(shown top right)*.

It is also possible to use the converging courses of two boats to tack into a lee bow position and force the opposition back with your disturbed air.

(Lower left) – in this the starboard tack boat would have passed marginally ahead. Instead of doing so he tacks just before they would cross and establishes the lee bow position. By then sailing as high as possible she pushes back the original port tacker. When the port tacker is going to pass marginally ahead *(lower right)*, he may use the same ploy, but in defence the windward boat may tack immediately.

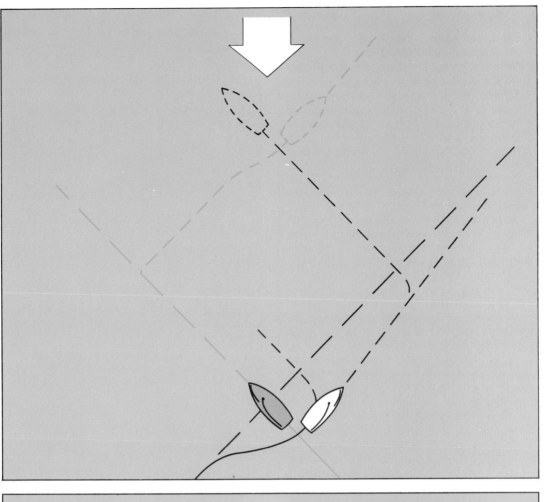

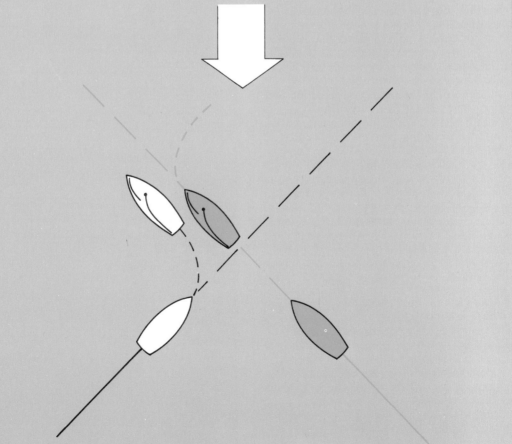

143

turbed air to stop the leeward boat from fetching the weather mark. It is also extremely difficult to judge, with any degree of accuracy, the exact lay-line from a distance. Only extreme tidal conditions can force the leading boat to a long lay-line and then the likelihood is that all her rivals will go at least as far as she does before making their final tack for the mark. In normal circumstances the approach should be to a point 110–220 yards (100–200 m) leeward of the marker buoy.

From there it is possible to control all the boats except those more than two lengths clear ahead, and even those can be shepherded in a way that does not affect you. This applies to boats on the same tack or on converging tacks. Different tactics apply to starboard roundings than to port roundings, but it is only the most foolish of race officers who will set courses with starboard roundings for large fleets. They can be the cause of considerable damage and put too much emphasis on luck and daring to be genuinely justified. If they are met with the overriding tactic is to herd your rival away beyond the lay-line on either tack and thus be in a position to tack so that you are between your rival and the mark.

The best approach is therefore a tack of around 50 yards (45 m) to the mark on the lay-line. In very shifting winds, even on this short distance, it pays to allow up to a length of overstanding to windward. In steady airs this is an unacceptable amount and could result in one or even two boats squeezing in at the mark. But few things are worse than getting a heading shift on the final approach with boats on your weather quarter that are then able to lay the mark while you are forced to gybe round and wait for a gap in the starboard tack lay-line queue.

Rarely, of course, will you have just one opponent to deal with on a windward leg and it may be that you can use other boats in order to get to, or keep at, the front of the fleet. If you are running level second in the fleet and converge with the level boat it is essential to go in the opposite direction to her in order that the lead boat is faced with a choice of which way to go. The leader must lose out to one or other of the pursuers because of the inevitable wind shifts. She will reduce her loss to a minimum by taking a series of short tacks between the paths of her closest rivals with the option to close with the one which appears to be most favoured. The leader then covers closest whichever of her two opponents comes to the fore.

There is need for caution in strategy in a series. You cannot go out on a limb as it may result in a placing that will badly affect your overall position. First-beat tactics therefore tend to favour middle-of-the-course strategy with a general observation as to what is going on on the wings. It is no use going for the middle of the course, however, when it is obvious from observation that the only way

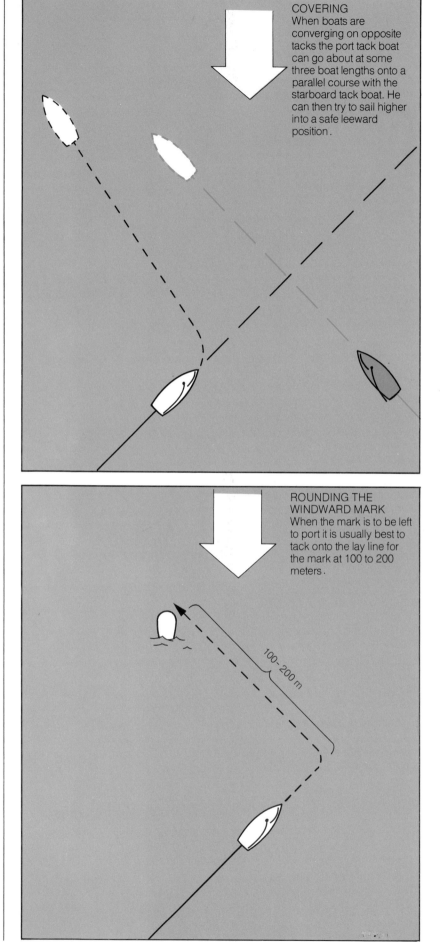

COVERING
When boats are converging on opposite tacks the port tack boat can go about at some three boat lengths onto a parallel course with the starboard tack boat. He can then try to sail higher into a safe leeward position.

ROUNDING THE WINDWARD MARK
When the mark is to be left to port it is usually best to tack onto the lay line for the mark at 100 to 200 meters.

100–200 m

When the boats are on parallel courses and level the windward boat may bear away to get a proper cover on the leeward boat by placing her in her wind shadow, which extends some six mast lengths down from the apparent wind. The leeward boat may bear away to escape the cover.

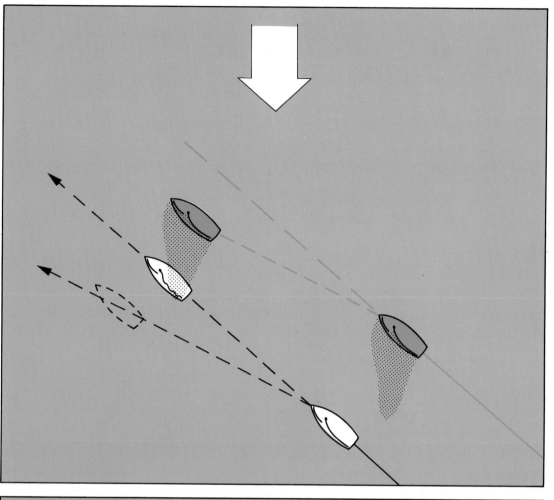

With a starboard hand mark , it is best to overstand the mark on the starboard tack, by about a boat's length, and to make the final tack much closer, some 45 meters to leeward of it.

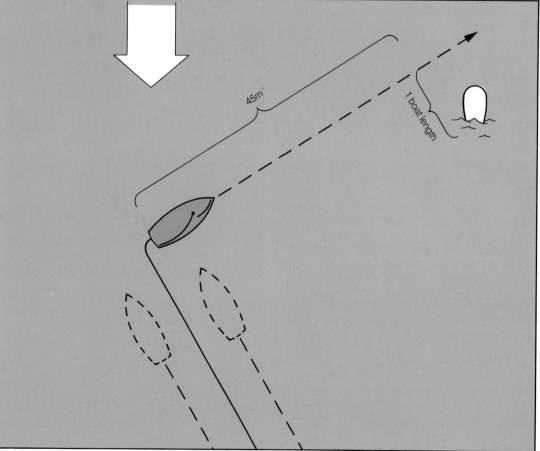

45m

1 boat length

to go is wide to the right or left. In a bay, for example, the leaders on almost all occasions will be those who first head into the shore. This applies 95 times out of 100. On the other five occasions when conditions dictate otherwise the unusual conditions will almost certainly be obvious to all, or else catch everyone napping. Conservative tactics are therefore to stay with the majority of the fleet. If a recognizable pattern emerges during the first windward leg the leader's consolidating course will be between that and the midline course whilst his attackers will go more towards the favoured part of the course. If they go that way to a man it makes the leader's choice of course that much easier.

Reaching

With the wind free far fewer opportunities exist for tactical manoeuvres than when going to windward. You attack by putting an opponent into your blanketing zone and the defence is by luffing. But in many cases these have little relevance as greater gains are to be made by sailing the boat to its full potential than by indulging in close-quarter tactical battles. This is particularly true for planing boats and in stronger winds.

The blanketing zone of a boat's sails is in the direction of the apparent wind of that boat, and not, as might be expected, to leeward of the true wind. It is possible to judge accurately the cone of interference from the masthead wind indicators of both boats.

The blanketing zone extends only six mast-lengths from the windward boat and beyond that distance a boat astern must sail faster to put her rival under pressure. That disturbance decreases both vertically as well as horizontally, so that even at six lengths away the disturbance is very small indeed. The attacker therefore should contain his desire to attack until he is sure that it will be effective, when he should concentrate fully on making the boat go as fast as possible.

The other major factor in passing a boat on a reach in close proximity for the blanketing zone to be effective, is the stern wave of the leading boat. The angle at which the attacking boat approaches the wake is important, since it can be used to the attacker's advantage as well as the defender's but the lesson is to keep the advantage with the attack.

An attack must be deliberate. Choose the right moment to move to windward – on a gust, preferably – and with the increased speed gained by luffing break through the stern wave of the boat ahead and then begin to interfere with her wind. To be effective the manoeuvre has to be close but the leeward boat has the right to luff to defend her position. If, therefore, the attacking boat is travelling noticeably faster than the one ahead, it is prudent for her to pass well to windward and avoid the risk of being luffed. The leeward boat would, in many cases, be foolish to detour to windward to prevent her passing by luffing.

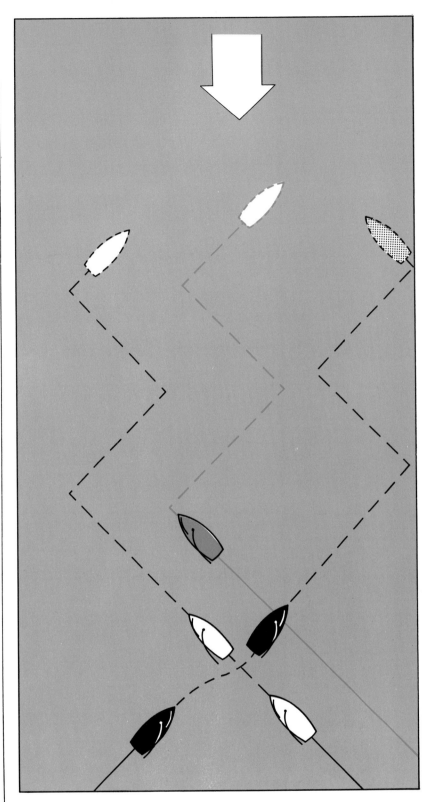

BREAKING COVER
Where two boats are competing for second place they may split the cover of the leading boat by going in opposite directions. The leading boat will then have to take short tacks between them, hoping to be in a position to cover whichever of them pulls ahead.

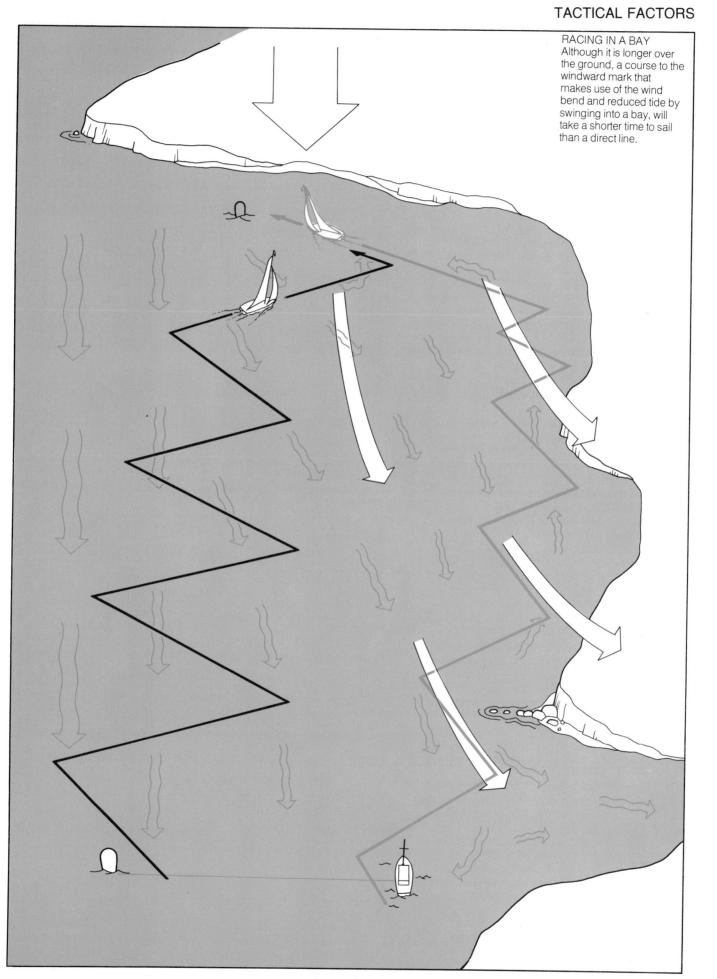

RACING IN A BAY
Although it is longer over the ground, a course to the windward mark that makes use of the wind bend and reduced tide by swinging into a bay, will take a shorter time to sail than a direct line.

If the attack is made to leeward it is a much longer manoeuvre. Gone is the weapon of interfering with the leading boat's wind; the only assistance that the attacker will obtain is the crest of the leader's stern wave and she must use this to the full. Because of the leader's cone of interference the attacking boat must go well to leeward. It is a move that will be dictated by the desire to go to leeward of the rhumb line course and is perhaps best used in light airs when the cone of interference is not great.

Generally, one of the most important effects that an attacking boat can have on the crew of the leading boat is a psychological one. Constantly riding astern of a boat and making the occasional dart either to windward or leeward will irritate the crew of the boat ahead. If carried out effectively it can reduce their concentration and lead them to make mistakes and slow up. The attacking boat has the advantage of being able to make the manoeuvres in her time and so the parrying of the defender must, of necessity, reduce her speed. Constant attacks will wear down the speed of the boat ahead and bring her within the range of her blanketing zone.

In defending, the leading boat should aim to stay between her closest opponent and the next mark. This can be done by luffing gently several times and then bearing away considerably to get back to the mark. Alternatively it can be done more effectively with a sharp luff which will stop the opponent. In this case the luff must be deliberate and go to the limit, head to wind. In responding the windward boat will slow more, probably going on to the other tack as she is on the inside of the turning circle of the pair. It is not such an effective tactic in planing dinghies where the 'mast abeam' position may be quickly reached by the windward boat, as on slower moving keelboats.

More often than not an attack or defence is made against more than one boat. If you estimate that the wind will free then it can pay to sail a course to leeward early on in the leg so that when you come back up to the mark your course is higher, and faster, than the boats to windward which have had to ease sheets further as the wind has freed. If the wind is likely to head then a windward course early is probably advisable. In either case these detours must, like any other free-wind tactic, be deliberate and get the boat outside the interference zone of the rest of the fleet. It must be done quickly.

A spinnaker will enhance the effectiveness of these manoeuvres. In a constant wind where it appears impossible to carry a spinnaker on a reach, it may be possible to gain extra room to windward. If this ploy is considered the move to windward must be made as quickly as possible to get clear of the rest of the fleet. It will almost certainly be necessary to bear away considerably to get the spinnaker to set before resuming your course for

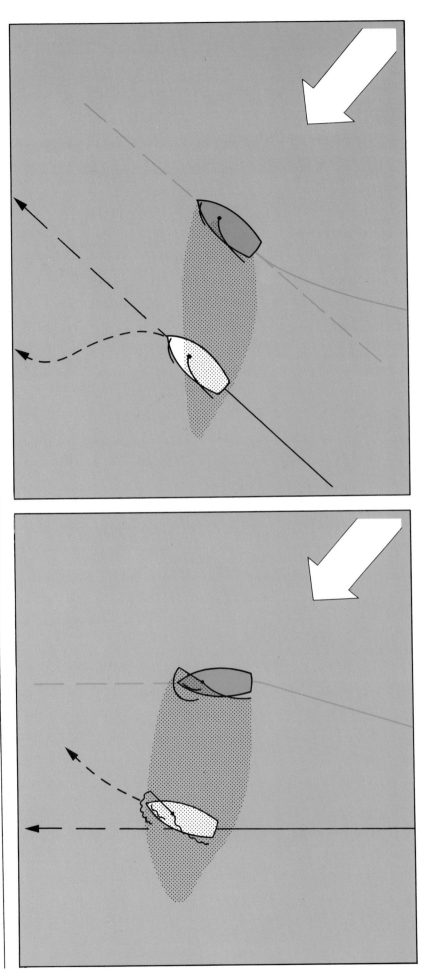

WIND SHADOW AND BLANKETING

The area of wind shadow extends about six mast lengths downwind in the direction of the apparent wind, that is a few degrees forward of the real wind. A windward boat may keep a boat to leeward covered by bearing down on it to keep it in the area of disturbance. To break the cover, when reaching the leeward boat may bear it away too (top left). The effectiveness of the disturbance is obviously strongest nearest to the sails (right). On a broad reach or run (lower left), the leeward boat may protect itself by luffing. The more determined the luff the more likely the cover will be broken, especially if the windward boat can be forced behind your stern wave again.

Apparent wind

True wind

the mark. In light weather it will pay to set the spinnaker early and, if necessary, go to leeward with it, planning to drop it and reach higher for the mark with more speed. If the wind frees or heads there is every advantage to be gained.

Always, when defending, there is the worry that the boat against which the immediate defence is taken may not eventually prove to be the greatest danger. Luffing one boat may allow another to slip through to leeward so overall strategy must be kept in mind.

Running

Most of the principles of attack and defence when reaching apply when running. The attacking boat, able to sail on the inside of the curve, should make consistent gains on the leading boat by endeavouring to instigate gybing duels on the run. Once again, constant challenges are likely to have the greatest effect and allow the attacker to get the leading boat into the cone of interference of her sails and thus slow her further. Planing boats are difficult to defend against and for this reason it is best to endeavour to sail the boat at its fastest without consideration for those astern.

Rounding Marks

More ground is won and lost in rounding marks than at any other moment in the race, except perhaps at the start. Practice in rounding marks correctly can assist immensely. It is bad enough to throw away a couple of lengths by incorrect rounding, but when this error is compounded by letting in four boats to windward, it can prove disastrous. Good skippers do not allow it to happen and as often as not will gain places at marks by their superior tactics. Much of the effort made towards the end of any leg of the course should be directed to obtaining the best position for rounding the mark.

REACHING RUNNING
Luffing your immediate opponent may allow other boats to slip through to leeward. The leading boat *(above)*, at the windward mark has tried to protect his position from the shadow of the second boat by luffing. At first he has tried a gentle luff, but this failed to shake off the cover. Later he tried a really determined luff but mistimed it and quickly found the windward boat calling "Mast Abeam" which obliged him to resume his proper course to the mark, unable to get out of the wind shadow of his opponent until the wind veered a little. The third boat around the windward mark did not anticipate the shift and decrease in the wind. By taking the direct line he was not able to get his spinnaker up until the wind had shifted and dropped five knots. The fourth boat round the windward mark decided to run off under spinnaker, hoping for a freeing shift later. He got it, and although it was not enough to reach for the mark all the way under spinnaker, his original spinnaker run put him far enough ahead to reach the mark first and with an inside overlap. The two who got locked into a luffing match lost out completely.

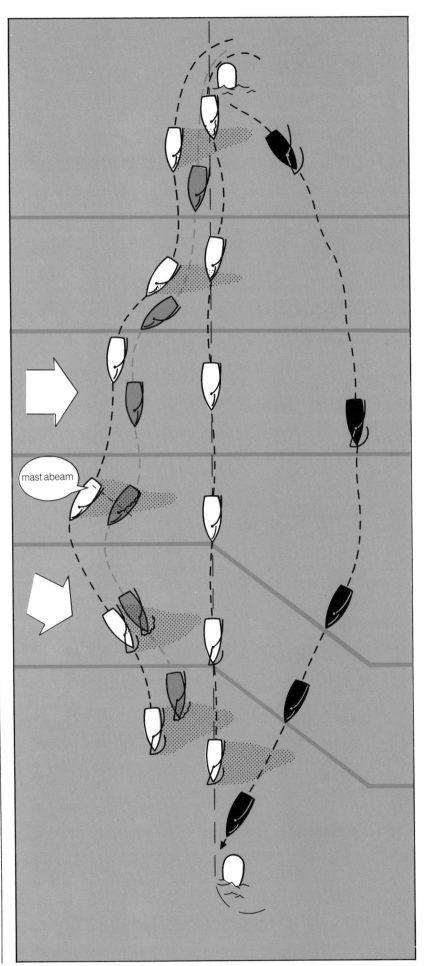

mast abeam

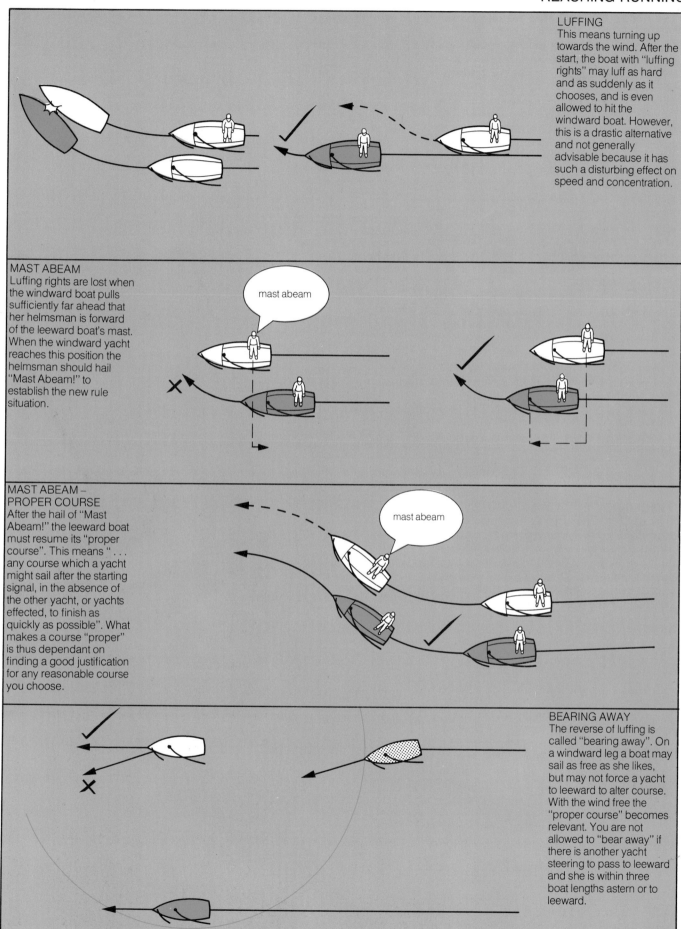

LUFFING
This means turning up towards the wind. After the start, the boat with "luffing rights" may luff as hard and as suddenly as it chooses, and is even allowed to hit the windward boat. However, this is a drastic alternative and not generally advisable because it has such a disturbing effect on speed and concentration.

MAST ABEAM
Luffing rights are lost when the windward boat pulls sufficiently far ahead that her helmsman is forward of the leeward boat's mast. When the windward yacht reaches this position the helmsman should hail "Mast Abeam!" to establish the new rule situation.

mast abeam

MAST ABEAM – PROPER COURSE
After the hail of "Mast Abeam!" the leeward boat must resume its "proper course". This means " . . . any course which a yacht might sail after the starting signal, in the absence of the other yacht, or yachts effected, to finish as quickly as possible". What makes a course "proper" is thus dependant on finding a good justification for any reasonable course you choose.

mast abeam

BEARING AWAY
The reverse of luffing is called "bearing away". On a windward leg a boat may sail as free as she likes, but may not force a yacht to leeward to alter course. With the wind free the "proper course" becomes relevant. You are not allowed to "bear away" if there is another yacht steering to pass to leeward and she is within three boat lengths astern or to leeward.

Rounding a mark after a windward leg is the least difficult of all manoeuvres. The helmsman's action should be smooth and, unless there is a gybe to follow, gradual so that maximum speed is maintained throughout the manoeuvre. The helmsman must concentrate on steering rather than worry about spinnaker hoisting, otherwise another boat will put the leading boat into its blanketing zone and get past. The opportunity for a boat astern to do so should not be missed. If the rounding is from a beat to a run on the opposite gybe the mark should be approached slightly wide and rounded with sheets eased. You should then go straight into an early gybe to protect your weather side. Care must be taken in a port rounding to avoid starboard-tack boats approaching the mark if you are running off on port gybe. This can lead to double gybe situation with the spinnaker half hoisted and a large loss of ground as well as the risk of collision.

When rounding from a reach or a run to a beat, the mark should be approached on a line one and a half boat lengths to leeward and the rounding begun when the boat is one and a half boat lengths from the buoy. In that way the boat will come on to a close-hauled course as her bow is at the mark and there is no opportunity for another boat to gain an advantage to windward of her. All tactics approaching the mark will be aimed at obtaining the ideal rounding position even if it means slowing the boat.

Finishing

One place or several may be gained close to the finishing line by correct tactical approach. When the finish is to windward the first thing to check is the bias of the line. Flags on the committee vessel will give the best indication of this and as a simple guide you should aim to finish at the opposite end to the one you would choose to start from, ie the leeward end of the line. Aim to go to that end as close as you can. It may be that there is a boat ahead and close to leeward unable to tack because of the windward boat's proximity. The windward boat should then take the advantage and sail her rival well beyond the lay-line to the finish before tacking, thus forcing the other boat to follow her to the line. The counter to this is for the leeward boat to bear off well before the finish and get into a position where she can tack and then, if on starboard put the windward boat about, or if on port dip the windward boat's stern closely and either sail hard for the right end of the line or hope when next tacked to catch her rival on port.

Downwind finishes are rare but when they occur the same principles apply. It is often necessary to sail a rival outside the limits of the line by luffing, and then beating them back to the line after gybing. All too often these manoeuvres fail, simply because they are executed with insufficient concentration, care and persistence.

Rounding the weather mark from a beat to a run (1) the helmsman's action should be smooth and gradual to maintain speed. But watch out for the boat behind trying to get you in his wind shadow. Gybing round the second mark from a reach to a run, or a broad reach, (2) the mark should be approached slightly wide and rounded with the sheets well eased. Go straight into an early gybe to protect the weather side. Rounding from a run to a beat (3) make the approach one and a half boat lengths to leeward and begin the rounding at the same distance from the buoy. When the bow is at the mark you should be close hauled on the new tack, leaving no space for another boat to slip in to windward.

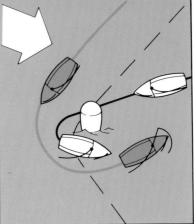

The Glossary

An international exchange of yachting terms.

APPARENT WIND
The wind that is experienced by the boat, made up of the true wind and the wind created by the boat's own forward motion.

BACKING
When the wind changes in an anticlockwise direction, for example from west to south west. When it changes in a clockwise direction it is said to veer.

BACKWIND
To deflect the wind from your sails onto those of another boat, giving it disturbed air.

BARBER HAUL
A temporary system for pulling the jib or genoa sheet further inboard or outboard from its normal sheeting angle.

BEAR AWAY
To turn away from the direction of the wind.

BEARING
The direction of an object from a boat, or between two objects. Compass Bearings express direction relative to the compass's magnetic north. Corrected for compass deviation they are known as Magnetic Bearings and relate to magnetic north. When further corrected for local magnetic variation in the earth's field they are True Bearings, relative to true north.

BEAUFORT SCALE
A scale which groups wind speeds up to 64 knots into forces – 1 to 12 – each group of wind speeds being recognisable by its effect on the appearance of the sea's surface. For example Force 8, Gale, wind velocity 34-40 knots, the sea is described as "Moderately high waves of greater length; edges of crests begin to break into the spindrift. The foam is blown in well marked streaks along the direction of the wind."

BLANKET
To blanket means to put another boat in your wind shadow. See backwind.

BLOOPER
A big baggy running sail used together with a spinnaker and set on the windward side without a stay or boom. Also known as a streaker, big boy, and shooter.

BOLT ROPE
A rope strengthening sewn on the luff and foot of a sail. Usually led into a groove on a boom, and on smaller boats into a groove in the mast. Also used with foresail headfoils set on the forestay.

BOOM VANG
See kicking strap.

BROACH
To turn out of control when running or reaching so that the boat is broadside to the waves and wind, and heavily heeled.

CE
Centre of Effort of a sail or sails.

CLR
Centre of Lateral Resistance: the point about which the boat pivots. The position of the CE in relation to the CLR determines the degree of weather or lee helm.

CHAIN PLATES
The metal plates to which the shrouds attach.

CLEW
See sail parts.

COCKED HAT
A triangle on a chart formed by three lines of bearing which do not intersect exactly.

CORRECTED TIME
The actual time taken to complete a race after it has been adjusted according to the rating or handicap system in use. Final placings are determined by corrected time, and not who crossed the line first.

CRINGLE
A reinforced hole on an edge or corner of a sail used for attaching and stretching out the sail.

CUNNINGHAM HOLE
A cringle near the bottom of the luff of a sail used to provide more tension on the luff when required.

DEAD RECKONING
DR is the method of keeping track of the boat's position, from the last known position, using course and distance sailed. When tides, currents, leeway and other factors are added in the result is known as the Estimated Position.

DEVIATION
The error in the compass caused by the various magnetic influences on board.

EASE
To ease away, or ease off means to slacken something.

ESTIMATED POSITION
See dead reckoning.

FAIRLEAD
A fitting through which a rope passes to give it a good lead without chaffing.

FALL OFF
To fall away or fall off means to steer further away from the direction of the wind.

FETCH
The distance over which the wind travels across open water creating waves. Also to reach a desired position on one tack.

FIX
The boat's position determined by taking bearings on known objects.

FOREGUY
A rope leading forward from the outer end of a boom to prevent it swinging in.

FRACTIONAL RIG
A rig designed so that the forestay attaches to the mast at some distance from the mast head. In a masthead rig it attaches at the top.

FRONT
An area where a warm air mass and a cold air mass meet. A cold front means that a cold air mass follows a mass of warm air.

GEL COAT
The polished coating on the outer surface of fibre glass. It is thin and may be coloured.

GENOA
A large headsail that overlaps the mainsail, cut so that the clew sets low near the deck.

GOOSENECK
The fitting connecting the boom to the mast allowing free movement horizontally and vertically.

GRP
Glass Reinforced Plastic, or glass fibre.

GUY
The control line through the outboard end of the spinnaker pole and onto the tack of the spinnaker. The terminology changes when the spinnaker is gybed with the boom on the other side. The guy becomes the sheet, and the sheet the guy. The tack becomes the new clew and the old clew becomes the tack.

GYBE
To gybe means to turn the boat so that the stern passes through the direction of the wind, bringing the wind onto the other side. When you tack the bow passes through the wind.

HALYARD
A rope or wire that hoists the sails.

HANK
A fitting to attach a headsail to its stay. A number of hanks are sewn on the luff of the sail.

HEAD
See sail parts.

HEADER
A shift in the wind towards the bow, forcing a sailing boat to bear away from her course.

HEADING
The boat's course.

HEEL
To tilt the boat sideways.

HEEL FITTING
The bottom of the mast; or the fitting on the bottom of a rudder hung on the back of the keel.

HELM
The steering wheel or tiller. Weather Helm means the boat tends to turn up towards the wind. Lee Helm means it tends to turn away from the wind. See CE and CLR.

HIKING
Sitting out.

HOUNDS
Where the stays attach to the mast.

JIB
A foresail that does not overlap the mast.

KICKING STRAP
Or boom vang, or kicker: a block and tackle, or wire, or hydraulic ram used to pull the boom down. The hydraulic ram may also lift it.

LEECH
See sail parts.

LEECH LINE
Line used to tension the leech of a sail.

LEE HELM
See helm.

LEEWARD
The side away from the wind.

LEEWAY
The sideways drift of the boat due to the wind.

LIFT
The opposite of heading. When the wind moves away from the bow it is said to free and to provide a lift. Also when the luff of the sails start to stall and flutter.

LOG
An instrument to record the distance sailed through the water. It may also show speed.

LOG BOOK
A book in which is recorded information about the boat's progress, course, log readings, bearings and fixes as well as weather observations.

LUFF
See sail parts. To luff, or luff up, means to turn up towards the wind. In racing this is sometimes used to prevent another boat from passing to windward.

MASTHEAD RIG
See fractional rig.

MARK
Usually a buoy or other object which serves as a turning point in the course of a race.

MAST RAM
Used to control the bend in the mast of a dinghy with a keel stepped mast. It pushes the mast fore or aft in the partners.

NULL
When the aerial of a direction finding radio is end-on to the transmitting beacon the signal is weakest. This is the null and a bearing on the station can be taken from it.

OFF THE WIND
To reach or run with the wind free. On the wind means close hauled or beating.

PARTNER
Reinforcement around the deck where the mast passes through. Also called the mast gate.

PAY OFF
To steer further away from the direction of the wind.

PINCH
To sail so close to the wind that the boat slows.

PITCH
The fore and aft plunging movement of a boat.

PLANE
When a light displacement boat picks up sufficient speed its hull shape causes it to rise up and plane – to skim over the top of the water something like a surf board.

POINT
To sail at a narrow angle to the wind, without pinching. To point up means to sail closer to the wind.

PROPER COURSE
Any course which a boat might sail after the start of a race, which, in the absence of other yachts would allow her to finish as quickly as possible.

RAKE
The fore or aft angle of the mast from the vertical.

RDF
Radio Direction Finder. A special radio and aerial used to get compass bearings from navigational radio beacons.

REACH
To sail with the wind coming more or less over the side of the boat. With a close reach the wind comes from further forward, but not close hauled. On a broad reach it is behind the beam to about 45 off the stern.

REEF
To reduce the area of a sail by rolling up or folding the foot, while keeping the remainder set.

RHUMB LINE
The shortest course between two points. A straight line on a Mercator chart.

RUN
To sail with the wind behind you. Also the distance covered in a given period of time.

SAIL PARTS

Head:	The top of the sail attached to the halyard.
Luff:	The leading edge.
Tack:	The bottom of the leading edge fixed to the deck or boom.
Foot:	The bottom or horizontal edge of the sail.
Clew:	The after corner of the sail to which the sheet is attached, or the clew outhaul if it is set on a boom.
Leech:	The trailing edge of a sail.

SEA BREEZE
A wind blowing from the sea to the land caused by the sun's heat.

SHEET TRAVELLER
A slide and track on which the lower block of a sheet tackle can be moved across the boat to alter the sheeting angle.

SHY
The spinnaker set as close to the wind as it can be kept filled.

SNAP SHACKLE
A quick release shackle.

SNATCH BLOCK
A block which can be opened so that a bight of rope can be put in, without having to reeve through the end.

SPREADERS
Horizontal struts attached to the sides of a mast to spread the shrouds further out from the mast. Also called cross trees.

STAY
A wire or rope supporting the mast in a fore and aft line.

TACK
See sail parts. Also to change direction by turning the bow through the wind. A port tack is with the wind coming over the port side, and a starboard tack is with the wind coming from the starboard side.

TANG
A metal fitting on a mast to which a shroud or stay is fixed.

TELL TALE
A thread or yarn fixed to a sail or shroud to show the apparent wind direction.

TOPPING LIFT
A rope or wire that raises or lowers the outer end of a boom. Sometimes called an uphaul.

TRANSIT LINE
When two known points are visibly 'in transit' as with leading marks. A transit bearing is very precise and useful for checking the compass deviation.

TRAPEZE
A wire rigged from the hounds to allow the helmsman or crew to hang his weight outside the hull with his feet on the gunwale. A more effective form of sitting out or hiking in dinghies.

TURNBUCKLE
Same as bottle screw or rigging screw.

VANG
See kicking strap.

VEER
See backing.

WATCH
The members of the crew working at any one time. Also the division of time on board ship.

WEATHER HELM
See helm.

WEATHER SIDE
The side towards the wind, also the windward side or to windward.

RATING AND CLASSES
Measuring offshore racing yachts of differing sizes and designs so that they may race together with equal chance under a handicap system has been a problem since the early part of this century.

This is in part because any measurement formula quickly influences design, sometimes in an undesirable way. In the USA the Cruising Club of America developed one rating rule, while in Britain the Royal Ocean Racing Club (RORC) developed another slightly different rule. Each was modified in the light of experience, but it became difficult for boats designed to race under one rating system to do well under the other. Finally to solve this problem an International Offshore Rule (IOR) was brought out in 1970. This too has been modified with experience. In most of the major races now held the boats are measured to the IOR Mark III, or Mark IIIA for boats of an early design. The measurement of a yacht for an IOR rating involves a complicated formula which takes account of the dimensions of the hull at various specified points, its flotation and stability, as well as its rig and sails. Other factors included in the calculation are engines, propellers and moveable keels.

Very approximately an IOR rating will be about 0.9 of a boat's actual waterline length, but this can vary considerably. Generally the proportion is lower in the smaller classes and larger with the larger boats, so that a big yacht may have an IOR rating that exceeds her real waterline length. The RORC classes are divided by IOR ratings.

Class I	33 to 70 feet
Class II	29 to 32.9 feet
Class III	25.5 to 28.9 feet
Class IV	23 to 25.4 feet
Class V	21 to 22.9 feet
Class VI	19.5 to 20.9 feet
Class VII	17.5 to 19.4 feet
Class VIII	16 to 17.4 feet

A few races included a Class Zero for yachts of 70 to 42.1 ft rating.

LEVEL RATING classes are based on the same IOR measurements. Two Tonners have an IOR rating of 32.0 ft or less, One Tonners 27.5 ft or less, Three Quarter Tonners 24.5 ft, Half Tonners 22.0 ft, Quarter Tonners 18.5 ft, and Mini Tonners 16.5 ft or less.

There is in addition a growing vogue for racing boats of One Design, which do not need this complicated and sometimes expensive measurement for rating, and are not effected by changes in the measurement rules.

Acknowledgments

The publishers wish to thank the following individuals and organizations for their kind permission to reproduce the pictures in this book: Beken of Cowes: 128–9: Alastair Black: 4–5, 76–7, 104–5, 112–13, 120–1; C.E.D.R.I. (Erwan Quemere): 2–3, 116–17, 130–1, (Roland de Greef): 124–5; Bob Fisher: Endpapers, 6–7, 10–11, 42–3, 69 inset, 68–9, 88–9, 108–9; John Watney: 64–5, 132–3, 140–1; Thomas Zimmermann: 36–7.
The following artists prepared the illustrations: Peter Milne; James Leech; Brian Mayor; Studio Briggs; Brian Watson.
Reference material was kindly supplied by: G. W. B. Gordon for the Navigators Log and Pre-Computed Data; Nauter for 'Swan 441' details; RORC and RYA; Westerly Marine Construction Ltd for J 24 details; Brookes and Gatehouse Ltd; Rediphone for Loran System; Channel Marine; George Philip and Son, London; Ambrose Greenway and Michael Busselle for photographic reference. Our particular thanks is also due to Michael Poole for editorial research.

INDEX

References in italics are to illustrations

Admiral's Cup races 66, 92
airfield weather data 70, 100
airflow *21*, 22, 40, *123*
America's Cup races 134
antifouling paint 60
apparent wind sheer *63*

Backstay 44, 54, 58
    hydraulic 76, *78*
barber-hauling 76, 78, *78*, 82, 124
bearing away *151*
bearings 96, *97*, 140
blanketing 72, 124, 132, 139, *148–9*
blanketing zone 148, *148–9*, 150, 152
blast reacher 82, *82–3*, 84
blooper *82–3*, 110
boat preparation 12, 60, 114, 116, 118
boat speed, in multihull racing 114, 120
boom positions 22, *34*, *60–61*, 76

Capsizing 34, 40
catamarans
    boat preparation 114, 116, 118,
        118–19, 128
    compared with monohulls 114, 124
    heeling angle 120, 122
    pitching 116, 122
    racing 114–31, *116–17*
    reaching in 124, 126, *126–7*
    sailing to windward 120, *120–21*, 122,
        124, 128
    in light winds 122, *123–5*
    starting 118, *118–19*, 120
celestial navigation 96, *96*, 98
centre of lateral resistance 24, 30, *59*, 132
centreboard 14, 40
    adjustment of *27*, 30, *33*, 34
    maintenance *14–15*, 18
    of catamaran 116
centreboard slot *13*, 14, 16
    keelstrip and gaskets 14, 16
clew outhaul *17*, *19*, *21*, 26, *27*, *33*,
        54–5, *56–7*, 58, *76–7*, 122, *122*
committee vessel starts 70, 135
compass 44, 72, *94*, 140
    hand bearing 74, *74–5*, 96
    tactical grid *51*, 126
compass deviation *94*, *97*
Coro Nero current 98, 100
course calculation *51*, *74–5*
covering *144–5*
crew positions
    in dinghies *18–19*, 24, 26, *27*, 32, *33*, 34
    in keel boats 44, 54, *56–7*
    in multihulls 122, *124–5*, 126
    in off-shore racing 74, *76–7*, 84
Cunningham
    in dinghies *19*, *21*, 26, *27*, 28, 32, *33*
    in keel boats 44, 54, *54–5*, *56–7*, 58
    in ocean racing *102–3*, 106
    in off-shore boats *76–7*
current flow *44*, 52, *58*, 70
currents 98, *98*, 132, 136

Dead reckoning (DR) 96, 98, *100*, 108
deck log *95*
depth sounding 96, *97*
dinghies 12–34
    boat preparation 12
    gybing in 34

reaching 30, 32, 34, 150
    roll tacking in *24–5*
    running 24, 34
    sailing to windward in 18, 20, 22, *22–3*,
        24, 26, 28, 30
        in heavy airs *26–7*, 28, 30, 80
        in light airs *18–19*, 20, 22, 24, 34
        in medium airs 26, *26–7*, 28
    tackling waves 28, 30, 32
    wave effects 26, 28, 30
dip-pole gybe *66–7*, 70, *70–71*
double head rig 82, *82–3*

470 dinghy 20
    rig adjustments to *17*
false tacking 144
Finn *24–5*, 140
Flying Dutchman 20, 140
foils 18, 116
food 92, 94
forestay 14, 44, 56
fractional rig 70, 78, 80, *80*, 82, 84

Gate starts *47*, 135, 139
genoa *76–7*, *78*, 82, *82–3*, 84
    in ocean racing 104
    in off-shore racing 74, 76, 78, 80
    on Flying Dutchman 20
glass reinforced plastic hulls (GRP) 12
gouges, filling of 12, 14
Gulf Stream current 98
gybing *34 5*, *107*, 108, 152
    in catamaran 126
    in dinghy 34
    in keelboat 60
    when running 152

Half-tonner 92, 108
halyards 18, 84
    mainsail 54
handicap allowances 68
headsails 74, 80, 82, 102, 104
    changing, reefing of 78, *79*, 80
    windseeker 106
heavy airs
    reaching in *33*, 34, 84
    sailing to windward in 28, 30, 56, 58, 80
    starting in 72
helmsman
    in multihulls 118, 122
    in ocean racing 90, 98, 106
helmsmanship 52, 54, 56, 72, 74, 78, 152
    in dinghy sailing 18, 20
    in multihulls 120, 122
    in ocean racing 92, 102, 134
hulls
    after-racing care 14
    glass reinforced plastic 12
    maintenance of 12, *14*, 60
    rigidity *13*, 14, 116
    wooden 12, 14
hydraulic controls 76, *78*

I.O.R. 74, 76, 82, 110
I.Y.R.U. rules 24, 32, 114, *116–17*, 126, 132
inland water sailing 20
instruments 70, 72, *99*

Jib 52, 58, 76, 78, *122*
    trimming of *19*, 44, 54, 58, *124–5*
        in catamaran 124, *124–5*, 126
        on dinghy 20, 22, 28
        on keelboats 54, 56, 58
jib fairlead *19*, 26, *27*, 54, 78
jib, self-tacking 54, *54–5*, *56–7*, 58
jiffy reef *79*, *102–3*

Keel, maintenance of 60
keel strips and gasket 14, 16
keelboat 40–63
    and dinghy compared 40
    crew duties in 40, 44, 46
    maintenance of 60
    racing in
        reaching and running 57, 58, *58*, *59*,
            60–61, 150
        starting 40, 46, 48, 50
        windward leg 50, 52, 54, 56, 58
            in light airs 52, 54, *54–5*, 56
            in medium and heavy airs 56, *56–7*,
    roll tacking in *24–5*
kicking strap 16, *19*, *21*, *27*, *30*, 32, *33*, 44,
        54, *56–7*, 60, *60–61*
    hydraulic 76, *78*

Laying the windward mark *74–5*
level raters 98, 110
level rating regattas 90
life jacket 110
light airs
    gybing in 34
    reaching in 32, *32–3*, 86
    running in 24, 34
    sailing to windward in 20, 22, 24, 52,
        54, 56
    starting in 72
luffing *102–3*, 148, 150, *150*, *151*
    at start *134–5*
    defensive racing tactic 148, 150
    in racing 52, 72, 134, 148
    to waves 26, 30, 32, 56, 78, 104, 122
    sailing to windward 78, 106, 120, 122
luffing rights *134–5*, *151*

Mainsail 78, 80, 84
    adjustments to 18, 26, *33*, *102–3*
    reefing 80
    trimming
        in catamaran 124, 126
        in ocean racing 104
        on dinghy 22, 24, 28, 32
        on keelboat 54, 58, 60, *60–61*
        on off-shore boat 74, 84
mainsheet 14, *27*, 58
mainsheet take-off points 14, 16
maintenance 12, 60
    of multihulls *116–17*, *118–19*
    see also boat preparation
man overboard 110, *110–11*
mark rounding 40, 132, 139, *144–5*, 146,
        152, *152—3*, 154
    port and starboard 146, 154
mast *17*
    and hull distortion 14
    calibration of 22
    in reaching 22
    in sailing to windward
        in heavy airs *56–7* 58
        in light airs 22, *54–5*
        in medium airs 56, *56–7*, *76–7*
    of catamaran 116, 122
    straightening 16, *20*, *33*
mast abeam position *134–5*, *150*, *151*
mast parterns *13*, 14, 16, *20*
masthead rig 74, 80, *80*
mast rake *59*, *60–61*, 78
mast ram *17*, *19*, *20–21*, 22, 26
mast rotation *114–15*, 116, 122, *123*
medium airs
    reaching in 32, 86
    sailing to windward in 26, 28, 56, 76, 78
    starting in 72
meteorology *48–9*

see also weather forecasts
multihulls
    compared with monohulls 114, 124
    two or three hull question 128
    see also catamaran
multipurpose staysails 82

Navigation 66, 74
    in ocean racing 92, 94, 94, 95, 96, 96,
        97, 98, 98, 99, 100, 108
    preplanning 100
navigator, in ocean racing 92, 98, 100, 108
    qualities of 96
navigator's log 100

Ocean racing 90–111
    food and diet for 90, 92, 94
    navigation in 92, 94, 94–100, 96, 98
    safety measures 110
    sailing to windward 102, 104, 106
        in heavy weather 102–3, 104, 106
        in light air 104–5, 106
    sail setting tabulation 150
    watch keeping 90, 92, 108–9
off-shore boats 66–87
    multihulls 114
    racing in 67, 68, 96, 108–9, 110, 140
        downwind leg 80, 82, 84
        reaching 82, 84
        sailing to windward 72, 74, 76, 78, 80
            in heavy airs 81
            in light airs 74, 76, 76–7
            in medium airs 76, 76–7, 78
        starting 70, 72, 72
Olympic courses 47, 58, 58, 59, 68, 102
Omega radio direction finder 95, 98
one design rating 68, 76, 110
one minute rule 46, 48, 136
oversheeting 22, 26, 84

Pitching 104, 116, 122
planing 30, 32, 58, 126
polar diagram 80, 80, 107, 150
pole gybing 66, 70
position lines 96, 97
premature start 46, 48
'pumping' 32, 126

Racing
    in keelboat 40, 46, 48, 50 52, 54,
        54–5, 56, 56–7, 58, 58–61
    off-shore 67, 70, 72, 72, 74, 76, 76–7,
        78, 80, 82, 84, 108–9, 110
    see also ocean racing
racing tactics 68, 132–55
    at the start 134, 134–5, 136, 136–7,
        138, 138–9
    attacking and defensive 132, 140, 142,
        144, 148, 150, 154
    finishing 154, 154–5
    in ocean racing 108
    on windward leg 54, 58, 139–46
    planning 132, 134
    reaching 148, 150, 150
    rounding the mark 152–3, 152–4
    running 150, 150–52
radio direction finding 94, 95, 96, 98
radius of gyration 12, 26
reaching
    helmsman and crew duties when 40–41
    in catamarans 124, 126, 126–7
    in dinghies 30, 32, 32–3, 34
    in keelboats 58, 60, 60–61
    in ocean racing 106, 108
    in off-shore racing 82, 84, 86, 148, 150
reefing 56, 78, 78, 80

rig adjustments
    for reaching 32–3
    for sailing to windward 26–7, 28
rigging, standing and running 16, 18, 118
right of way 72, 132
    advantage in starting 139
roll tacking 24, 24–5, 54
rudder
    maintenance of 14, 18, 60
    of catamaran 116
    use of in light air 20
    use of in medium airs 26
rudder blades 18, 116
rudder fittings 13, 14
running
    helmsman and crew duties when 40–41
    in catamarans 126, 128
    in dinghies 24, 34
    in keelboats 58, 60
    in ocean racing 108
    in off-shore racing 150, 152
    with waves 30–31

Safety 110
sail adjustments 21, 26–7, 32–3
sail configuration 74, 76, 80
sail trim
    in dinghies 20
    in heavy airs 28, 58, 104, 106
    in keelboats 40, 42, 44, 52, 60–61
    in light air 20, 22, 24, 32, 54, 74, 76
    in medium airs 26, 28, 32, 56, 78
    in multihulls 114, 120, 122
    in ocean racing 92, 102, 104, 106
    in off-shore racing 74, 76, 78
    pump action 32, 126
sail trimmer 66, 92, 104
sea breezes 45, 48, 49, 50
self-tacking jib 54, 54–5, 56–7, 58
sextant 96, 96, 98
shooter (blooper) 82–3
shore-based start 70, 135, 138, 138–9
shoreline, and starting position 70, 72
shroud anchorages 13, 14
skipper, role of 40, 66, 70, 74, 74–5, 80
    in ocean racing 90, 100, 108
slab reefing 78, 79, 102–3
Soling class 39, 44, 54, 54–5, 56, 70
spars 16, 118
spinnaker 34, 44, 58, 59, 66–7, 70,
        70–71, 72, 82, 82–3, 84
    changing under way 44, 86
    dropping 84–5, 86
    gybing with 34
    in catamarans 128
    in ocean racing 102, 106, 108
    in off-shore racing 84, 150, 150
    order of hoisting 84, 84–5
    spinnaker peel 82, 86, 86–7
    starts with 74
    trim of 32, 33, 58, 60, 60–61, 84, 86, 108
spinnaker pole 32, 33, 34, 46, 60, 60–61, 84
spinnaker trimmer 58, 60, 70–71, 84
spreaders 16, 18, 19, 22
    adjustment of 20–21, 26, 27
starting 134–9
    in dinghy racing 40
    in keelboat racing 40, 46, 48, 50
    in off-shore racing 70, 72, 72
    tactics 50, 134–8, 134–9
starting line 46, 135
    shore-based 70, 135, 138, 138–9
starting line bias 45, 46, 46, 50, 51, 136
starts
    committee vessel 70, 135

gate starts 135, 139
    on port tack 138
    pin end starts 52, 52, 118
    planning required 44, 45, 47, 48, 48, 124,
        135–6
    premature 46, 48
    reaching, running 70, 139
    shore-based 70, 135, 138, 138–9
    standing starts 52
    timing of 48, 50, 118, 120
staysails 82, 84, 86, 102
    multipurpose 82
strategy 66, 68, 90, 94, 98, 100, 108, 114
    fundamental considerations 132
streaker (blooper) 82–3

Tacking
    decisions on 20, 24, 44, 48, 52, 56, 72,
        74, 76, 140
    in dinghy 24
    in keelboat 50, 54, 56
    in off-shore boats 72, 74, 76, 140, 142, 144
tacking duels in racing 124
tactics 18, 20, 40, 44, 66, 78
teamwork 12, 46, 66, 90, 126–7
tell-tales
    on headsail 72, 82
    on jib 20, 40, 54
    on mainsail 40
    on spinnaker 32
through pole gybing 86
tidal atlas 70, 96, 98, 136
tidal gradient 70, 72
tides 73, 74–5, 98, 98
    in selecting starting position 44, 46, 70,
        72, 72, 74
Tornado catamaran 114–15, 116, 121
training and practice, importance of 18,
        28, 34, 66, 68, 78, 80, 84, 120, 152
trapeze 26, 27, 126
triangular courses 47, 68
trimaran 114, 116–17, 128
twin pole gybe 70, 70–71

Watch keeping 90, 92, 108–9
waves, effect of 26, 28
    in ocean racing 102–3, 104
    when reaching 30, 32
    when running 30–31
    when sailing to windward 28, 30, 56, 58,
        74, 78, 102–3, 104, 122
weather forecasts 48, 70, 100
weather mark, layline to 140, 144
weight 12, 14, 114, 116, 128
wind bends 45, 48, 49, 124, 136, 136–7, 139
wind, deflection over sails 132
wind gusts 22, 30
wind oscillation plot 48, 136
wind shadow 148–9
wind sheer and sail twist 62
wind shifts 22, 34, 48–9, 54, 58, 60–61,
        104, 107, 132
    in sailing to windward 18, 20, 30, 124
    on runs 60, 108
    tacking to 24, 48, 54, 124, 126, 140
windseeker head sail 104–5, 106
windward, sailing to
    duties of helmsman and crew 40–41
    in catamaran 120, 122, 124
    in dinghy 18, 20, 22, 22–3, 24, 26, 28, 30
    in keelboats 50, 52, 54, 54–5, 56, 56–7, 58
    in ocean racing 102, 104, 106, 102–5
    in off-shore boats 72, 74, 76, 76–7, 78, 80
    through waves 28–9, 30, 56, 58, 74, 78,
        102–3, 104, 122
wooden hulls 12, 14